CASENOTE LEGAL BRIEFS

CONTRACTS

Adaptable to courses utilizing Murphy and Speidel's casebook on Contract Law

Buy a E.Z. Rules for Contracts

NORMAN S. GOLDENBERG, SENIOR EDITOR
PETER TENEN, MANAGING EDITOR

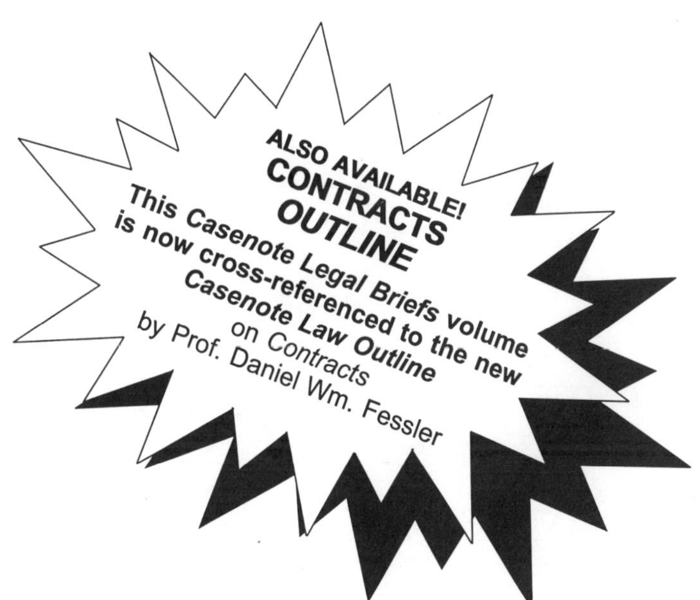

STAFF WRITERS
TERRY MOLLOY
ROBERT J. SWITZER
RICHARD A. LOVICH
JAMES I. ROSENTHAL
MATT HARDY
CLAUDIA NORBY
JERRY SMILOWITZ
DAVID KYLER
MARGIE PELTON
HOWARD SCOTT LEVIANT

PUBLISHED BY **CASENOTES PUBLISHING CO., INC. 1640 5th ST., SUITE 208 SANTA MONICA, CA 90401**

ISBN 0-87457-041-7

FORMAT OF THE CASENOTE LEGAL BRIEF

CASE CAPSULE: This bold-faced section (first three paragraphs) highlights the procedural nature of the case, a short summary of the facts, and the rule of law. This is an invaluable quick-review device designed to refresh the student's memory for classroom discussion and exam preparation.

NATURE OF CASE: This section identifies the form of action (e.g., breach of contract, negligence, battery), the type of proceeding (e.g., demurrer, appeal from trial court's jury instructions) and the relief sought (e.g., damages, injunction, criminal sanctions).

FACT SUMMARY: The fact summary is included to refresh the student's memory. It can be used as a quick reminder of the facts when the student is chosen by an instructor to brief a case.

CONCISE RULE OF LAW: This portion of the brief summarizes the general principle of law that the case illustrates. Like the fact summary, it is included to refresh the student's memory. It may be used for instant recall of the court's holding and for classroom discussion or home review.

FACTS: This section contains all relevant facts of the case, including the contentions of the parties and the lower court holdings. It is written in a logical order to give the student a clear understanding of the case. The plaintiff and defendant are identified by their proper names throughout and are always labeled with a (P) or (D).

ISSUE: The issue is a concise question that brings out the essence of the opinion as it relates to the section of the casebook in which the case appears. Both substantive and procedural issues are included if relevant to the decision.

HOLDING AND DECISION: This section offers a clear and in-depth discussion of the rule of the case and the court's rationale. It is written in easy-to-understand language. When relevant, it includes a thorough discussion of the exceptions listed by the court, the concurring and dissenting opinions, and the names of the judges.

CONCURRENCE / DISSENT: All concurrences and dissents are briefed whenever they are included by the casebook editor.

EDITOR'S ANALYSIS: This last paragraph gives the student a broad understanding of where the case "fits in" with other cases in the section of the book and with the entire course. It is a hornbook-style discussion indicating whether the case is a majority or minority opinion and comparing the principal case with other cases in the casebook. It may also provide analysis from restatements, uniform codes, and law review articles. The editor's analysis will prove to be invaluable to classroom discussion.

CROSS-REFERENCE TO OUTLINE: Wherever possible, following each case is a cross-reference linking the subject matter of the issue to the appropriate place in the *Casenote Law Outline,* which provides further information on the subject.

WINTER v. G.P. PUTNAM'S SONS

938 F.2d 1033 (1991).

NATURE OF CASE: Appeal from summary judgment in a products liability action.

FACT SUMMARY: Winter (P) relied on a book on mushrooms published by Putnam (D) and became critically ill after eating a poisonous mushroom.

CONCISE RULE OF LAW: Strict products liability is not applicable to the expressions contained within a book.

FACTS: Winter (P) purchased The Encyclopedia of Mushrooms, a book published by Putnam (D), to help in collecting and eating wild mushrooms. In 1988, Winter (P), relying on descriptions in the book, ate some wild mushrooms which turned out to be poisonous. Winter (P) became so ill he required a liver transplant. He brought a strict products liability action against Putnam (D), alleging that the book contained erroneous and misleading information that caused his injury. Putnam (D) responded that the information in the book was not a product for purposes of strict products liability, and the trial court granted its motion for summary judgment. The trial court also rejected Winter's (P) actions for negligence and misrepresentation. Winter (P) appealed.

ISSUE: Is strict products liability applicable to the expressions contained within a book?

HOLDING AND DECISION: (Sneed, J.) No. Strict products liability is not applicable to the expressions contained within a book. Products liability is geared toward tangible objects. The expression of ideas is governed by copyright, libel, and misrepresentation laws. The Restatement (Second) of Torts lists examples of the items that are covered by §402A strict liability. All are tangible items, such as tires or automobiles. There is no indication that the doctrine should be expanded beyond this area. Furthermore, there is a strong public interest in the unfettered exchange of ideas. The threat of liability without fault could seriously inhibit persons who wish to share thoughts and ideas with others. Although some courts have held that aeronautical charts are products for purposes of strict liability, these charts are highly technical tools which resemble compasses. The Encyclopedia of Mushrooms, published by Putnam (D), is a book of pure thought and expression and therefore does not constitute a product for purposes of strict liability. Additionally, publishers do not owe a duty to investigate the contents of books that they distribute. Therefore, a negligence action may not be maintained by Winter (P) against Putnam (D). Affirmed.

EDITOR'S ANALYSIS: This decision is in accord with the rulings in most jurisdictions. See Alm v. Nostrand Reinhold Co., Inc., 480 N.E. 2d 1263 (Ill. 1985). The court also stated that since the publisher is not a guarantor of the accuracy of an author's statements, an action for negligent misrepresentation could not be maintained. The elements of negligent misrepresentation are stated in § 311 of the Restatement (Second) of Torts.

[For more information on misrepresentation, see Casenote Law Outline on Torts, Chapter 12, § III, Negligent Misrepresentation.]

NOTE TO THE STUDENT

OUR GOAL. It is the goal of Casenotes Publishing Company, Inc. to create and distribute the finest, clearest and most accurate legal briefs available. To this end, we are constantly seeking new ideas, comments and constructive criticism. As a user of *Casenote Legal Briefs,* your suggestions will be highly valued. With all correspondence, please include your complete name, address, and telephone number, including area code and zip code.

THE TOTAL STUDY SYSTEM. Casenote Legal Briefs are just one part of the Casenotes TOTAL STUDY SYSTEM. Most briefs are (wherever possible) cross-referenced to the appropriate *Casenote Law Outline,* which will elaborate on the issue at hand. By purchasing a Law Outline together with your Legal Brief, you will have both parts of the Casenotes TOTAL STUDY SYSTEM. (See the advertising in the front of this book for a list of Law Outlines currently available.)

A NOTE ABOUT LANGUAGE. Please note that the language used in *Casenote Legal Briefs* in reference to minority groups and women reflects terminology used within the historical context of the time in which the respective courts wrote the opinions. We at Casenotes Publishing Co., Inc. are well aware of and very sensitive to the desires of all people to be treated with dignity and to be referred to as they prefer. Because such preferences change from time to time, and because the language of the courts reflects the time period in which opinions were written, our case briefs will not necessarily reflect contemporary references. We appreciate your understanding and invite your comments.

A NOTE REGARDING NEW EDITIONS. As of our press date, this Casenote Legal Brief is current and includes briefs of all cases in the current version of the casebook, divided into chapters that correspond to that edition of the casebook. However, occasionally a new edition of the casebook comes out in the interim, and sometimes the casebook author will make changes in the sequence of the cases in the chapters, add or delete cases, or change the chapter titles. Should you be using this Legal Brief in conjuction with a casebook that was issued later than this book, you can receive all of the newer cases, which are available free from us, by sending in the "Supplement Request Form" in this section of the book (please follow all instructions on that form). The Supplement(s) will contain all the missing cases, and will bring your Casenote Legal Brief up to date.

EDITOR'S NOTE. Casenote Legal Briefs are intended to supplement the student's casebook, not replace it. There is no substitute for the student's own mastery of this important learning and study technique. If used properly, *Casenote Legal Briefs* are an effective law study aid that will serve to reinforce the student's understanding of the cases.

REV 4-97

REF. # 1012-97 -797

SUPPLEMENT REQUEST FORM

At the time this book was printed, a brief was included for every major case in the casebook and for every existing supplement to the casebook. However, if a new supplement to the casebook (or a new edition of the casebook) has been published since this publication was printed and if that casebook supplement (or new edition of the casebook) was available for sale at the time you purchased this Casenote Legal Briefs book, we will be pleased to provide you the new cases contained therein AT NO CHARGE when you send us a stamped, self-addressed envelope.

TO OBTAIN YOUR FREE SUPPLEMENT MATERIAL, **YOU MUST FOLLOW THE INSTRUCTIONS BELOW PRECISELY** OR YOUR REQUEST WILL NOT BE ACKNOWLEDGED!

1. Please check if there is in fact an existing supplement and, if so, that the cases are not already included in your Casenote Legal Briefs. Check the main table of cases as well as the supplement table of cases, if any.

2. **REMOVE THIS ENTIRE PAGE FROM THE BOOK.** You MUST send this ORIGINAL page to receive your supplement. This page acts as your proof of purchase and contains the reference number necessary to fill your supplement request properly. No photocopy of this page or written request will be honored or answered. Any request from which the reference number has been removed, altered or obliterated will not be honored.

✶ 3. Prepare a STAMPED self-addressed envelope for return mailing. Be sure to use a FULL SIZE (9 X 12) ENVELOPE (MANILA TYPE) so that the supplement will fit and AFFIX ENOUGH POSTAGE TO COVER 3 OZ. **ANY SUPPLEMENT REQUEST NOT ACCOMPANIED BY A STAMPED SELF-ADDRESSED ENVELOPE WILL ABSOLUTELY NOT BE FILLED OR ACKNOWLEDGED.**

4. MULTIPLE SUPPLEMENT REQUESTS: If you are ordering more than one supplement, we suggest that you enclose a stamped, self-addressed envelope for each supplement requested. If you enclose only one envelope for a multiple request, your order may not be filled immediately should any supplement which you requested still be in production. In other words, your order will be held by us until it can be filled completely.

5. Casenotes prints two kinds of supplements. A "New Edition" supplement is issued when a new edition of your casebook is published. A "New Edition" supplement gives you all major cases found in the new edition of the casebook which did not appear in the previous edition. A regular "supplement" is issued when a paperback supplement to your casebook is published. If the box at the lower right is stamped, then the "New Edition" supplement was provided to your bookstore and is *not* available from Casenotes; however, Casenotes will still send you any regular "supplements" which have been printed either before or after the new edition of your casebook appeared and which, according to the reference number at the top of this page, have not been included in this book. If the box is not stamped, Casenotes will send you any supplements, "New Edition" and/or regular, needed to completely update your Casenote Legal Briefs.

✶☞ ***NOTE:* REQUESTS FOR SUPPLEMENTS WILL NOT BE FILLED UNLESS THESE INSTRUCTIONS ARE COMPLIED WITH!**

6. Fill in the following information:

Full title of CASEBOOK **CONTRACTS**

____

CASEBOOK author's name **Murphy**
and Speidel

Date of new supplement you are requesting ______________________________

____

Name and location of bookstore where this Casenote Legal Brief was purchased ______________________________

____

Name and location of law school you attend ______________________________

____

Any comments regarding Casenote Legal Briefs ______________________________

____

NOTE: IF THIS BOX IS STAMPED, NO NEW EDITION SUPPLEMENT CAN BE OBTAINED BY MAIL.

PUBLISHED BY **CASENOTES PUBLISHING CO., INC. 1640 5th ST, SUITE 208 SANTA MONICA, CA 90401**

PLEASE PRINT

NAME ______________________________ **PHONE** ______________________________

ADDRESS/CITY/STATE/ZIP ______________________________

Announcing the First *Totally Integrated* Law Study System

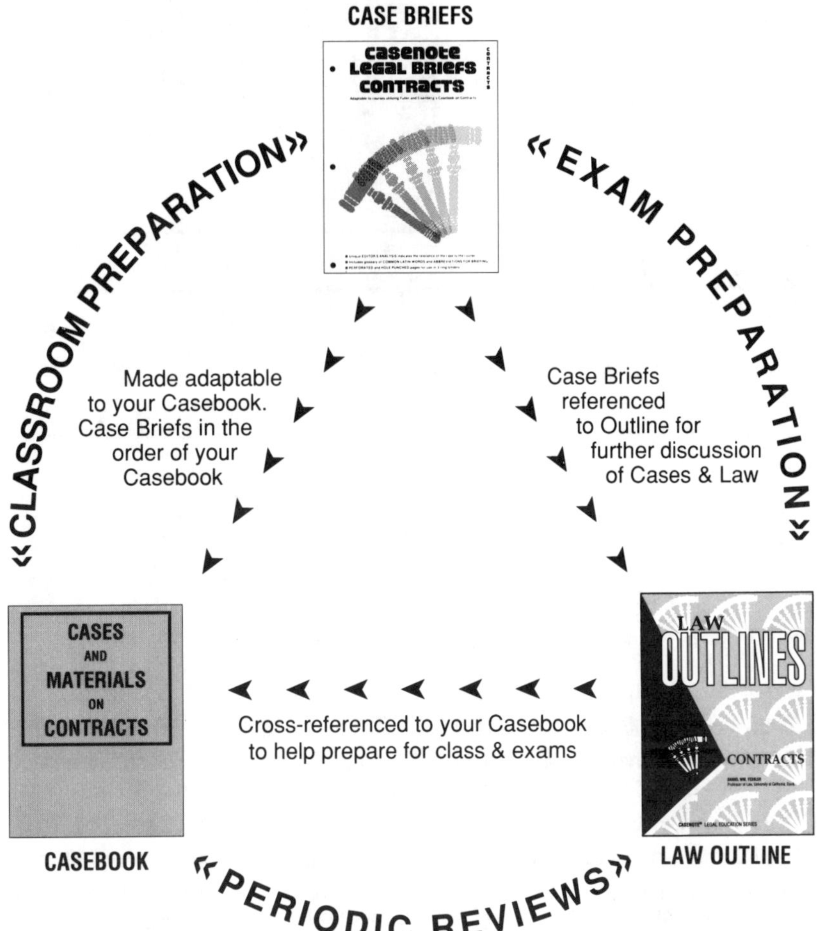

Casenotes Integrated Study System Makes Studying Easier and More Effective Than Ever!

Casenotes has just made studying easier and more effective than ever before, because we've done the work for you! Through our exclusive integrated study system, most briefs found in this volume of Casenote Legal Briefs are cross-referenced to the corresponding area of law in the Casenote Law Outline series. The cross-reference immediately follows the Editor's Analysis at the end of the brief, and it will direct you to the corresponding chapter and section number in the Casenote Law Outline for further information on the case or the area of law.

This cross-referencing feature will enable you to make the most effective use of your time. While each Casenote Law Outline focuses on a particular subject area of the law, each legal briefs volume is adapted to a specific casebook. Now, with cross-referencing of Casenote Legal Briefs to Casenote Law Outlines, you can have the best of both worlds – briefs for all major cases in your casebooks and easy-to-find, easy-to-read explanations of the law in our Law Outline series. Casenote Law Outlines are authored exclusively by law professors who are nationally recognized authorities in their field. So using Casenote Law Outlines is like studying with the top law professors.

Try Casenotes new totally integrated study system and see just how easy and effective studying can be.

Casenotes Integrated Study System Does The Work For You!

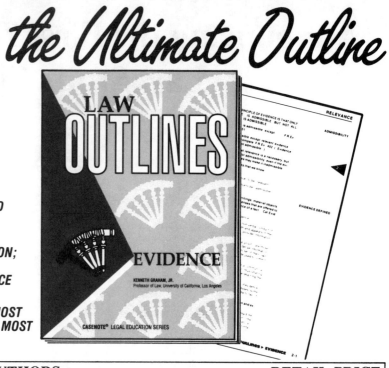

CASENOTE™ LEGAL BRIEFS

PRICE LIST — EFFECTIVE JULY 1, 1997 • PRICES SUBJECT TO CHANGE WITHOUT NOTICE

Ref. No.	Course	Adaptable to Courses Utilizing	Retail Price
1265	ADMINISTRATIVE LAW	BONFIELD & ASIMOV	17.00
1263	ADMINISTRATIVE LAW	BREYER, STEWART & SUNSTEIN	19.00
1266	ADMINISTRATIVE LAW	CASS, DIVER & BEERMAN	17.00
1260	ADMINISTRATIVE LAW	GELLHORN, B., S., R., S. & F.	17.00
1264	ADMINISTRATIVE LAW	MASHAW, MERRILL & SHANE	18.50
1267	ADMINISTRATIVE LAW	REESE	17.00
1262	ADMINISTRATIVE LAW	SCHWARTZ	18.00
1290	ADMIRALTY	HEALY & SHARPE	21.00
1350	AGENCY & PARTNERSHIP (ENT.ORG)	CONARD, KNAUSS & SIEGEL	21.00
1351	AGENCY & PARTNERSHIP	HYNES	20.00
1281	ANTITRUST (TRADE REGULATION)	HANDLER, P., G., & W.	17.50
1283	ANTITRUST	SULLIVAN & HOVENKAMP	18.00
1611	BANKING LAW	MACEY & MILLER	17.00
1303	BANKRUPTCY (DEBTOR-CREDITOR)	EISENBERG	19.00
1040	CIVIL PROCEDURE	COUND, F., M. & S	20.00
1043	CIVIL PROCEDURE	FIELD, KAPLAN & CLERMONT	20.00
1041	CIVIL PROCEDURE	HAZARD, TAIT & FLETCHER	19.00
1047	CIVIL PROCEDURE	MARCUS, REDISH & SHERMAN	19.00
1044	CIVIL PROCEDURE	ROSENBERG, S. & D.	20.00
1046	CIVIL PROCEDURE	YEAZELL	17.00
1311	COMM'L LAW	FARNSWORTH, H., R., H. & M.	19.00
1312	COMM'L LAW	JORDAN & WARREN	19.00
1310	COMM'L LAW (SALES/SEC.TR./PAY.LAW [Sys.])	SPEIDEL, SUMMERS & WHITE	22.00
1313	COMM'L LAW (SALES/SEC.TR./PAY.LAW)	WHALEY	19.00
1320	COMMUNITY PROPERTY	BIRD	17.50
1630	COMPARATIVE LAW	SCHLESINGER, B., D., & H.	16.00
1048	COMPLEX LITIGATION	MARCUS & SHERMAN	17.00
1072	CONFLICTS	BRILMAYER	17.00
1071	CONFLICTS	CRAMTON, C. K., & K.	17.00
1070	CONFLICTS	ROSENBERG, HAY & W.	20.00
1086	CONSTITUTIONAL LAW	BREST & LEVINSON	18.00
1082	CONSTITUTIONAL LAW	COHEN & VARAT	21.00
1088	CONSTITUTIONAL LAW	FARBER, ESKRIDGE & FRICKEY	18.00
1080	CONSTITUTIONAL LAW	GUNTHER & SULLIVAN	20.00
1081	CONSTITUTIONAL LAW	LOCKHART, K., C., S. & F.	18.00
1085	CONSTITUTIONAL LAW	ROTUNDA	20.00
1087	CONSTITUTIONAL LAW	STONE, S., S. & T.	19.00
1102	CONTRACTS	BURTON	20.00
1017	CONTRACTS	CALAMARI, PERILLO & BENDER	23.00
1101	CONTRACTS	CRANDALL & WHALEY	20.00
1014	CONTRACTS	DAWSON, HARVEY & H.	19.00
1010	CONTRACTS	FARNSWORTH & YOUNG	18.00
1011	CONTRACTS	FULLER & EISENBERG	20.00
1100	CONTRACTS	HAMILTON, RAU & WEINTRAUB	19.00
1013	CONTRACTS	KESSLER, GILMORE & KRONMAN	23.00
1016	CONTRACTS	KNAPP & CRYSTAL	20.50
1012	CONTRACTS	MURPHY & SPEIDEL	22.00
1018	CONTRACTS	MURRAY	22.00
1015	CONTRACTS	ROSETT	21.00
1019	CONTRACTS	VERNON	20.00
1502	COPYRIGHT	GOLDSTEIN	18.00
1501	COPYRIGHT	NIMMER, M., M., & N.	19.50
1218	CORPORATE TAXATION	LIND, S. L. & R	14.00
1050	CORPORATIONS	CARY & EISENBERG	19.00
1054	CORPORATIONS	CHOPER,COFFEE, & GILSON	21.50
1350	CORPORATIONS (ENTERPRISE ORG.)	CONARD, KNAUSS & SIEGEL	21.00
1053	CORPORATIONS	HAMILTON	19.00
1057	CORPORATIONS	O'KELLEY & THOMPSON	18.00
1056	CORPORATIONS	SOLOMON, S., B., & W.	19.00
1052	CORPORATIONS	VAGTS	17.00
1300	CREDITOR'S RIGHTS (DEBTOR-CREDITOR)	RIESENFELD	21.00
1550	CRIMINAL JUSTICE	WEINREB	18.00
1029	CRIMINAL LAW	BONNIE, C., J., & L.	17.00
1020	CRIMINAL LAW	BOYCE & PERKINS	22.00
1028	CRIMINAL LAW	DRESSLER	21.00
1027	CRIMINAL LAW	JOHNSON	20.00
1021	CRIMINAL LAW	KADISH & SCHULHOFER	19.00
1026	CRIMINAL LAW	KAPLAN, WEISBERG & BINDER	18.00
1023	CRIMINAL LAW	LAFAVE	19.00
1205	CRIMINAL PROCEDURE	ALLEN, KUHNS & STUNTZ	17.00
1202	CRIMINAL PROCEDURE	HADDAD, Z., S. & B.	20.00
1200	CRIMINAL PROCEDURE	KAMISAR, LAFAVE & ISRAEL	19.00
1204	CRIMINAL PROCEDURE	SALTZBURG & CAPRA	17.00
1203	CRIMINAL PROCEDURE (PROCESS)	WEINREB	18.50
1303	DEBTOR-CREDITOR	EISENBERG	19.00
1300	DEBTOR-CREDITOR (CRED. RTS.)	RIESENFELD	21.00
1304	DEBTOR-CREDITOR	WARREN & WESTBROOK	19.00
1224	DECEDENTS ESTATES	RITCHIE, ALFORD, EFFLAND & D.	21.00
1222	DECEDENTS ESTATES	SCOLES & HALBACH	21.50
1231	DECEDENTS ESTATES (TRUSTS)	WAGGONER, A. & F.	20.00
	DOMESTIC RELATIONS (*see* FAMILY LAW)		
3000	EDUCATION LAW (COURSE OUTLINE)	AQUILA & PETZKE	25.50
1670	EMPLOYMENT DISCRIMINATION	FRIEDMAN & STRICKLER	17.00
1671	EMPLOYMENT DISCRIMINATION	ZIMMER, SULLIVAN, R. & C.	18.00
1660	EMPLOYMENT LAW	ROTHSTEIN, KNAPP & LIEBMAN	19.50
1350	ENTERPRISE ORGANIZATION	CONARD, KNAUSS & SIEGEL	21.00
1342	ENVIRONMENTAL LAW	ANDERSON, MANDELKER & T.	16.00
1341	ENVIRONMENTAL LAW	FINDLEY & FARBER	18.00
1345	ENVIRONMENTAL LAW	MENELL & STEWART	17.00
1344	ENVIRONMENTAL LAW	PERCIVAL, MILLER, S. & L.	18.00
1343	ENVIRONMENTAL LAW	PLATER, ABRAMS & GOLDFARB	17.00
	EQUITY (*see* REMEDIES)		
1217	ESTATE & GIFT TAXATION	BITTKER, CLARK & McCOUCH	15.00
	ETHICS (*see* PROFESSIONAL RESPONSIBILITY)		
1065	EVIDENCE	GREEN & NESSON	20.00

Ref. No.	Course	Adaptable to Courses Utilizing	Retail Price
1066	EVIDENCE	MUELLER & KIRKPATRICK	17.00
1064	EVIDENCE	STRONG, BROUN & M..	22.50
1062	EVIDENCE	SUTTON & WELLBORN	22.00
1061	EVIDENCE	WALTZ & PARK	20.00
1060	EVIDENCE	WEINSTEIN, M., A. & B.	22.50
1244	FAMILY LAW (DOMESTIC RELATIONS)	AREEN	22.00
1242	FAMILY LAW (DOMESTIC RELATIONS)	CLARK & GLOWINSKY	19.00
1245	FAMILY LAW (DOMESTIC RELATIONS)	ELLMAN, KURTZ & BARTLETT	20.00
1243	FAMILY LAW (DOMESTIC RELATIONS)	KRAUSE	24.00
1240	FAMILY LAW (DOMESTIC RELATIONS)	WADLINGTON	20.00
1231	FAMILY PROPERTY LAW (WILLS/TRUSTS)	WAGGONER, A. & F.	20.00
1362	FEDERAL COURTS	CURRIE	17.00
1360	FEDERAL COURTS	FALLON, M. & S. (HART & W.)	19.00
1360	FEDERAL COURTS	HART & WECHSLER (FALLON)	19.00
1363	FEDERAL COURTS	LOW & JEFFRIES	16.00
1361	FEDERAL COURTS	McCORMICK, C. & W.	20.00
1364	FEDERAL COURTS	REDISH & NICHOL	17.00
1510	GRATUITOUS TRANSFERS	CLARK, LUSKY & MURPHY	18.00
1650	HEALTH LAW	FURROW, J., J., & S.	17.50
1640	IMMIGRATION LAW	ALEINIKOFF, MARTIN & M.	16.00
1641	IMMIGRATION LAW	LEGOMSKY	18.00
1371	INSURANCE LAW	KEETON	21.00
1372	INSURANCE LAW	YORK, WHELAN & MARTINEZ	19.00
1370	INSURANCE LAW	YOUNG & HOLMES	17.00
1394	INTERNATIONAL BUSINESS TRANSACTIONS	FOLSOM, GORDON & SPANOGLE	15.00
1393	INTERNATIONAL LAW	CARTER & TRIMBLE	16.00
1392	INTERNATIONAL LAW	HENKIN, P., S. & S.	17.00
1390	INTERNATIONAL LAW	OLIVER, F., B., S., & W.	22.00
1331	LABOR LAW	COX, BOK, GORMAN & FINKIN	19.00
1332	LABOR LAW	HARPER & ESTREICHER	20.00
1333	LABOR LAW	LESLIE	18.50
1330	LABOR LAW	MERRIFIELD, S. & C.	19.00
1471	LAND FINANCE (REAL ESTATE TRANS)	BERGER & JOHNSTONE	18.00
1620	LAND FINANCE (REAL ESTATE TRANS)	NELSON & WHITMAN	19.00
1452	LAND USE	CALLIES, FREILICH & ROBERTS	17.00
1450	LAND USE	WRIGHT & GITELMAN	23.00
1421	LEGISLATION	ESKRIDGE & FRICKEY	15.00
1480	MASS MEDIA	FRANKLIN & ANDERSON	15.00
1312	NEGOTIABLE INSTRUMENTS (COMM. LAW)	JORDAN & WARREN	19.00
1313	NEGOTIABLE INSTRUMENTS (COMM. LAW)	WHALEY	18.00
1541	OIL & GAS	KUNTZ, L., A. & S.	18.00
1540	OIL & GAS	MAXWELL, WILLIAMS, M. & K.	18.00
1560	PATENT LAW	FRANCIS & COLLINS	23.00
1310	PAYMENT LAW [SYST.][COMM. LAW]	SPEIDEL, SUMMERS & WHITE	22.00
1313	PAYMENT LAW (COMM.LAW / NEG. INST.)	WHALEY	19.00
1431	PRODUCTS LIABILITY	OWEN, MONTGOMERY & K.	20.00
1091	PROF. RESPONSIBILITY (ETHICS)	GILLERS	13.00
1093	PROF. RESPONSIBILITY (ETHICS)	HAZARD, KONIAK, & CRAMTON	18.00
1092	PROF. RESPONSIBILITY (ETHICS)	MORGAN & ROTUNDA	13.00
1030	PROPERTY	CASNER & LEACH	21.00
1031	PROPERTY	CRIBBET, J., F. & S.	21.50
1037	PROPERTY	DONAHUE, KAUPER & MARTIN	18.00
1035	PROPERTY	DUKEMINIER & KRIER	18.00
1034	PROPERTY	HAAR & LIEBMAN	20.50
1036	PROPERTY	KURTZ & HOVENKAMP	19.00
1033	PROPERTY	NELSON, STOEBUCK, & W.	20.50
1032	PROPERTY	RABIN & KWALL	20.00
1038	PROPERTY	SINGER	18.50
1621	REAL ESTATE TRANSACTIONS	GOLDSTEIN & KORNGOLD	18.00
1471	REAL ESTATE TRANS. & FIN. (LAND FINANCE)	BERGER & JOHNSTONE	18.00
1620	REAL ESTATE TRANSFER & FINANCE	NELSON & WHITMAN	18.00
1254	REMEDIES (EQUITY)	LAYCOCK	20.00
1253	REMEDIES (EQUITY)	LEAVELL, L., N. & K/F.	21.00
1252	REMEDIES (EQUITY)	RE & RE	23.00
1255	REMEDIES (EQUITY)	SHOBEN & TABB	22.50
1250	REMEDIES (EQUITY)	YORK, BAUMAN & RENDLEMAN	25.00
1312	SALES (COMM. LAW)	JORDAN & WARREN	19.00
1310	SALES (COMM. LAW)	SPEIDEL, SUMMERS & WHITE	22.00
1313	SALES (COMM. LAW)	WHALEY	19.00
1312	SECURED TRANS. (COMM. LAW)	JORDAN & WARREN	19.00
1310	SECURED TRANS.	SPEIDEL, SUMMERS & WHITE	22.00
1313	SECURED TRANS. (COMM. LAW)	WHALEY	19.00
1272	SECURITIES REGULATION	COX, HILLMAN, LANGEVOORT	18.00
1270	SECURITIES REGULATION	JENNINGS, MARSH & COFFEE	18.00
1680	SPORTS LAW	WEILER & ROBERTS	17.50
1217	TAXATION (ESTATE & GIFT)	BITTKER, CLARK & McCOUCH	15.00
1219	TAXATION (INDIV. INC.)	BURKE & FRIEL	19.00
1212	TAXATION (FED. INC.)	FREELAND, LIND & STEPHENS	18.00
1211	TAXATION (FED. INC.)	GRAETZ & SCHENK	17.00
1210	TAXATION (FED. INC.)	KLEIN & BANKMAN	18.00
1218	TAXATION (CORPORATE)	LIND, S., L. & R.	14.00
1006	TORTS	DOBBS	19.00
1003	TORTS	EPSTEIN	20.50
1004	TORTS	FRANKLIN & RABIN	17.50
1001	TORTS	HENDERSON, P. & S.	20.50
1000	TORTS	PROSSER, W., S., K., & P.	24.00
1005	TORTS	SHULMAN, JAMES & GRAY	22.00
1281	TRADE REGULATION (ANTITRUST)	HANDLER, P., G., & W.	17.50
1230	TRUSTS	BOGERT, O., H., & H.	20.50
1231	TRUSTS/WILLS (FAMILY PROPERTY LAW)	WAGGONER, A. & F.	20.00
1410	U.C.C	EPSTEIN, MARTIN, H. & N.	15.00
1223	WILLS, TRUSTS & ESTATES	DUKEMINIER & JOHANSON	19.00
1220	WILLS	MECHEM & ATKINSON	20.00
1231	WILLS/TRUSTS (FAMILY PROPERTY LAW)	WAGGONER, A. & F.	20.00

(SERIES XI.)

CASENOTES PUBLISHING CO. INC. ● 1640 FIFTH STREET, SUITE 208 ● SANTA MONICA, CA 90401 ● (310) 395-6500

E-Mail Address- casenote@westworld.com

Website-http://www.casenotes.com

PLEASE PURCHASE FROM YOUR LOCAL BOOKSTORE. IF UNAVAILABLE, YOU MAY ORDER DIRECT.*

4TH CLASS POSTAGE (ALLOW TWO WEEKS) $1.00 PER ORDER; 1ST CLASS POSTAGE $3.00 (ONE BOOK), $2.00 EACH (TWO OR MORE BOOKS)

*CALIF. RESIDENTS PLEASE ADD 8¼% SALES TAX

Notes

A GLOSSARY OF COMMON LATIN WORDS AND PHRASES ENCOUNTERED IN THE LAW

A FORTIORI: Because one fact exists or has been proven, therefore a second fact that is related to the first fact must also exist.

A PRIORI: From the cause to the effect. A term of logic used to denote that when one generally accepted truth is shown to be a cause, another particular effect must necessarily follow.

AB INITIO: From the beginning; a condition which has existed throughout, as in a marriage which was void ab initio.

ACTUS REUS: The wrongful act; in criminal law, such action sufficient to trigger criminal liability.

AD VALOREM: According to value; an ad valorem tax is imposed upon an item located within the taxing jurisdiction calculated by the value of such item.

AMICUS CURIAE: Friend of the court. Its most common usage takes the form of an amicus curiae brief, filed by a person who is not a party to an action but is nonetheless allowed to offer an argument supporting his legal interests.

ARGUENDO: In arguing. A statement, possibly hypothetical, made for the purpose of argument, is one made arguendo.

BILL QUIA TIMET: A bill to quiet title (establish ownership) to real property.

BONA FIDE: True, honest, or genuine. May refer to a person's legal position based on good faith or lacking notice of fraud (such as a bona fide purchaser for value) or to the authenticity of a particular document (such as a bona fide last will and testament).

CAUSA MORTIS: With approaching death in mind. A gift causa mortis is a gift given by a party who feels certain that death is imminent.

CAVEAT EMPTOR: Let the buyer beware. This maxim is reflected in the rule of law that a buyer purchases at his own risk because it is his responsibility to examine, judge, test, and otherwise inspect what he is buying.

CERTIORARI: A writ of review. Petitions for review of a case by the United States Supreme Court are most often done by means of a writ of certiorari.

CONTRA: On the other hand. Opposite. Contrary to.

CORAM NOBIS: Before us; writs of error directed to the court that originally rendered the judgment.

CORAM VOBIS: Before you; writs of error directed by an appellate court to a lower court to correct a factual error.

CORPUS DELICTI: The body of the crime; the requisite elements of a crime amounting to objective proof that a crime has been committed.

CUM TESTAMENTO ANNEXO, ADMINISTRATOR (ADMINISTRATOR C.T.A.): With will annexed; an administrator c.t.a. settles an estate pursuant to a will in which he is not appointed.

DE BONIS NON, ADMINISTRATOR (ADMINISTRATOR D.B.N.): Of goods not administered; an administrator d.b.n. settles a partially settled estate.

DE FACTO: In fact; in reality; actually. Existing in fact but not officially approved or engendered.

DE JURE: By right; lawful. Describes a condition that is legitimate "as a matter of law," in contrast to the term "de facto," which connotes something existing in fact but not legally sanctioned or authorized. For example, de facto segregation refers to segregation brought about by housing patterns, etc., whereas de jure segregation refers to segregation created by law.

DE MINIMUS: Of minimal importance; insignificant; a trifle; not worth bothering about.

DE NOVO: Anew; a second time; afresh. A trial de novo is a new trial held at the appellate level as if the case originated there and the trial at a lower level had not taken place.

DICTA: Generally used as an abbreviated form of obiter dicta, a term describing those portions of a judicial opinion incidental or not necessary to resolution of the specific question before the court. Such nonessential statements and remarks are not considered to be binding precedent.

DUCES TECUM: Refers to a particular type of writ or subpoena requesting a party or organization to produce certain documents in their possession.

EN BANC: Full bench. Where a court sits with all justices present rather than the usual quorum.

EX PARTE: For one side or one party only. An ex parte proceeding is one undertaken for the benefit of only one party, without notice to, or an appearance by, an adverse party.

EX POST FACTO: After the fact. An ex post facto law is a law that retroactively changes the consequences of a prior act.

EX REL.: Abbreviated form of the term ex relatione, meaning, upon relation or information. When the state brings an action in which it has no interest against an individual at the instigation of one who has a private interest in the matter.

FORUM NON CONVENIENS: Inconvenient forum. Although a court may have jurisdiction over the case, the action should be tried in a more conveniently located court, one to which parties and witnesses may more easily travel, for example.

GUARDIAN AD LITEM: A guardian of an infant as to litigation, appointed to represent the infant and pursue his/her rights.

HABEAS CORPUS: You have the body. The modern writ of habeas corpus is a writ directing that a person (body) being detained (such as a prisoner) be brought before the court so that the legality of his detention can be judicially ascertained.

IN CAMERA: In private, in chambers. When a hearing is held before a judge in his chambers or when all spectators are excluded from the courtroom.

IN FORMA PAUPERIS: In the manner of a pauper. A party who proceeds in forma pauperis because of his poverty is one who is allowed to bring suit without liability for costs.

INFRA: Below, under. A word referring the reader to a later part of a book. (The opposite of supra.)

IN LOCO PARENTIS: In the place of a parent.

IN PARI DELICTO: Equally wrong; a court of equity will not grant requested relief to an applicant who is in pari delicto, or as much at fault in the transactions giving rise to the controversy as is the opponent of the applicant.

IN PARI MATERIA: On like subject matter or upon the same matter. Statutes relating to the same person or things are said to be in pari materia. It is a general rule of statutory construction that such statutes should be construed together, i.e., looked at as if they together constituted one law.

IN PERSONAM: Against the person. Jurisdiction over the person of an individual.

IN RE: In the matter of. Used to designate a proceeding involving an estate or other property.

IN REM: A term that signifies an action against the res, or thing. An action in rem is basically one that is taken directly against property, as distinguished from an action in personam, i.e., against the person.

INTER ALIA: Among other things. Used to show that the whole of a statement, pleading, list, statute, etc., has not been set forth in its entirety.

INTER PARTES: Between the parties. May refer to contracts, conveyances or other transactions having legal significance.

INTER VIVOS: Between the living. An inter vivos gift is a gift made by a living grantor, as distinguished from bequests contained in a will, which pass upon the death of the testator.

IPSO FACTO: By the mere fact itself.

JUS: Law or the entire body of law.

LEX LOCI: The law of the place; the notion that the rights of parties to a legal proceeding are governed by the law of the place where those rights arose.

MALUM IN SE: Evil or wrong in and of itself; inherently wrong. This term describes an act that is wrong by its very nature, as opposed to one which would not be wrong but for the fact that there is a specific legal prohibition against it (malum prohibitum).

MALUM PROHIBITUM: Wrong because prohibited, but not inherently evil. Used to describe something that is wrong because it is expressly forbidden by law but that is not in and of itself evil, e.g., speeding.

MANDAMUS: We command. A writ directing an official to take a certain action.

MENS REA: A guilty mind; a criminal intent. A term used to signify the mental state that accompanies a crime or other prohibited act. Some crimes require only a general mens rea (general intent to do the prohibited act), but others, like assault with intent to murder, require the existence of a specific mens rea.

MODUS OPERANDI: Method of operating; generally refers to the manner or style of a criminal in committing crimes, admissible in appropriate cases as evidence of the identity of a defendant.

NEXUS: A connection to.

NISI PRIUS: A court of first impression. A nisi prius court is one where issues of fact are tried before a judge or jury.

N.O.V. (NON OBSTANTE VEREDICTO): Notwithstanding the verdict. A judgment n.o.v. is a judgment given in favor of one party despite the fact that a verdict was returned in favor of the other party, the justification being that the verdict either had no reasonable support in fact or was contrary to law.

NUNC PRO TUNC: Now for then. This phrase refers to actions that may be taken and will then have full retroactive effect.

PENDENTE LITE: Pending the suit; pending litigation underway.

PER CAPITA: By head; beneficiaries of an estate, if they take in equal shares, take per capita.

PER CURIAM: By the court; signifies an opinion ostensibly written "by the whole court" and with no identified author.

PER SE: By itself, in itself; inherently.

PER STIRPES: By representation. Used primarily in the law of wills to describe the method of distribution where a person, generally because of death, is unable to take that which is left to him by the will of another, and therefore his heirs divide such property between them rather than take under the will individually.

PRIMA FACIE: On its face, at first sight. A prima facie case is one that is sufficient on its face, meaning that the evidence supporting it is adequate to establish the case until contradicted or overcome by other evidence.

PRO TANTO: For so much; as far as it goes. Often used in eminent domain cases when a property owner receives partial payment for his land without prejudice to his right to bring suit for the full amount he claims his land to be worth.

QUANTUM MERUIT: As much as he deserves. Refers to recovery based on the doctrine of unjust enrichment in those cases in which a party has rendered valuable services or furnished materials that were accepted and enjoyed by another under circumstances that would reasonably notify the recipient that the rendering party expected to be paid. In essence, the law implies a contract to pay the reasonable value of the services or materials furnished.

QUASI: Almost like; as if; nearly. This term is essentially used to signify that one subject or thing is almost analogous to another but that material differences between them do exist. For example, a quasi-criminal proceeding is one that is not strictly criminal but shares enough of the same characteristics to require some of the same safeguards (e.g., procedural due process must be followed in a parol hearing).

QUID PRO QUO: Something for something. In contract law, the consideration, something of value, passed between the parties to render the contract binding.

RES GESTAE: Things done; in evidence law, this principle justifies the admission of a statement that would otherwise be hearsay when it is made so closely to the event in question as to be said to be a part of it, or with such spontaneity as not to have the possibility of falsehood.

RES IPSA LOQUITUR: The thing speaks for itself. This doctrine gives rise to a rebuttable presumption of negligence when the instrumentality causing the injury was within the exclusive control of the defendant, and the injury was one that does not normally occur unless a person has been negligent.

RES JUDICATA: A matter adjudged. Doctrine which provides that once a court of competent jurisdiction has rendered a final judgment or decree on the merits, that judgment or decree is conclusive upon the parties to the case and prevents them from engaging in any other litigation on the points and issues determined therein.

RESPONDEAT SUPERIOR: Let the master reply. This doctrine holds the master liable for the wrongful acts of his servant (or the principal for his agent) in those cases in which the servant (or agent) was acting within the scope of his authority at the time of the injury.

STARE DECISIS: To stand by or adhere to that which has been decided. The common law doctrine of stare decisis attempts to give security and certainty to the law by following the policy that once a principle of law as applicable to a certain set of facts has been set forth in a decision, it forms a precedent which will subsequently be followed, even though a different decision might be made were it the first time the question had arisen. Of course, stare decisis is not an inviolable principle and is departed from in instances where there is good cause (e.g., considerations of public policy led the Supreme Court to disregard prior decisions sanctioning segregation).

SUPRA: Above. A word referring a reader to an earlier part of a book.

ULTRA VIRES: Beyond the power. This phrase is most commonly used to refer to actions taken by a corporation that are beyond the power or legal authority of the corporation.

ADDENDUM OF FRENCH DERIVATIVES

IN PAIS: Not pursuant to legal proceedings.

CHATTEL: Tangible personal property.

CY PRES: Doctrine permitting courts to apply trust funds to purposes not expressed in the trust but necessary to carry out the settlor's intent.

PER AUTRE VIE: For another's life; in property law, an estate may be granted that will terminate upon the death of someone other than the grantee.

PROFIT A PRENDRE: A license to remove minerals or other produce from land.

VOIR DIRE: Process of questioning jurors as to their predispositions about the case or parties to a proceeding in order to identify those jurors displaying bias or prejudice.

HOW TO BRIEF A CASE

A. DECIDE ON A FORMAT AND STICK TO IT

Structure is essential to a good brief. It enables you to arrange systematically the related parts that are scattered throughout most cases, thus making manageable and understandable what might otherwise seem to be an endless and unfathomable sea of information. There are, of course, an unlimited number of formats that can be utilized. However, it is best to find one that suits your needs and stick to it. Consistency breeds both efficiency and the security that when called upon you will know where to look in your brief for the information you are asked to give.

Any format, as long as it presents the essential elements of a case in an organized fashion, can be used. Experience, however, has led *Casenotes* to develop and utilize the following format because of its logical flow and universal applicability.

NATURE OF CASE: This is a brief statement of the legal character and procedural status of the case (e.g., "Appeal of a burglary conviction").

There are many different alternatives open to a litigant dissatisfied with a court ruling. The key to determining which one has been used is to discover *who is asking this court for what.*

This first entry in the brief should be kept as *short as possible.* The student should use the court's terminology if the student understands it. But since jurisdictions vary as to the titles of pleadings, the best entry is the one that apprises the student of who wants what in this proceeding, not the one that sounds most like the court's language.

CONCISE RULE OF LAW: A statement of the general principle of law that the case illustrates (e.g., "An acceptance that varies any term of the offer is considered a rejection and counteroffer").

Determining the rule of law of a case is a procedure similar to determining the issue of the case. Avoid being fooled by red herrings; there may be a few rules of law mentioned in the case excerpt, but usually only one is *the* rule with which the casebook editor is concerned. The techniques used to locate the issue, described below, may also be utilized to find the rule of law. Generally, your best guide is simply the chapter heading. It is a clue to the point the casebook editor seeks to make and should be kept in mind when reading every case in the respective section.

FACTS: A synopsis of only the essential facts of the case, i.e., those bearing upon or leading up to the issue.

The facts entry should be a short statement of the events and transactions that led one party to initiate legal proceedings against another in the first place. While some cases conveniently state the salient facts at the beginning of the decision, in other instances they will have to be culled from hiding places throughout the text, even from concurring and dissenting opinions. Some of the "facts" will often be in dispute and should be so noted. Conflicting evidence may be briefly pointed up. "Hard" facts must be included. Both must be *relevant* in order to be listed in the facts entry. It is impossible to tell what is relevant until the entire case is read, as the ultimate determination of the rights and liabilities of the parties may turn on something buried deep in the opinion.

The facts entry should never be longer than one to three *short* sentences.

It is often helpful to identify the role played by a party in a given context. For example, in a construction contract case the identification of a party as the "contractor" or "builder" alleviates the need to tell that that party was the one who was supposed to have built the house.

It is always helpful, and a good general practice, to identify the "plaintiff" and the "defendant." This may seem elementary and uncomplicated, but, especially in view of the creative editing practiced by some casebook editors, it is sometimes a difficult or even impossible task. Bear in mind that the *party presently* seeking something from this court may not be the plaintiff, and that sometimes only the cross-claim of a defendant is treated in the excerpt. Confusing or misaligning the parties can ruin your analysis and understanding of the case.

ISSUE: A statement of the general legal question answered by or illustrated in the case. For clarity, the issue is best put in the form of a question capable of a "yes" or "no" answer. In reality, the issue is simply the Concise Rule of Law put in the form of a question (e.g., "May an offer be accepted by performance?").

The major problem presented in discerning what is *the* issue in the case is that an opinion usually purports to raise and answer several questions. However, except for rare cases, only one such question is really the issue in the case. Collateral issues not necessary to the resolution of the matter in controversy are handled by the court by language known as *"obiter dictum"* or merely *"dictum."* While dicta may be included later in the brief, it has no place under the issue heading.

To find the issue, the student again asks *who wants what* and then goes on to ask *why did that party succeed or fail in getting it.* Once this is determined, the "why" should be turned into a question.

The complexity of the issues in the cases will vary, but in all cases a single-sentence question should sum up the issue. *In a few cases,* there will be two, or even more rarely, three issues of equal importance to the resolution of the case. Each should be expressed in a single-sentence question.

Since many issues are resolved by a court in coming to a final disposition of a case, the casebook editor will reproduce the portion of the opinion containing the issue or issues most relevant to the area of law under scrutiny. A noted law professor gave this advice: "Close the book; look at the title on the cover." Chances are, if it is Property, the student need not concern himself with whether, for example, the federal government's treatment of the plaintiff's land really raises a federal question sufficient to support jurisdiction on this ground in federal court.

The same rule applies to chapter headings designating sub-areas within the subjects. They tip the student off as to what the text is designed to teach. The cases are arranged in a casebook to show a progression or development of the law, so that the preceding cases may also help.

It is also most important to remember to *read the notes and questions* at the end of a case to determine what the editors wanted the student to have gleaned from it.

HOLDING AND DECISION: This section should succinctly explain the rationale of the court in arriving at its decision. In capsulizing the "reasoning" of the court, it should always include an application of the general rule or rules of law to the specific facts of the case. Hidden justifications come to light in this entry; the reasons for the state of the law, the public policies, the biases and prejudices, those considerations that influence the justices' thinking and, ultimately, the outcome of the case. At the end, there should be a short indication of the disposition or procedural resolution of the case (e.g., "Decision of the trial court for Mr. Smith (P) reversed").

The foregoing format is designed to help you "digest" the reams of case material with which you will be faced in your law school career. Once mastered by practice, it will place at your fingertips the information the authors of your casebooks have sought to impart to you in case-by-case illustration and analysis.

B. BE AS ECONOMICAL AS POSSIBLE IN BRIEFING CASES

Once armed with a format that encourages succinctness, it is as important to be economical with regard to the time spent on the actual reading of the case as it is to be economical in the writing of the brief itself. This does not mean "skimming" a case. Rather, it means reading the case with an "eye" trained to recognize into which "section" of your brief a particular passage or line fits and having a system for quickly and precisely marking the case so that the passages fitting any one particular part of the brief can be easily identified and brought together in a concise and accurate manner when the brief is actually written.

It is of no use to simply repeat everything in the opinion of the court; the student should only record enough information to trigger his or her recollection of what the court said. Nevertheless, an accurate statement of the "law of the case," i.e., the legal principle applied to the facts, is absolutely essential to class preparation and to learning the law under the case method.

To that end, it is important to develop a "shorthand" that you can use to make margin notations. These notations will tell you at a glance in which section of the brief you will be placing that particular passage or portion of the opinion.

Some students prefer to underline all the salient portions of the opinion (with a pencil or colored underliner marker), making marginal notations as they go along. Others prefer the color-coded method of underlining, utilizing different colors of markers to underline the salient portions of the case, each separate color being used to represent a different section of the brief. For example, blue underlining could be used for passages relating to the concise rule of law, yellow for those relating to the issue, and green for those relating to the holding and decision, etc. While it has its advocates, the color-coded method can be confusing and time-consuming (all that time spent on changing colored markers). Furthermore, it can interfere with the continuity and concentration many students deem essential to the reading of a case for maximum comprehension. In the end, however, it is a matter of personal preference and style. Just remember, whatever method you use, underlining must be used sparingly or its value is lost.

For those who take the marginal notation route, an efficient and easy method is to go along underlining the key portions of the case and placing in the margin alongside them the following "markers" to indicate where a particular passage or line "belongs" in the brief you will write:

N (NATURE OF CASE)
CR (CONCISE RULE OF LAW)
I (ISSUE)
HC (HOLDING AND DECISION, relates to the CONCISE RULE OF LAW behind the decision)
HR (HOLDING AND DECISION, gives the RATIONALE or reasoning behind the decision)
HA (HOLDING AND DECISION, APPLIES the general principle(s) of law to the facts of the case to arrive at the decision)

Remember that a particular passage may well contain information necessary to more than one part of your brief, in which case you simply note that in the margin. If you are using the color-coded underlining method instead of margin notation, simply make asterisks or checks in the margin next to the passage in question in the colors that indicate the additional sections of the brief where it might be utilized.

The economy of utilizing "shorthand" in marking cases for briefing can be maintained in the actual brief writing process itself by utilizing "law student shorthand" within the brief. There are many commonly used words and phrases for which abbreviations can be substituted in your briefs (and in your class notes also). You can develop abbreviations that are personal to you and which will save you a lot of time. A reference list of briefing abbreviations will be found elsewhere in this book.

C. USE BOTH THE BRIEFING PROCESS AND THE BRIEF AS A LEARNING TOOL

Now that you have a format and the tools for briefing cases efficiently, the most important thing is to make the time spent in briefing profitable to you and to make the most advantageous use of the briefs you create. Of course, the briefs are invaluable for classroom reference when you are called upon to explain or analyze a particular case. However, they are also useful in reviewing for exams. A quick glance at the fact summary should bring the case to mind, and a rereading of the concise rule of law should enable you to go over the underlying legal concept in your mind, how it was applied in that particular case, and how it might apply in other factual settings.

As to the value to be derived from engaging in the briefing process itself, there is an immediate benefit that arises from being forced to sift through the essential facts and reasoning from the court's opinion and to succinctly express them in your own words in your brief. The process ensures that you understand the case and the point that it illustrates, and that means you will be ready to absorb further analysis and information brought forth in class. It also ensures you will have something to say when called upon in class. The briefing process helps develop a mental agility for getting to the *gist* of a case and for identifying, expounding on, and applying the legal concepts and issues found there. Of most immediate concern, that is the mental process on which you must rely in taking law school examinations. Of more lasting concern, it is also the mental process upon which a lawyer relies in serving his clients and in making his living.

Notes

TABLE OF CASES

A

B

C

D

E

F

G

H

I

Continued on next page

TABLE OF CASES (Continued)

TABLE OF CASES (Continued)

W

Z

CHAPTER 1
INTRODUCTION TO THE STUDY OF CONTRACT LAW

QUICK REFERENCE RULES OF LAW

1. **Introductory Cases and Problems.** A party who volunteers his services to another is not normally entitled to restitution for their reasonable value. (Bailey v. West)

   [For more information on mutual assent requirement, see Casenote Law Outline on Contracts, Chapter 1, § I, The Agreement Process — Manifesting Mutual Consent.]

2. **Introductory Cases and Problems.** Forbearance is valuable consideration. (Hamer v. Sidway)

   [For more information on the concept of legal detriment, see Casenote Law Outline on Contracts, Chapter 2, § I, Valuable Consideration: The Bargained-for Incursion of Legal Detriment.]

3. **Introductory Cases and Problems.** A promise may be legally binding without consideration if it reasonably induced action or forbearance and if injustice will be avoided by its enforcement. (Ricketts v. Scothorn)

   [For more information on promissory estoppel, see Casenote Law Outline on Contracts, Chapter 2, § II, Substitutes for Valuable Consideration as Grounds for Imparting Liability Consequences for Breaching a Promise.]

4. **Introductory Cases and Problems.** One who signs a contract has a duty to read it or, if it is written in a language which he cannot read, to have someone read it to him before he signs it, and "one who refrains from reading a contract and in ignorance of its terms voluntarily assents thereto will not be relieved from his bad bargain" (i.e., will be obligated according to the terms of the contract). (Williams v. Walker-Thomas Furniture Co.)

   [For more information on adhesion contracts, see Casenote Law Outline on Contracts, Chapter 3, § IV, Defenses Centered on the Deceptive or Coercive Formation Tactics of One of the Parties.]

5. **Introductory Cases and Problems.** Where, in light of the general commercial background of a particular case, it appears that gross inequality of bargaining power between the parties has led to the formation of a contract on terms to which one party has had no meaningful choice, a court should refuse to enforce such a contract on the ground that it is unconscionable. (Williams v. Walker-Thomas Furniture Co.)

   [For more information on unconscionability, see Casenote Law Outline on Contracts, Chapter 3, § IV, Defenses Centered on the Deceptive or Coercive Formation Tactics of One of the Parties.]

6. **Introductory Cases and Problems.** A physician who breaches his contractual obligation to effect a particular result is liable to his patient for the cost of any measures or treatment necessitated by the physician's breach and for any pain and suffering resulting therefrom. (Sullivan v. O'Connor)

   [For more information on compensatory damages, see Casenote Law Outline on Contracts, Chapter 7, § III, Remedies for Breach of Contract.]

BAILEY v. WEST

105 R.I. 61, 249 A.2d 414 (1969).

NATURE OF CASE: Action for value of services.

FACT SUMMARY: Bascom's Folly, a racehorse, was purchased by West (D). He arrived lame, and West (D) had him shipped back to the owner.

CONCISE RULE OF LAW: A party who volunteers his services to another is not normally entitled to restitution for their reasonable value.

FACTS: West (D) purchased a racehorse from Strauss. When the horse arrived, it was lame. West (D) sent the horse back, but Strauss refused it. The driver telephoned West's (D) trainer for instructions. The trainer said the horse was not West's (D) and West (D) would not pay anything for its care. The driver delivered the horse to Bailey (P). He informed Bailey (P) that there was a dispute over ownership. Bailey (P) cared for the horse for a number of months, sending bills to both Strauss and West (D). After Strauss prevailed against West (D) in a suit for the purchase price, Bailey (P) brought suit against West (D) for the reasonable value of the services rendered the horse. The court found that there was a contract "implied in fact" between the parties and that West (D) was liable for the services. West (D) appealed on the basis that the parties had never intended a contract be formed, so there was no "implied in fact" contract. Bailey (P) also could not recover in quasi-contract since he was a mere volunteer.

ISSUE: May a mere volunteer recover for the value of services gratuitously rendered?

HOLDING AND DECISION: (Paolino, J.) No. A quasi-contract is imposed by law, generally to avoid unjust enrichment. Where a benefit is conferred which aids the defendant, courts hold that it is inequitable for him not to pay for it. However, where the service was gratuitously rendered without being requested, the plaintiff is a mere volunteer and will normally be denied restitution for the reasonable value of the services. Here, Bailey (P) was never authorized to perform a service for West (D). They had had no prior dealings. Bailey (P) knew of the disputed ownership claims. Further, Bailey (P) knew from the bill of lading that the horse was being returned by West (D). Under these circumstances, Bailey (P) could not reasonably believe that West (D) would either authorize or pay for his services. West (D) is not liable in quasi-contract. With respect to the trial court's finding of a contract "implied in fact," the court apparently ignored the requirement that it must have appeared that the parties intended to enter into a contractual relationship. There was no mutual agreement or misleading conduct between the parties. Indeed, Bailey (P) never even spoke to West (D) or one of his agents. Since the intent of the parties is an essential element to recovery in an "implied in fact" contract, Bailey (P) cannot recover. Reversed.

EDITOR'S ANALYSIS: A mere volunteer may recover when the benefits are conferred by mistake and the defendant accepted them knowing of plaintiff's error. For example, if plaintiff paints defendant's house by mistake, thinking it belongs to another, and the defendant, realizing a mistake has been made, allows plaintiff to complete the work, he will be estopped from denying the existence of a contract and will be liable for the reasonable value of the services.

[For more information on mutual assent requirement, see Casenote Law Outline on Contracts, Chapter 1, § I, The Agreement Process — Manifesting Mutual Consent.]

NOTES:

HAMER v. SIDWAY

N.Y. Ct. App., 124 N.Y. 538, 27 N.E. 256 (1891).

NATURE OF CASE: Action on appeal to recover upon a contract which is supported by forbearance of a right as consideration.

FACT SUMMARY: William Story (D) promised to pay $5,000 to William Story 2d (P) if he would forbear in the use of liquor, tobacco, swearing, or playing cards or billiards for money until he became 21 years of age.

CONCISE RULE OF LAW: Forbearance is valuable consideration.

FACTS: William Story (D) agreed with his nephew William Story 2d (P) that if W. Story 2d (P) would refrain from drinking liquor, using tobacco, swearing, and playing cards or billiards for money until he became 21 years of age, W. Story (D) would pay him $5,000. Upon becoming 21 years of age, W. Story 2d (P) received a letter from W. Story (D) stating he had earned the $5,000, and it would be kept at interest for him. Twelve years later, W. Story (D) died, and this action was brought by the assignee of W. Story 2d (P) against the executor (D) of the estate of W. Story (D). Judgment was entered in favor of W. Story 2d (P) at the trial at special term and was reversed at general term of the supreme court. The assignee of W. Story 2d (P) appealed.

ISSUE: Is forbearance on the part of a promisee sufficient consideration to support a contract?

HOLDING AND DECISION: (Parker, J.) Yes. Valuable consideration may consist either of some right, interest, profit, or benefit accruing to the one party or some forbearance, detriment, loss, or responsibility given, suffered, or undertaken by the other.

EDITOR'S ANALYSIS: The surrendering or forgoing of a legal right constitutes a sufficient consideration for a contract if the minds of the parties meet on the relinquishing of the right as a consideration. Consideration may be forbearance to sue on a claim, extension of time, or any other giving up of a legal right in consideration of a promise.

[For more information on the concept of legal detriment, see Casenote Law Outline on Contracts, Chapter 2, § I, Valuable Consideration: The Bargained-for Incursion of Legal Detriment.]

NOTES:

RICKETTS v. SCOTHORN

Neb. Sup. Ct., 57 Neb 51, 77 N.W. 365 (1898).

NATURE OF CASE: Action to compel payment on a promissory note given without consideration.

FACT SUMMARY: In reliance on her grandfather's promise to pay money, Scothorn (P) quit her employment.

CONCISE RULE OF LAW: A promise may be legally binding without consideration if it reasonably induced action or forbearance and if injustice will be avoided by its enforcement.

FACTS: J.C. Ricketts gave his granddaughter, Scothorn (P), a promissory note for $2,000 on demand. Ricketts indicated that the note was for the purpose of freeing Scothorn (P) from the necessity of working. Scothorn (P) immediately quit her employment. J.C. Ricketts thereafter died, and Scothorn (P) sued A.D. Ricketts (D), executor of the estate, for the amount due on the note.

ISSUE: Is the abandonment — induced by a promise — of a job sufficient reliance to estop the promisor from refuting that promise on the ground that it was given without consideration?

HOLDING AND DECISION: (Sullivan, J.) Yes. When a promisee is induced by a promise to change his position in accordance with the real or apparent intention of the promisor, the doctrine of estoppel precludes the promisor from later claiming that the promise was not supported by consideration. This remedy is equitable in nature and is designed to prevent the gross injustice which would otherwise result.

EDITOR'S ANALYSIS: In this leading case, the court recognizes that Scothorn's (P) abandoning her job was not consideration for the note. Rather, the note was a pure gift and, thus, absent reliance, would ordinarily not be enforced because of lack of a bargained-for consideration. Traditionally, the estoppel doctrine had been limited to cases where one party had represented a fact to another party who then relied on the fact as represented. In the present case, the court for the first time extended the estoppel doctrine to promissory expressions (hence, "promissory estoppel"). (Cf. Rest. (2d) § 90, which states the most recent version of the doctrine.) Caveat: Courts have often confused and blended the doctrine of estoppel with the doctrine of consideration, resulting in such statements as: "The reliance on the promise serves as the consideration for that promise." This is conceptually misleading since the promissory estoppel doctrine is basically a twentieth-century exception to the general rule which requires every enforceable promise to be supported by a bargained-for consideration.

[For more information on promissory estoppel, see Casenote Law Outline on Contracts, Chapter 2, § II, Substitutes for Valuable Consideration as Grounds for Imparting Liability Consequences for Breaching a Promise.]

WILLIAMS v. WALKER-THOMAS FURNITURE CO.

D.C. Ct. App., 198 A.2d 914 (1964).

NATURE OF CASE: Appeal from decision upholding a contract.

FACT SUMMARY: After Williams (D) purchased items from the Walker-Thomas Furniture Co. (P) under installment contracts providing that payments, after the first purchase, would be prorated on all outstanding purchases, she defaulted in payments.

CONCISE RULE OF LAW: One who signs a contract has a duty to read it or, if it is written in a language which he cannot read, to have someone read it to him before he signs it, and "one who refrains from reading a contract and in ignorance of its terms voluntarily assents thereto will not be relieved from his bad bargain" (i.e., will be obligated according to the terms of the contract).

FACTS: Williams (D), a woman with little education, was separated from her husband and maintained herself and her seven children, on $218 a month from welfare. During the period from 1957–1962, she purchased several household items on an installment plan from the Walker-Thomas Furniture Co. (P). In all, Williams (D) signed 14 contracts for these purchases, with each containing a long paragraph in "extremely fine print" providing that all payments, after the first purchase, were to be prorated on all purchases then outstanding. This clause had the effect of keeping a balance due on all items until the time balance was completely eliminated (i.e., the Furniture Co. (P) retained title to the first purchase until all 14 purchases were completely paid for). After she purchased the 14th item, Williams (D) defaulted on her time payments, and the Furniture Co. (P) filed a complaint in replevin for possession of all 14 items. After the Furniture Co. (P) obtained, through this writ, a bed, chest of drawers, washing machine, and stereo set purchased by Williams (D), Williams (D) brought this appeal, claiming that she had not read the contract before she signed it and, therefore, did not understand its terms.

ISSUE: Is a party to a contract excused from his performance under that contract if he did not read it and, therefore, did not understand its terms?

HOLDING AND DECISION: (Quinn, J.) No. One who signs a contract has a duty to read it or, if it is written in a language which he cannot read, to have someone read it to him before he signs it, and "one who refrains from reading a contract and in ignorance of its terms voluntarily assents thereto will not be relieved from his bad bargain" (i.e., will be obligated according to the terms of the contract). Of course, if a person is induced to sign a contract through fraud or misrepresentation, he is relieved from any obligations under that contract. Here, though, there was no fraud or misrepresentation, and Williams (D) cannot be relieved of her obligations under the contract merely because she did not read its terms. Furthermore, even though the actions of the Furniture Co. (P) (i.e., selling expensive items while knowing about Williams' (D) limited income) should be condemned, there is no ground for declaring the contract void as contrary to public policy. Affirmed.

EDITOR'S ANALYSIS: This case was later remanded by the United States Court of Appeals and the result reversed on the basis that the contract involved was "unconscionable." Section 2-302 of the U.C.C. provides that "if a court finds a contract or any clause of a contract to have been unconscionable at the time it was made, the court may refuse to enforce it." However, the U.C.C. does not define unconscionability, and many factors have been used in considering whether a contract is unconscionable. Unequal bargaining power has been recognized as an important element, but it has not in itself usually been held to render a contract unconscionable. Some courts, though, have held that where a stronger party has control of negotiations over a weaker, more ignorant, unsophisticated party, there is a presumption that any unreasonable, contested terms are unconscionable.

[For more information on adhesion contracts, see Casenote Law Outline on Contracts, Chapter 3, § IV, Defenses Centered on the Deceptive or Coercive Formation Tactics of One of the Parties.]

NOTES:

WILLIAMS v. WALKER-THOMAS FURNITURE CO.

350 F.2d 445 (D.C. Cir. 1965).

NATURE OF CASE: Action in replevin.

FACT SUMMARY: Williams (D) made a series of purchases, on credit, from Walker-Thomas (P) but defaulted on her payments.

CONCISE RULE OF LAW: Where, in light of the general commercial background of a particular case, it appears that gross inequality of bargaining power between the parties has led to the formation of a contract on terms to which one party has had no meaningful choice, a court should refuse to enforce such a contract on the ground that it is unconscionable.

FACTS: Beginning about 1957, Walker-Thomas (P), a retail furniture company, began using a standard form contract for all credit transactions which contained, inter alia, a clause by which the company (P) reserved the right, upon default by a purchaser, to repossess all items contemporaneously being purchased by the buyer at the time of the repossession. This clause was accompanied by one which stated that all credit purchases made from Walker-Thomas (P) were to be handled through one account, with each installment payment spread pro rata over all items purchased (even where purchased separately and at different times) until all items were paid for. Williams (D) began purchasing items from Walker-Thomas (P) in 1957. In 1962, she bought a stereo set there. When she defaulted on a payment soon thereafter, Walker-Thomas (P) filed this action to replevy (i.e., repossess) all items she had purchased (and was still paying for) since 1957. From judgment for Walker-Thomas (P), this appeal followed.

ISSUE: May a court refuse to enforce an unreasonable contract, even though no evidence of fraud can be produced?

HOLDING AND DECISION: (Wright, J.) Yes. Where, in light of the general commercial background of a particular case, it appears that gross inequality of bargaining power between the parties has led to the formation of a contract on terms to which one party has had no meaningful choice, a court should refuse to enforce such a contract on the ground that it is unconscionable. It is true that the common law, operating by the caveat emptor rationale, refused to look into the essential fairness of a contract absent evidence of out-and-out fraud. The U.C.C., however, notably § 2-302, as adopted in this jurisdiction, has accepted the rule that courts should seek to prevent overreaching in contracts of adhesion such as the one at bar. Williams (D), and others, comes from a socioeconomic class for which credit is difficult to obtain. To permit Walker-Thomas (P) to exploit this condition with provisions such as those pointed out above is clearly unconscionable. Judgment reversed, and the trial court is ordered to undertake an examination of these provisions, in light of this opinion.

DISSENT: (Danaher, J.) The court ignores many policy considerations in its decision today. For one, the high risk of granting credit to the poor for companies like Walker-Thomas (P) is not even addressed. A more cautious approach is warranted.

EDITOR'S ANALYSIS: This case points up the major application which the U.C.C. § 2-302 concept of unconscionability has had to date: adhesion (i.e., form) contracts. Note that the general common law rule regarding such contracts remains the general rule today. That rule is that a person who signs a contract will be held responsible for any clauses or conditions which a reasonable man making a reasonable inspection would have discovered. The U.C.C. rule merely qualifies this to say that where one party to a form contract has no real choice over whether to accept the terms because of his relative economic position, then the fact he knows of the terms will not be enough to constitute a "meeting of the minds" on his part necessary to form a valid contract.

[For more information on unconscionability, see Casenote Law Outline on Contracts, Chapter 3, § IV, Defenses Centered on the Deceptive or Coercive Formation Tactics of One of the Parties.]

NOTES:

SULLIVAN v. O'CONNOR

Mass. Sup. Jud. Ct., 363 Mass. 579, 296 N.E.2d 183 (1973).

NATURE OF CASE: Negligence and breach of contract.

FACT SUMMARY: O'Connor (D), a doctor, promised to improve Sullivan's (P) appearance by cosmetic surgery. In fact, O'Connor's (D) efforts left Sullivan (P) with more of a disfigurement than previously.

CONCISE RULE OF LAW: A physician who breaches his contractual obligation to effect a particular result is liable to his patient for the cost of any measures or treatment necessitated by the physician's breach and for any pain and suffering resulting therefrom.

FACTS: Dr. O'Connor (D) expressly promised to enhance and improve the appearance of Sullivan (P), an entertainer, by performing cosmetic surgery on her nose. However, after two operations, Sullivan's (P) nose looked worse than it had previously. As a result of the surgery, the nose was disfigured, apparently permanently. Sullivan (P) sued to recover damages from O'Connor (D), alleging both breach of contract and medical malpractice, the latter theory of recovery being based on negligence. A jury trial resulted in a verdict for Sullivan (P) on the contract count and for O'Connor (D) on the count alleging malpractice. On appeal, O'Connor (D) took exception to the trial judge's instruction that Sullivan (P) could recover all out-of-pocket expenses occasioned by O'Connor's (D) breach of his promise, plus any pain and suffering caused by her condition or by a third operation which Sullivan (P) endured in a vain attempt to restore her nose to its previous shape.

ISSUE: If a doctor contracts to achieve a particular result for a patient, is the patient's recovery for breach limited to the amount of his out-of-pocket expenditures?

HOLDING AND DECISION: (Kaplan, J.) No. A physician who breaches his contractual obligation to effect a particular result is liable to his patient for the cost of any measures or treatment necessitated by the physician's breach and for any pain and suffering resulting therefrom. Because contracts involving promises by physicians are necessarily predicated on matters which can be no more certain than medical science itself, it does not seem fair to award a patient the difference in value between the actual condition of his bodily part after treatment and the condition which the physician promised to bring about. But the patient should be entitled to recover more than just the money he expended on the doctor's treatment. It is a reasonable compromise which permits the patient to recover all his out-of-pocket expenses, including additional costs incurred in trying to remedy the doctor's failure to perform his promise, plus an amount which compensates him for any pain and suffering, physical or mental, occasioned by the physician's breach.

EDITOR'S ANALYSIS: Ordinarily, a nonbreaching party is entitled to recover such compensatory damages as will place him in the same situation as he would have enjoyed had the contract never been breached. Under some circumstances, the nonbreaching party will be awarded restitution only of whatever he has given in performance of the contract, i.e., he will be restored to the position he occupied prior to execution.

[For more information on compensatory damages, see Casenote Law Outline on Contracts, Chapter 7, § III, Remedies for Breach of Contract.]

NOTES:

CHAPTER 2
THE BASES OF PROMISSORY LIABILITY

QUICK REFERENCE RULES OF LAW

1. **Bargain Requirement.** To be legally enforceable, an executory promise must be supported by sufficient, bargained-for consideration. (Kirksey v. Kirksey)

    [For more information on donative transactions, see Casenote Law Outline on Contracts, Chapter 2, § I, Valuable Consideration: The Bargained-for Incursion of Legal Detriment.]

2. **Bargain Requirement.** A good consideration exists if one refrains from doing anything that he has a right to do. (Langer v. Superior Steel Corp.)

    [For more information on the concept of the legal detriment, see Casenote Law Outline on Contracts, Chapter 2, § I, Valuable Consideration: The Bargained-for Incursion of Legal Detriment.]

3. **Bargain Requirement.** A consideration is deemed valid only when it consists of a bargained-for exchange between the contracting parties. (Bogigian v. Bogigian)

    [For more information on bargained-for consideration, see Casenote Law Outline on Contracts, Chapter 2, § I, Valuable Consideration: The Bargained-for Incursion of Legal Detriment.]

4. **Bargain Requirement.** Motive is not sufficient consideration for a contract. (Thomas v. Thomas)

    [For more information on legal considerations, see Casenote Law Outline on Contracts, Chapter 2, § I, Valuable Consideration: The Bargained-for Incursion of Legal Detriment.]

5. **Sufficiency of Exchange in General.** Consideration must have value to the buyer; however, there is no requirement that an idea used as consideration must have novelty. (Apfel v. Prudential-Bache Securities, Inc.)

    [For more information on value of consideration, see Casenote Law Outline on Contracts, Chapter 2, § I, Valuable Consideration: The Bargained-for Incursion of Legal Detriment.]

6. **Sufficiency of Exchange in General.** A court may refuse to enforce a contract for the sale of goods on the ground that an excessive price term renders the contract unconscionable. (Jones v. Star Credit Corp.)

    [For more information on substantive unconscionability, see Casenote Law Outline on Contracts, Chapter 3, § III, Defenses Rooted in Social Objection to the Content of the Bargain.]

7. **Sufficiency of Exchange in General.** A consideration given by one party which is only token or nominal does not constitute sufficient consideration. (In re Greene)

    [For more information on token considerations, see Casenote Law Outline on Contracts, Chapter 2, § I, Valuable Consideration: The Bargained-for Incursion of Legal Detriment.]

8. **Sufficiency of Exchange in General.** Forbearance to assert an invalid claim may serve as consideration for a return promise if the parties at the time of the settlement reasonably believed in good faith that the claim was valid. (Fiege v. Boehm)

    [For more information on promise to forbear the assertion or abandon the prosecution of a legal claim, see Casenote Law Outline on Contracts, Chapter 2, § I, Valuable Consideration: The Bargained-for Incursion of Legal Detriment.]

9. **Pre-Existing Duty Rule.** Neither economic disasters nor acceptance of partial payments will be considered adequate consideration for the modification of contractual obligations. (Levine v. Blumenthal)

[For more information on modification, see Casenote Law Outline on Contracts, Chapter 2, § I, Valuable Consideration: The Bargained-for Incursion of Legal Detriment.]

10. **Pre-Existing Duty Rule.** A promise to pay a man for doing that which he is already under contract to do is without consideration. (Alaska Packers' Association v. Domenico)

[For more information on preexisting duty, see Casenote Law Outline on Contracts, Chapter 2, § I, Valuable Consideration: The Bargained-for Incursion of Legal Detriment.]

11. **Pre-Existing Duty Rule.** An agreement by which a party is promised additional compensation for performing a duty which he is already contractually obligated to undertake may be enforced if the new agreement was voluntarily entered into and was prompted by the occurrence of events which were not anticipated when the original contract was executed. (Angel v. Murray)

[For more information on modifications which pass muster under the preexisting duty rule, see Casenote Law Outline on Contracts, Chapter 2, § I, Valuable Consideration: The Bargained-for Incursion of Legal Detriment.]

12. **Mutuality of Obligation.** Where in a purchase agreement the buyer has reserved an alternative by which he may, at his own discretion, buy nothing at all, the contract lacks mutuality and may be enforced by neither party. (Rehm-Zeiher Co. v. F.G. Walker Co.)

[For more information on the illusory promise, see Casenote Law Outline on Contracts , Chapter 2, § I, Valuable Consideration: The Bargained-for Incursion of Legal Detriment.]

13. **Mutuality of Obligation.** Where one party promises to sell to another all that the latter can use, the obligation of the parties to sell and buy must be mutual to render the contract binding. (McMichael v. Price)

[For more information on requirement contracts, see Casenote Law Outline on Contracts, Chapter 2, § I, Valuable Consideration: The Bargained-for Incursion of Legal Detriment.]

14. **Mutuality of Obligation.** While an express promise may be lacking, the whole writing may be instinct with an obligation — an implied promise — imperfectly expressed so as to form a valid contract. (Wood v. Lucy, Lady Duff-Gordon)

[For more information on implication of promises and U.C.C. § 2-306(2), see Casenote Law Outline on Contracts, Chapter 2, § I, Valuable Consideration: The Bargained-for Incursion of Legal Detriment.]

15. **Mutuality of Obligation.** A contractual condition calling for the subjective satisfaction of a party imposes a duty of good faith in the exercise of the party's discretion and is not illusory. (Omni Group, Inc. v. Seattle-First National Bank)

[For more information on illusory promises, see Casenote Law Outline on Contracts, Chapter 2, § I, Valuable Consideration: The Bargained-for Incursion of Legal Detriment.]

16. **Moral Obligation.** A moral obligation is insufficient as consideration for a promise. (Mills v. Wyman)

[For more information on moral obligation, see Casenote Law Outline on Contracts, Chapter 2, § I, Valuable Consideration: The Bargained-for Incursion of Legal Detriment.]

17. **Moral Obligation.** Moral obligations alone are not adequate consideration to support a contract. (Manwill v. Oyler)

[For more information on moral consideration, see Casenote Law Outline on Contracts, Chapter 2, § I, Valuable Consideration: The Bargained-for Incursion of Legal Detriment.]

18. **Moral Obligation.** A moral obligation is a sufficient consideration to support a subsequent promise to pay where the promisor has received a material benefit. (Webb v. McGowin)

[For more information on enforcement of moral obligation, see Casenote Law Outline on Contracts, Chapter 2, § II, Substitutes for Valuable Consideration as Grounds for Imparting Liability Consequences for Breaching a Promise.]

19. **Moral Obligation.** A voluntary action of a humanitarian nature will not be adequate consideration for a subsequent promise. (Harrington v. Taylor)

[For more information on donative transactions, see Casenote Law Outline on Contracts, Chapter 2, § I, Valuable Consideration: The Bargained-for Incursion of Legal Detriment.]

20. **Promissory Estoppel.** When the promisor requires that the promisee do anything in exchange for the promise, there is adequate consideration present when dealing with charitable contributors. (Allegheny College v. National Chautaugua County Bank of Jamestown)

[For more information on "economic adequacy" of consideration, see Casenote Law Outline on Contracts, Chapter 2, § I, Valuable Consideration: The Bargained-for Incursion of Legal Detriment.]

21. **Promissory Estoppel.** A promise which the promisor should reasonably expect to induce action or forbearance of a definite and substantial character on the part of the promisee and which does induce such action or forbearance is binding if injustice can be avoided only by enforcement of the promise. (Feinberg v. Pfeiffer Co.)

[For more information on promissory estoppel, see Casenote Law Outline on Contracts, Chapter 2, § II, Substitutes for Valuable Consideration as Grounds for Imparting Liability Consequences for Breaching a Promise.]

22. **Promissory Estoppel.** One resigning employment in reliance on a job offer may recover damages if the offer is withdrawn. (Grouse v. Group Health Plan, Inc.)

[For more information on promissory estoppel, see Casenote Law Outline on Contracts, Chapter 2, § II, Substitutes for Valuable Consideration as Grounds for Imparting Liability Consequences for Breaching a Promise.]

23. **Promissory Estoppel.** Under the doctrine of promissory estoppel, a court should consider all aspects of a transaction's substance in determining whether enforcement is necessary to prevent an injustice. (Cohen v. Cowles Media Co.)

24. **"Within the Statute:" The "One Year" Clause.** The Statute of Frauds, requiring a writing for an agreement that is not to be performed within one year from the making thereof, will not render unenforceable an oral contract that fails to specify explicitly the time for performance, even when performance will likely take more than one year. (C.R. Klewin, Inc. v. Flagship Properties, Inc.)

[For more information on the Statute of Frauds, see Casenote Law Outline on Contracts, Chapter 3, § V, Defenses Arising from the Form of the Bargain.]

25. "Within the Statute:" The "One Year" Clause. An oral agreement which may, by its terms, be performed within one year is not within the Statute of Frauds. (North Shore Bottling Co. v. C. Schmidt & Sons, Inc.)

[For more information on the Statute of Frauds, see Casenote Law Outline on Contracts, Chapter 3, § V, Defenses Arising from the Form of the Bargain.]

26. "Within the Statute:" The "One Year" Clause. The complete performance of one party to an oral agreement takes the agreement out of the one-year provision of the Statute of Frauds. (Mason v. Anderson)

[For more information on the Statute of Frauds and equitable estoppel, see Casenote Law Outline on Contracts, Chapter 3, § V, Defenses Arising from the Form of the Bargain.]

27. Compliance with the Statute: The "One Year" Clause. The Statute of Frauds does not require the memorandum expressing the contract to be in one document. It may be pieced together out of separate writings, connected with one another either expressly or by the internal evidence of subject matter and occasion. (Crabtree v. Elizabeth Arden Sales Corp.)

[For more information on the Statute of Frauds and extrinsic evidence, see Casenote Law Outline on Contracts, Chapter 3, § V, Defenses Arising from the Form of the Bargain.]

28. Effective of Noncompliance. A party asserting the Statute of Frauds as a defense may not be deposed for the sole purpose of eliciting an admission that a contract was made. (DF Activities Corporation v. Brown)

[For more information on the Statute of Frauds, see Casenote Law Outline on Contracts, Chapter 3, § V, Defenses Arising from the Form of the Bargain.]

KIRKSEY v. KIRKSEY

Ala. Sup. Ct., 8 Ala. 131 (1845).

NATURE OF CASE: Action to recover damages for breach of a promise.

FACT SUMMARY: Kirksey (D) promised "Sister Antillico" (P) a place to raise her family "if you come down and see me."

CONCISE RULE OF LAW: To be legally enforceable, an executory promise must be supported by sufficient, bargained-for consideration.

FACTS: Kirksey (D) wrote to "Sister Antillico" (P) a letter containing the following clause: "If you will come down and see me, I will let you have a place to raise your family." "Sister Antillico" (P) moved 60 miles to Kirksey's (D) residence, where she remained for over two years. Kirksey (D) then required her to leave, although her family was not yet "raised." "Sister Antillico" (P) contended that the loss which she sustained in moving was sufficient consideration to support Kirksey's (D) promise to furnish her with "a place" until she could raise her family.

ISSUE: Is a promise on the condition "If you will come down and see me" given as a bargained exchange for the promisee's "coming down and seeing" the promisor?

HOLDING AND DECISION: (Ormond, J.) No. Such a promise is a promise to make a gift. Any expenses incurred by the promisee in "coming down and seeing" are merely conditions necessary to acceptance of the gift. In this case, Kirksey (D) did not appear to be bargaining either for "Sister Antillico's" presence or for her 60-mile move. Instead, Kirksey (D) merely wished to assist her out of what he perceived as a grievous and difficult situation.

EDITOR'S ANALYSIS: This well-known case demonstrates the court's insistence on finding a bargained-for exchange before it will enforce an executory promise. A promise to make a gift is generally not legally binding until it is executed. Compare Williston's famous hypothetical in which a benevolent man says to a tramp: "If you go around the corner to the clothing shop there, you may purchase an overcoat on my credit." This hypo highlights the conceptual problem of the present case in that it is unreasonable to construe the walk around the corner as the price of the promise, yet it is a legal detriment to the tramp to make the walk. Perhaps a reasonable (though not conclusive) guideline is the extent to which the happening of the condition will benefit the promisor. The present case might be decided differently today under the doctrine of promissory estoppel which had not yet been developed in 1845.

[For more information on donative transactions, see Casenote Law Outline on Contracts, Chapter 2, § I, Valuable Consideration: The Bargained-for Incursion of Legal Detriment.]

X

BOGIGIAN v. BOGIGIAN

Ind. Ct. of App., 551 N.E.2d 1149 (1990).

NATURE OF THE CASE: Appeal from refusal to release judgment unsupported by consideration.

FACT SUMMARY: After Bogigian (P) was misled to release the judgment she had obtained against her husband Bogigian (D) in a divorce decree, the release was ruled voidable since it was not supported by valid consideration.

CONCISE RULE OF LAW: A consideration is deemed valid only when it consists of a bargained-for exchange between the contracting parties.

FACTS: Bogigian (P) obtained a $10,300 judgment on the family home against her husband, David Bogigian (D), in a divorce action. One year later, Bogigian (P) signed documents releasing her husband (D) from the judgment, believing she was releasing the mortgage on the house so that it could be sold. Subsequently, Bogigian (P) received $5 as her share of the sale's proceeds. Bogigian (P) sought to enforce the $10,300 judgment against her husband (D) claiming that the release was not supported by valid consideration. Bogigian (D) argued that his wife benefited from the satisfaction of the mortgage obligation and such a benefit is sufficient consideration to support the judgment release she had signed. From judgment for Bogigian (P), her husband (D) appealed.

ISSUE: Can a benefit or detriment that is not a bargained-for exchange by the contractual parties be deemed a valid consideration?

HOLDING AND DECISION: (Buchanan, J.) No. A contract must be supported by a valid "bargained-for" consideration. The parties have to agree on the benefits and detriments that would be deemed as consideration. Thus, the benefits that merely "flow" from the contract are insufficient consideration to support the enforceability of an agreement. The benefit received by Bogigian (P) from her release of the mortgage obligation was not a bargained-for-exchange rendering the judgment release of Bogigian (D) a voidable document. Therefore, the reinstatement of the judgment against Bogigian (D) was affirmed.

DISSENT: (Sullivan, J.) It is sufficient for a consideration to flow from the bargain. Lack of consideration and not inadequacy of consideration should be the reason to set aside an agreement.

EDITOR'S ANALYSIS: The purpose of the bargain requirement is to prevent the enforcement of promises that are promises to make gifts. To decide whether a condition was bargained for, one must determine whether the occurrence of the condition is of benefit to the promisor.

[For more information on bargained-for consideration, see Casenote Law Outline on Contracts, Chapter 2, § I, Valuable Consideration: The Bargained-for Incursion of Legal Detriment.]

LANGER v. SUPERIOR STEEL CORP.

Pa. Sup. Ct., 105 Pa. Super. 579, 161 A. 571 (1932).

NATURE OF CASE: Action of assumpsit to recover damages for breach of contract.

FACT SUMMARY: Superior (D) promised Langer (P), who was retiring from its employ, a lifetime pension if Langer (P) would refrain from seeking competitive employment.

CONCISE RULE OF LAW: A good consideration exists if one refrains from doing anything that he has a right to do.

FACTS: Superior Steel Corp. (D) promised Langer (P), upon his retirement as a superintendent with the company, that he "will receive a pension of $100 per month as long as you live and preserve your present attitude of loyalty to the company and its officers and are not employed in any competitive position." Superior (D) paid the sum of $100 a month for four years when it discontinued payments. Langer (P) brought an action in assumpsit for an alleged breach of contract, and in defense, Superior (D) argued that the offer of a pension was merely gratuitous.

ISSUE: Is sufficient consideration present where one performing party has given up the right to do anything which he otherwise would have had the right to do?

HOLDING AND DECISION: (Baldrige, J.) Yes. Good consideration exists if one refrains from doing anything that he has a right to do, whether there is any actual loss or detriment to him or actual benefit to the promisor or not. Such forbearance involves a detriment to the performing party. While it is helpful to determine whether the promisor will also be benefited, in doubtful cases, a showing that the promisee has, as a result of the promise, incurred a detriment is usually sufficient to prevent the promise from being interpreted as a mere gratuity. In the present case, by receiving the monthly payments, Langer (P) also impliedly accepted the conditions imposed and thus was prevented from securing other employment. Unlike in Kirksey v. Kirksey, here there was a benefit to be derived by the promisor. An alternative basis for regarding this case as involving an enforceable contract, rather than a mere gratuity, is promissory estoppel. A promise which the promisor should reasonably expect to induce action or forbearance of a definite and substantial character on the part of the promisee and which does induce same is binding if injustice can be avoided only by enforcement of the promise. Under either theory, Langer (P) is entitled to enforce Superior's (D) promise.

EDITOR'S ANALYSIS: A majority of courts have embraced the "legal detriment" rule for determining the sufficiency of consideration. Under the approach, proof that one party's act or performance results in a legal benefit being conferred on the other is not, by itself, sufficient to establish consideration. Restatement, 384(a) adopts the minority view in positing in the alternative that either legal detriment or legal benefit is sufficient.

[For more information on the concept of the legal detriment, see Casenote Law Outline on Contracts, Chapter 2, § I, Valuable Consideration: The Bargained-for Incursion of Legal Detriment.]

NOTES:

ELEANOR THOMAS v. BENJAMIN THOMAS

Queen's Bench, 2 Q.B. Rep. 851, 114 Eng. Rep. 330 (1842).

NATURE OF CASE: Assumpsit upon an agreement to convey a dwelling.

FACT SUMMARY: Eleanor Thomas (P) was given a choice by her now-deceased husband to take upon his death either the use of their dwelling house so long as she remain a widow or £100 from his personal estate. She chose the dwelling, but the executor of the estate, Benjamin Thomas (D), refused to convey the dwelling, stating lack of consideration to support the promise of the husband as his reason.

CONCISE RULE OF LAW: Motive is not sufficient consideration for a contract.

FACTS: Eleanor Thomas (P) was given a choice by her now-deceased husband to take upon his death either the use of their dwelling house so long as she remain a widow or £100 from his personal estate. After the husband's death, the executors of the estate, Samuel Thomas and Benjamin Thomas (D), agreed to allow the choice, stating the consideration for the agreement between Eleanor Thomas (P) and her deceased husband had been the motive of the husband. The executors also added a provision to the conveyance of the dwelling in that E. Thomas (P) would pay to them the sum of £1 annually for ground rent. Executor Samuel Thomas died, and executor Benjamin Thomas (D) refused to make the conveyance of the dwelling, stating that there actually did not exist any consideration for the conveyance.

ISSUE: Is motive acceptable consideration?

HOLDING AND DECISION: (Coltman, J.) No. Motive is not the same as consideration. Consideration means something which is of some value in the eye of the law moving from the plaintiff. That which is suggested as consideration here, a pious respect for the wishes of the testator, does not move from the plaintiff; it moves from the testator. Therefore, legally speaking, it forms no part of the consideration. However, payment of £1 annually is more than good consideration; it is valuable consideration. It is clearly a thing newly created. Even though the motive is insufficient as consideration, the requested £1 annually is sufficient consideration to bind Benjamin Thomas (D) to his agreement to convey the dwelling house.

CONCURRENCE: (Denman, J.) This is an express agreement supported by adequate legal consideration wholly irrespective of any "moral" feelings involved.

CONCURRENCE: (Coleridge, J.) The mere fact that the consideration for this agreement does not appear in the normal place for the recitation of such is immaterial.

EDITOR'S ANALYSIS: In this case the court is agreeing with the defendant in saying motive is not sufficient consideration for a promise. However, the court also finds that the defendant, in requiring the plaintiff to pay the sum of £1 annually, had actually bargained for an exchange, that is, the unobstructed right to choose the dwelling house in return for the annual payment of £1. The court determined that the £1 was a benefit moving from the plaintiff to the defendant.

[For more information on legal considerations, see Casenote Law Outline on Contracts, Chapter 2, § I, Valuable Consideration: The Bargained-for Incursion of Legal Detriment.]

NOTES:

APFEL v. PRUDENTIAL-BACHE SECURITIES, INC.

N.Y. Ct. of App., 81 N.Y.2d 470, 616 N.E.2d 1095 (1993).

NATURE OF CASE: Appeal in a suit for breach of contract.

FACT SUMMARY: Apfel (P) sold a method for computerized securities transactions to Prudential-Bache (D), which paid on the agreement for a few years before reneging.

CONCISE RULE OF LAW: Consideration must have value to the buyer; however, there is no requirement that an idea used as consideration must have novelty.

FACTS: Apfel (P) approached Prudential-Bache (D) with a proposal for issuing municipal securities through a computerized system. After negotiating, Apfel (P) conveyed his idea for a stipulated rate based on use for a term from October 1982 to January 1988. Prudential-Bache (D) was to pay even if the idea became public knowledge. For the first year, Prudential-Bache (D) was the only underwriter using such a system. In 1985, Prudential-Bache (D) refused to make further payments. Apfel (P) filed suit. On motions for summary judgment, the trial court dismissed all causes of action except a claim for breach of contract. The ruling was immediately appealed. The appellate division modified the ruling and held that novelty was required for consideration based on an idea, but the issue was factual. Prudential-Bache (D) appealed, seeking certification of the question of whether novelty was required for consideration based upon an idea.

ISSUE: Must an idea be novel to serve as consideration in a contract selling the idea to another?

HOLDING AND DECISION: (Simons, J.) No. Consideration must have value to the buyer; however, there is no requirement that an idea used as consideration must have novelty. Contract law has long held that consideration exchanged may be grossly unequal and still suffice. Ideas, however, pose a special problem. Since they lack tangibility, it is often difficult to prove the source of an idea. Where the idea is novel, the seller can conclusively show that there was no other source for the idea. In this case, Prudential-Bache (D) does not deny that Apfel (P) conveyed the idea. Instead, Prudential-Bache (D) cites cases where novelty was required to find an idea was conveyed in a contract. However, these cases have been misconstrued. Novelty was only required to prove the source of the idea. Here, the source is admitted. And Prudential-Bache (D) clearly received something of value since for one year it was the only underwriter using the method. The answer to the certified question is that novelty is not required for an idea to suffice as consideration.

EDITOR'S ANALYSIS: The intangible nature of ideas makes their sale a difficult proposition. To negotiate a contract, the idea must be expressed to the other party; however, that party then also knows the idea. The idea may have tremendous value, more than sufficient to serve as the basis for a contract. Proving that the idea belonged to the seller can be quite a different matter altogether.

[For more information on value of consideration, see Casenote Law Outline on Contracts, Chapter 2, § I, Valuable Consideration: The Bargained-for Incursion of Legal Detriment.]

NOTES:

JONES v. STAR CREDIT CORP.

N.Y. Sup. Ct., 59 Misc. 2d 189, 298 N.Y.S.2d 264 (1969).

NATURE OF CASE: Action to reform a contract on grounds of unconscionability.

FACT SUMMARY: Jones (P) purchased a freezer from Star Credit (D) for $900 plus credit charges, but the actual retail value of the freezer was only $300.

CONCISE RULE OF LAW: A court may refuse to enforce a contract for the sale of goods on the ground that an excessive price term renders the contract unconscionable.

FACTS: Jones (P), a welfare recipient, purchased a freezer from Star Credit (D) for $900 ($1,439.69, including credit charges and $18 sales tax). Jones (P) had already paid $619.88 toward the purchase, but the freezer had a maximum retail value of only $300.

ISSUE: May a court refuse to enforce a contract for the sale of goods on the ground that the price term was "unconscionable"?

HOLDING AND DECISION: (Wachtter, J.) Yes. U.C.C. § 2-302 allows a court to refuse enforcement of a contract containing an unconscionable price term. The sale of a freezer having a retail value of $300 for $900 ($1,439.69, including credit charges and $18 sales tax) is unconscionable as a matter of law. But U.C.C. § 2-302 is not simply a mathematical ratio formula. Other factors in the balance include: (1) financial resources of the buyer known to the seller at the time of sale; (2) "knowing advantage" taken of the buyer; and (3) a gross inequality of bargaining power. Accordingly, the contract should be reformed by changing the payments called for therein to equal the amount already paid by Jones (P).

EDITOR'S ANALYSIS: It is not convincing for the court simply to assert, as it does: "There is no reason to doubt . . . that U.C.C. § 2-302 is intended to encompass the price term of an agreement." The court's paternalistic recognition of a kind of so-called substantive unconscionability, in which the court's valuation of the goods is substituted for that of the parties, needs further justification than it receives in this case. [See also Williams v. Walker-Thomas, 350 F. 2d 445 (D.C. Cir., 1965).] Most courts have stopped short of taking this step and have required some sort of procedural unconscionability ("bargaining nastiness") before refusing to enforce a contract. Further, the court's remedy of reformation of the contract to the amount already paid seems most suspect. How does this amount reflect anything other than pure fortuity?

[For more information on substantive unconscionability, see Casenote Law Outline on Contracts, Chapter 3, § III, Defenses Rooted in Social Objection to the Content of the Bargain.]

NOTES:

IN RE GREENE

45 F.2d 428 (S.D. N.Y. 1930).

NATURE OF CASE: Claim against bankrupt's estate.

FACT SUMMARY: Preamble to instrument signed by Greene (D), in which he promised to pay his former mistress (P) hundreds of thousands of dollars, recited that the consideration was $1.

CONCISE RULE OF LAW: A consideration given by one party which is only token or nominal does not constitute sufficient consideration.

FACTS: Prior to 1926, Greene (D) had lived in adultery with claimant (P). Greene (D) gave her substantial sums of money and a $70,000 house. In 1926, their relationship ended, and they executed a written, sealed agreement in which Greene (D) promised to pay the claimant (P) $1,000 a month, to assign to her a $100,000 life insurance policy and to maintain the premiums on it, and to pay the rent for four years on an apartment she had leased. The agreement recited that Greene (D) would no longer be liable for mortgage interest, taxes, or other charges on the house he had given the claimant (P). The preamble to the instrument stated that consideration was $1 by the claimant (P) to Greene (D) "and other good and valuable considerations." Greene (D) made payments only up to 1928, and when he went bankrupt, the claimant (P) sought to enforce the agreement against his bankrupt estate.

ISSUE: Will a merely nominal consideration support a promise?

HOLDING AND DECISION: (Woolsey, J.) No. A $1 consideration, being nominal, will not support an executory promise to pay, in the present case, hundreds of thousands of dollars. The promise is unenforceable since there appears no other sufficient consideration in the written agreement. Past illicit intercourse is not consideration. "Other good and valuable considerations" is plausible, but there is no proof that in fact anything good or valuable had been given at the time the contract was made. Greene's (D) purported immunity from having to pay taxes and other charges on the claimant's (P) house is not enough since he was never chargeable with these expenses; his previous payments were gratuitous. Finally, although the parties here may have intended to make a valid agreement, the most solemn and formal document possible cannot disguise what is in reality a gift. A seal is only presumptive evidence of consideration on an executory instrument. The agreement is unenforceable.

EDITOR'S ANALYSIS: Although, in a standard contract, a recital of a token or nominal consideration indicates that a gift, rather than a bargain, was intended, a $1 sum, or less, may be adequate to sustain certain types of agreements. In option and guaranty contracts, the party giving the nominal or token consideration is bargaining for something of a speculatory nature or value. Thus, in one case, a consideration of $0.25 for a 4-month option to purchase land for $100,000 was held sufficient to render the contract enforceable.

[For more information on token considerations, see Casenote Law Outline on Contracts, Chapter 2, § I, Valuable Consideration: The Bargained-for Incursion of Legal Detriment.]

NOTES:

FIEGE v. BOEHM

Md. Ct. App., 210 Md. 352, 123 A.2d 316 (1956).

NATURE OF CASE: Action to recover damages for breach of contract.

FACT SUMMARY: Fiege (D) promised to pay money if Boehm (P) would refrain from instituting bastardy proceedings, but Fiege (D), after blood tests, determined that Boehm's (P) bastardy claim was invalid and refused to pay.

CONCISE RULE OF LAW: Forbearance to assert an invalid claim may serve as consideration for a return promise if the parties at the time of the settlement reasonably believed in good faith that the claim was valid.

FACTS: Boehm (P), an unmarried woman, became pregnant and believed in good faith that Fiege (D) was the father. Fiege (D) promised to pay expenses incident to the birth and make regular payments for the raising of the child on condition that Boehm (P) would not institute bastardy proceedings against him. Subsequent to the child's birth, Fiege (D) had blood tests made which demonstrated that he could not have been the father. Fiege (D) then stopped making payments whereupon Boehm (P) unsuccessfully instituted bastardy proceedings against him. Boehm (P) sought to recover the balance of the expenses as promised.

ISSUE: May one party's promise not to assert a claim which she reasonably believes in good faith to be valid but which in fact is invalid serve as consideration for a return promise by another party?

HOLDING AND DECISION: (Delaplaine, J.) Yes. Although forbearance to assert a claim known to be invalid will not support a return promise, if the parties to a settlement agreement reasonably believe in good faith that the claim forgone is valid (or if there is at least a bona fide dispute), the forbearance is consideration for a return promise. (The subjective requisite that the claim be bona fide is combined with the objective requisite that the claim have a reasonable basis of support.)

EDITOR'S ANALYSIS: Basic public policy underlies this decision. The law seeks to encourage out-of-court settlements which are not coerced. Such settlements (1) tend to promote goodwill, (2) are much less expensive for the parties to pursue than a full-blown court battle, and (3) help relieve unnecessary (and expensive) congestion on court dockets. However, a settlement based on forbearance to assert a claim known to be invalid is likely to be coercive and in bad faith, and courts will not enforce it.

[For more information on promise to forbear the assertion or abandon the prosecution of a legal claim, see Casenote Law Outline on Contracts, Chapter 2, § I, Valuable Consideration: The Bargained-for Incursion of Legal Detriment.]

ALASKA PACKERS' ASSOCIATION v. DOMENICO

54 C.C.A. 485, 117 F. 99 (9th Cir. 1902).

NATURE OF CASE: Libel action for breach of contract.

FACT SUMMARY: A group of seamen (P), who had agreed to ship from San Francisco to Alaska at a fixed pay, refused to continue working once they reached Alaska and demanded a new contract with more compensation.

CONCISE RULE OF LAW: A promise to pay a man for doing that which he is already under contract to do is without consideration.

FACTS: A group of seamen (P) entered into a written contract with Alaska Packers' Association (D) to go from San Francisco to Alaska on the Packers' (D) ships and to work as sailors and fishermen. Compensation was fixed at $60 for the season and $0.02 for each salmon caught. Once they had reached port in Alaska, the seamen (P) refused to continue work and demanded that compensation be increased to $100. A superintendent for Packers' (D), unable to hire a new crew, drew up a new contract, substituted in the sum of $100, and signed it, although he expressed doubt at the time that he had the authority to do so. The seamen (P) resumed work, but upon the ship's return to San Francisco, Packers' (D) refused to honor the new contract. The seamen (P) filed a libel action for breach of contract.

ISSUE: Is a promise to pay a man for performing a duty he is already under contract to perform without consideration?

HOLDING AND DECISION: (Ross, C.J.) Yes. The performance of a preexisting legal duty guaranteed by contract is not sufficient consideration to support a promise. No astute reasoning can change the plain fact that the party who refuses to perform and thereby coerces a promise from the other party to pay him an increased compensation for doing that which he is legally bound to do takes an unjustifiable advantage of the necessities of the other party. The parties in the present case have not voluntarily rescinded or modified their contract. The Packers' (D) second contract with the seamen is unenforceable, although the seamen completed their performance in reliance on it.

EDITOR'S ANALYSIS: A few cases have held that the promise to pay additional compensation is enforceable. Consideration is found in the promisee's giving up of his power to breach the first contract. In other words, by refusing to continue work, the promisee has invoked the option to pay money damages rather than to invest his labor in further performance. This view has been questioned on the ground that a promisee may have the power to breach a contract but certainly not the legal right, and in any event, he should not be encouraged to do so.

[For more information on preexisting duty, see Casenote Law Outline on Contracts, Chapter 2, § I, Valuable Consideration: The Bargained-for Incursion of Legal Detriment.]

LEVINE v. BLUMENTHAL

117 N.J.L. 23, 186 A. 457 (1936).

NATURE OF CASE: Action to recover on lease.

FACT SUMMARY: Blumenthal (D) told Levine (P) that he could not afford to pay the higher rental called for by the lease for the second year of occupancy. Levine (P) accepted a lower rental for one year and then sued for the deficiency.

CONCISE RULE OF LAW: Neither economic disasters nor acceptance of partial payments will be considered adequate consideration for the modification of contractual obligations.

FACTS: Blumenthal (D) rented a store from Levine (P) for two years. The lease required Blumenthal to pay $175 per month the first year, $200 per month the second year. At the end of the first year, Blumenthal (D) told Levine (P) that economic conditions were so bad he couldn't afford to pay the higher rent and would have to leave or maybe go out of business. Levine (P) agreed to allow Blumenthal (D) to remain if he continued to pay $175 per month. Blumenthal (D) left at the end of the second year, having paid $175 the entire second year, except for the last month's rent, which was never paid. Levine (P) sued for the last month's rent plus $25 per month for the last 11 months of the contract. Blumenthal (D) argued accord and satisfaction as to the $175 payments paid under the oral modification. He also argued that his remaining as a tenant during the economic crisis was adequate consideration to support the modification. The trial judge held that there was no consideration for the modification and found for Levine (P).

ISSUE: Is either a poor economic climate or the acceptance of partial payments consideration for an oral modification to a contract?

HOLDING AND DECISION: (Hener, J.) No. The payment of part of an obligation is not consideration for excusing repayment of the whole debt. Some additional type of consideration is required. General economic adversity will never supply the needed consideration nor will Blumenthal's (D) claim of accord and satisfaction. The debt is totally liquidated. There was no dispute as to amount owed. Blumenthal (D) did no more than he was legally obligated to do. This was no consideration for a reduced rental. Since there was no dispute as to the amount due, there was no accord and satisfaction. Judgment affirmed.

EDITOR'S ANALYSIS: In Watkins & Son v. Carrig, 91 N.H. 459 (1941), the court came to the opposite conclusion. There, it held that a promise in adjustment of a contractual promise already outstanding (i.e., a modification) may be enforceable. If the parties are acting to meet changed conditions and circumstances, the court should enforce the agreement if it is a reasonable practice or understanding in business and commerce.

[For more information on modification, see Casenote Law Outline on Contracts, Chapter 2, § I, Valuable Consideration: The Bargained-for Incursion of Legal Detriment.]

NOTES:

ANGEL v. MURRAY

R.I. Sup. Ct., 113 R.I. 482, 332 A.2d 630 (1974).

NATURE OF CASE: Suit seeking repayment of money allegedly paid improperly.

FACT SUMMARY: Angel (P) objected when the City of Newport (D) paid Maher (D) $10,000 per year more than the original contract price for collecting refuse in the City (D).

CONCISE RULE OF LAW: An agreement by which a party is promised additional compensation for performing a duty which he is already contractually obligated to undertake may be enforced if the new agreement was voluntarily entered into and was prompted by the occurrence of events which were not anticipated when the original contract was executed.

FACTS: Maher (D) entered into a series of contracts to collect refuse for the City of Newport (D). One of these contracts, executed in 1964, obligated Maher (D) to pick up all refuse generated within the City (D). The contract entitled Maher (D) to receive $137,000 per year for five years. On two occasions, however, Maher (D) appeared before the city council and was awarded an additional $10,000 per year. In each instance, Maher (D) cited the fact that the city's dwelling units had increased by 400 instead of by the 10 to 25 new units which had been anticipated. After the additional payments had been made, Angel (P) and others (P) sued Maher (D), the City (D), and Murray (D), who was the Director of Finance for the City (D). The suit sought repayment of the $20,000 which had been paid over and above the original contract price. The trial judge, reasoning that Maher (D) had had a preexisting duty to collect the City's (D) refuse and therefore was not entitled to additional compensation for performing that service, granted the relief sought. Maher (D) then appealed.

ISSUE: May an agreement by which a party is to receive additional compensation for performing a preexisting duty ever be enforced?

HOLDING AND DECISION: (Roberts, C.J.) Yes. An agreement by which a party is promised additional compensation for performing a duty which he is already contractually obligated to undertake may be enforced if the new agreement was voluntarily entered into and was prompted by the occurrence of events which were not anticipated when the original contract was executed. The trial court erred in concluding that the $20,000 could not be allocated without the approval of the city manager. But it was also error to apply the preexisting duty rule to this case. Recently, courts have come to realize that that rule should be applied cautiously. It is true that Maher (D) was already obligated to collect the City's (D) refuse and thus gave no new consideration in exchange for the City's (D) promises to pay him additional amounts totaling $20,000. But, those promises were made before either party had fully performed the original refuse collection contract, and the new agreement was entered into voluntarily. Moreover, the modification was fair and equitable and was motivated by events which were not anticipated at the time of the original contract. Under these circumstances, § 89D(a) of the Restatement (Second) of Contracts clearly entitles Maher (D) to retain the $20,000 paid pursuant to the City's (D) promises.

EDITOR'S ANALYSIS: Countless cases have recognized and applied the preexisting duty rule. However, the rule has, over the years, become riddled with exceptions. Perhaps the most important of these exceptions is that which renders a modification enforceable if it appends any additional condition, no matter how insignificant, to the preexisting duty of the party seeking to enforce the new agreement. Thus, a requirement changing the time or place of delivery or the mode of payment may make the preexisting duty rule inapplicable. In fact, the present viability of the rule is questionable in light of §2-209 of the Uniform Commercial Code, which provides, "[a]n agreement modifying a contract within this Article needs no consideration to be binding."

[For more information on modifications which pass muster under the preexisting duty rule, see Casenote Law Outline on Contracts, Chapter 2, § I, Valuable Consideration: The Bargained-for Incursion of Legal Detriment.]

NOTES:

REHM-ZEIHER CO. v. F.G. WALKER CO.

Ky. Ct. App., 156 Ky. 6, 160 S.W. 777 (1913).

NATURE OF CASE: Action to recover damages for breach of contract.

FACT SUMMARY: Buyer (P) agreed to purchase from Seller (D) a given number of whisky cases a year for five years but reserved the right to refuse acceptance at any time for "any unforeseen reason."

CONCISE RULE OF LAW: Where in a purchase agreement the buyer has reserved an alternative by which he may, at his own discretion, buy nothing at all, the contract lacks mutuality and may be enforced by neither party.

FACTS: Rehm-Zeiher (P), a seller of whiskey, agreed to purchase from F.G. Walker (D), a distiller, 2,000 cases of whiskey in 1909, 3,000 in 1910, 4,000 in 1911, and 5,000 in 1912. The contract recited that "If for any unforeseen reason [Rehm-Zeiher (P)] find that they cannot use the full amount . . . [F.G. Walker (D)] agrees to release them from the contract for the amount desired by [Rehm-Zeiher (P)]." In 1909, Rehm-Zeiher (P) only ordered and received 786 cases of the 2,000 called for by the contract, and in 1910 it only ordered and received 1,200 cases of the 3,000 called for by the contract. In 1911, whiskey having advanced in price, F.G. Walker (D) refused to make any further deliveries. Rehm-Zeiher (P) thereupon brought a suit for breach of contract.

ISSUE: Does a reservation in a purchase agreement by the buyer under which he may, at his own discretion, refuse to make any purchase void the contract?

HOLDING AND DECISION: (Carroll, J.) Yes. Where a buyer in a purchase contract has reserved unto himself the right to evade his obligation for any "unforeseen reason" and left the meaning of these words to his own discretion, the contract is void for lack of mutuality. Any reason Rehm-Zeiher (P) might assign for not taking the whiskey would relieve it of any obligation to do so; the reason need not be a good one or reasonable. Thus, the fact that Rehm-Zeiher (P) accepted a part of the whiskey in 1909 and 1910 did not oblige them to take any of it in the subsequent years. Mutuality being lacking, the contract may be distinguished from one in which A has agreed to furnish B all the goods that B will require in the operation of his business. This form of an output contract is not lacking in mutuality. Courts, in recognition of the fluctuating needs of business, have upheld such contracts despite their indefiniteness. While the quantity under contract is incapable of exact measurements, it is capable of an approximately accurate forecast ascertainable by the vendor.

EDITOR'S ANALYSIS: A promise to buy "all that I want" is termed illusory and is unenforceable by either party for want of mutuality. However, a promise to buy "all that I need" encumbers the promisor with a legal detriment since he must purchase from the promisee-supplier or not at all. Similarly, a promise to sell "all that I produce" is enforceable because the promisor, in being restricted to sell his goods to only one purchaser, has suffered a legal detriment.

[For more information on the illusory promise, see Casenote Law Outline on Contracts , Chapter 2, § I, Valuable Consideration: The Bargained-for Incursion of Legal Detriment.]

NOTES:

McMICHAEL v. PRICE

Okla. Sup. Ct., 177 Okla. 186, 58 P.2d 549 (1936).

NATURE OF CASE: Action for damages for breach of a requirements contract.

FACT SUMMARY: Price (P), a salesman of sand doing business as Sooner Sand Company, agreed to purchase all the sand he could sell for out-of-city shipment from McMichael (D), who agreed to furnish all the sand Price (P) could sell for out-of-city shipment at 60% of the current market price of sand at place of destination of shipment.

CONCISE RULE OF LAW: Where one party promises to sell to another all that the latter can use, the obligation of the parties to sell and buy must be mutual to render the contract binding.

FACTS: Price (P), doing business as Sooner Sand Company, made the following agreement with McMichael (D): Price (P) agreed to purchase and accept from McMichael (D) all the sand of various grades and quality that Price (P) could sell for shipment outside the city of Tulsa provided McMichael (D) furnished and loaded sand at least equal in quality with the sand sold by other companies in the Tulsa area for a sum per ton representing 60% of the current market price per ton at the place of destination of shipment. McMichael (D) agreed to furnish all sand of various grades and quality that Price (P) could sell for shipment outside of Tulsa and load all sand in suitable railway cars within a reasonable time after receiving a verbal or written order from Price (P). McMichael (D) failed to deliver, alleging Price (P) was not bound to any promise.

ISSUE: Is there mutuality of consideration to uphold both parties' promises so as to enforce the contract?

HOLDING AND DECISION: (Osborne, V.C.J.) Yes. The contract is specific in requiring Price (P) to buy all sand he can sell from McMichael (D), and McMichael (D) is to furnish all sand Price (P) can sell to Price (P). While McMichael (D) claims that Price (P) had no established business at the time, the contract states Price (P) is engaged in the business of selling and shipping sand. Even so, Price (P) was an experienced sand salesman, which McMichael (D) knew. The parties anticipated that on account of Price's (P) experience, acquaintances, and connections, he would be able to sell a substantial amount to their mutual profit.

EDITOR'S ANALYSIS: This was a "requirement" contract, that is, McMichael (D) was to provide according to Price's (P) needs. An "output" contract is one where buyer agrees to take all the goods seller produces. The court looks to see if buyer has "a free way out" of the contract. The modern view is to find the requirement of mutuality satisfied without a commitment by the buyer to take a fixed quantity of goods. U.C.C. § 2-306 states the essential test to be whether the buyer is acting in good faith. Some courts will not find a contract where the buyer is a middleman or does not have an established business. There are cases on both sides, but those courts which would determine this case oppositely would find the lack of an established business to make the requirements of the buyer indefinite and, hence, his promise illusory.

[For more information on requirement contracts, see Casenote Law Outline on Contracts, Chapter 2, § I, Valuable Consideration: The Bargained-for Incursion of Legal Detriment.]

NOTES:

WOOD v. LUCY, LADY DUFF-GORDON

N.Y. Ct. App., 222 N.Y. 88, 118 N.E. 214 (1907).

NATURE OF CASE: Action for damages for breach of a contract for an exclusive right.

FACT SUMMARY: Wood (P), in a complicated agreement, received the exclusive right for one year, renewable on a year-to-year basis if not terminated by 90-day notice, to endorse designs with Lucy's (D) name and to market all her fashion designs, for which she would receive one-half the profits derived. Lucy (D) broke the contract by placing her endorsement on designs without Wood's (P) knowledge.

CONCISE RULE OF LAW: While an express promise may be lacking, the whole writing may be instinct with an obligation — an implied promise — imperfectly expressed so as to form a valid contract.

FACTS: Lucy (D), a famous-name fashion designer, contracted with Wood (P) that for her granting to him an exclusive right to endorse designs with her name and to market and license all of her designs, they were to split the profits derived by Wood (P) in half. The exclusive right was for a period of one year, renewable on a year-to-year basis and terminable upon 90 days' notice. Lucy (D) placed her endorsement on fabrics, dresses, and millinery without Wood's (P) knowledge and in violation of the contract. Lucy (D) claimed that the agreement lacked the elements of a contract, as Wood (P) allegedly was not bound to do anything.

ISSUE: If a promise may be implied from the writing even though it is imperfectly expressed, is there a valid contract?

HOLDING AND DECISION: (Cardozo, J.) Yes. While the contract did not precisely state that Wood (P) had promised to use reasonable efforts to place Lucy's (D) endorsement and market her designs, such a promise can be implied. The implication arises from the circumstances. Lucy (D) gave an exclusive privilege, and the acceptance of the exclusive agency was an acceptance of its duties. Lucy's (D) sole compensation was to be one-half the profits resulting from Wood's (P) efforts. Unless he gave his efforts, she could never receive anything. Without an implied promise, the transaction could not have had such business efficacy as they must have intended it to have. Wood's (P) promise to make monthly accountings and to acquire patents and copyrights as necessary showed the intention of the parties that the promise has value by showing that Wood (P) had some duties. The promise to pay Lucy (D) half the profits and make monthly accountings was a promise to use reasonable efforts to bring profits and revenues into existence.

EDITOR'S ANALYSIS: A bilateral contract can be express, implied in fact, or a little of each. The finding of an implied promise for the purpose of finding sufficient consideration to support an express promise is an important technique of the courts in order to uphold agreements which seem to be illusory and to avoid problems of mutuality of obligation. This case is the leading case on the subject. It is codified in U.C.C. § 2-306(2), where an agreement for exclusive dealing in goods imposes, unless otherwise agreed, an obligation to use best efforts by both parties.

[For more information on implication of promises and U.C.C. § 2-306(2), see Casenote Law Outline on Contracts, Chapter 2, § I, Valuable Consideration: The Bargained-for Incursion of Legal Detriment.]

NOTES:

OMNI GROUP, INC. v. SEATTLE FIRST NATIONAL BANK

Wash. Ct. App., 32 Wash. App. 22, 645 P.2d 727 (1982).

NATURE OF CASE: Appeal from the denial of enforcement of a contract for the sale of realty.

FACT SUMMARY: The Clarks (D) contended that by making their contractual obligations subject to a satisfactory engineer's and architect's feasibility report, Omni (P) rendered its promise to purchase the Clarks' (D) land illusory and the contract unenforceable.

CONCISE RULE OF LAW: A contractual condition calling for the subjective satisfaction of a party imposes a duty of good faith in the exercise of the party's discretion and is not illusory.

FACTS: Omni (P) signed an earnest money agreement to purchase the Clarks' (D) land. The agreement provided that Omni's (P) performance was subject to its receiving a satisfactory engineer's and architect's feasibility report concerning the land's development potential. Subsequently, Omni (P) notified the Clarks (D) it would forgo the study. After further negotiations, the Clarks (D) refused to go through with the transaction, and Omni (P) sued for breach of contract. The Clarks (D) defended on the basis that by making its performance conditional upon receipt of a satisfactory feasibility report, Omni (P) rendered its promise illusory, and, therefore, the contract lacked consideration and was unenforceable. The trial court entered judgment for the Clarks (D), and Omni (P) appealed.

ISSUE: Does a contract condition calling for a party's satisfaction with the performance of an act render that party's promise to perform illusory and the contract unenforceable?

HOLDING AND DECISION: (James, J.) No. A contract condition which requires a party's satisfaction with the performance of an act imposes on that party the duty to exercise his judgment, concerning whether the performance is satisfactory, in good faith. In this case, Omni's (P) acceptance of the feasibility report was not left to its unfettered discretion. It was bound to act in good faith in either accepting it or rejecting it. Therefore, the promise was not illusory; it supplied sufficient consideration for the Clarks' (D) promise to sell, and a valid contract was formed. Reversed.

EDITOR'S ANALYSIS: This case illustrates the requirement of good faith in contracts calling for the satisfaction of a party as a condition precedent to his obligations under the contract. This requirement exists where the performance must meet the subjective satisfaction of the party. In such a case, some courts allow evidence of the unreasonableness of the rejection of performance to show a lack of good faith. The good faith rule is codified in Restatement Second, Contracts, §254, and is derived from the Case of Devoine Co. v. International Co., 136 A. 37 (Md. 1927).

[For more information on illusory promises, see Casenote Law Outline on Contracts, Chapter 2, § I, Valuable Consideration: The Bargained-for Incursion of Legal Detriment.]

NOTES:

MILLS v. WYMAN

Mass. Sup. Jud. Ct., 3 Pick. 207 (1825).

NATURE OF CASE: Action on appeal to recover upon alleged promise.

FACT SUMMARY: Mills (P) took care of Wyman's (D) son without being requested to do so, and for so doing Wyman (D) promised compensation for expenses arising out of the rendered care. Wyman (D) later refused to compensate Mills (P).

CONCISE RULE OF LAW: A moral obligation is insufficient as consideration for a promise.

FACTS: Mills (P) nursed and cared for Levi Wyman, the son of Wyman (D). Upon learning of Mills' (P) acts of kindness toward his son, Wyman (D) promised to repay Mills (P) his expenses incurred in caring for Levi Wyman. Later, Wyman (D) refused to compensate Mills (P) for his expenses. Mills (P) filed an action in the Court of Common Pleas, where Wyman (D) was successful in obtaining a nonsuit against Mills (P). Mills (P) appealed.

ISSUE: Is a moral obligation sufficient consideration for a promise?

HOLDING AND DECISION: (Parker, C.J.) No. It is said a moral obligation is a sufficient consideration to support an express promise. However, the universality of the rule cannot be supported. Therefore, there must be some other preexisting obligation which will suffice as consideration.

EDITOR'S ANALYSIS: In cases such as this one, the nearly universal holding is that the existing moral obligation is not a sufficient basis for the enforcement of an express promise to render the performance that it requires. The general statement is that it is not sufficient consideration for the express promise. The difficulties and differences of opinion involved in the determination of what is a moral obligation are probably much greater than those involved in determining the existence of a legal obligation. This tends to explain the attitude of the majority of courts on the subject and justifies the generally stated rule.

[For more information on moral obligation, see Casenote Law Outline on Contracts, Chapter 2, § I, Valuable Consideration: The Bargained-for Incursion of Legal Detriment.]

NOTES:

MANWILL v. OYLER

11 Utah 2d 433 (1961).

NATURE OF CASE: Interlocutory appeal from a denial of a motion to dismiss for failure to state a cause of action.

FACT SUMMARY: Manwill (P) claimed that Oyler (D) agreed to pay a debt which was barred by the statute of limitations.

CONCISE RULE OF LAW: Moral obligations alone are not adequate consideration to support a contract.

FACTS: Manwill (P) made payments on behalf of the Oylers (D) amounting to $5,500. Subsequently, the debt became barred by the statute of limitations. Manwill (P) brought an action, alleging that Oyler (D) had promised to pay the debt in 1957 and that this constituted a legally binding contract on which the limitations period had not yet run. The consideration for the contract was the antecedent debt, a moral obligation. Oyler (D) moved to dismiss for failure to state a cause of action since moral obligations are considered inadequate consideration. The court denied the motion but allowed an interlocutory appeal to be made. Manwill (P) argued that the modern trend was to hold that where the defendant received value from the plaintiff under such circumstances as would create a moral obligation to pay for it, a promise to pay is binding ("material benefit rule").

ISSUE: Will moral consideration, standing alone, constitute consideration for a contract?

HOLDING AND DECISION: (Crockett, J.) No. Most authorities state that moral consideration, standing alone, will not be deemed adequate consideration to support a contract. A barred antecedent debt is only considered a moral obligation for a promise to repay the obligation. If there was a contract to repay that which has been barred by the statute of limitations, the debt may only be revived by a writing acknowledging the debt and signed by the party to be charged. If the promise was to pay for a gift, in order for the material benefit rule to apply, all of the facts surrounding the transaction must be set out by the plaintiff. It must appear from these facts that a legal obligation to repay was created in order to find valid consideration for the promise. No such facts are adduced by Manwill (P), and no writing was signed by Oyler (D). Therefore, the promise to pay is not supported by adequate consideration and is unenforceable. Motion to dismiss is granted.

EDITOR'S ANALYSIS: In many jurisdictions moral obligations will be deemed binding on the promisor's estate. If payments under the promise were made to plaintiff during the decedent's life, and no superior claimants exist, the estate will be obligated to continue making payments under the terms of the promise.

[For more information on moral consideration, see Casenote Law Outline on Contracts, Chapter 2, § I, Valuable Consideration: The Bargained-for Incursion of Legal Detriment.]

WEBB v. McGOWIN

Ala. Ct. App., 27 Ala. App. 82, 168 So. 196 (1935); cert. denied, 232 Ala. 374, 168 So. 199 (1936).

NATURE OF CASE: Action on appeal to collect on a promise.

FACT SUMMARY: Webb (P) saved the now-deceased J. McGowin from grave bodily injury or death by placing himself in grave danger and subsequently suffering grave bodily harm. J. McGowin, in return, promised Webb (P) compensation. McGowin's executors (D) refused to pay the promised compensation.

CONCISE RULE OF LAW: A moral obligation is a sufficient consideration to support a subsequent promise to pay where the promisor has received a material benefit.

FACTS: Webb (P), while in the scope of his duties for the W. T. Smith Lumber Co., was clearing the floor, which required him to drop a 75-lb. pine block from the upper floor of the mill to the ground. Just as Webb (P) was releasing the block, he noticed J. McGowin below and directly under where the block would have fallen. In order to divert the fall of the block, Webb (P) fell with it, breaking an arm and leg and ripping his heel off. The fall left Webb (P) a cripple and incapable of either mental or physical labor. In return for Webb's (P) act, J. McGowin promised to pay Webb (P) $15 every two weeks for the rest of Webb's (P) life. J. McGowin paid the promised payments until his death eight years later. Shortly after J. McGowin's death, the payments were stopped, and Webb (P) brought an action against N. McGowin (D) and J. F. McGowin (D) as executors of J. McGowin's estate for payments due him. The executors (D) of the estate were successful in obtaining a nonsuit against Webb (P) in the lower court. Webb (P) appealed.

ISSUE: Was the moral obligation to compensate as promised sufficient consideration?

HOLDING AND DECISION: (Bricken, J.) Yes. It is well settled that a moral obligation is a sufficient consideration to support a subsequent promise to pay where the promisor has received a material benefit, although there was no original duty or liability resting on the promisor.

EDITOR'S ANALYSIS: In most cases where the moral obligation is asserted, the court feels that the promise ought not be enforced; instead of going into the uncertain field of morality, the court chooses to rely upon the rule that moral obligation is not a sufficient consideration. On the other hand, in cases where the promise is one which would have been kept by most citizens, and the court feels that enforcement is just, a few courts will enforce the promise using the Webb v. McGowin rule. In general, the Webb v. McGowin rule is the minority rule and the Mills v. Wyman the majority rule.

[For more information on enforcement of moral obligation, see Casenote Law Outline on Contracts, Chapter 2, § II, Substitutes for Valuable Consideration as Grounds for Imparting Liability Consequences for Breaching a Promise.]

HARRINGTON v. TAYLOR

255 N.C. 690 (1945).

NATURE OF CASE: Action to enforce oral promise to pay damages.

FACT SUMMARY: Harrington (P) saved Taylor's (D) life by deflecting an ax blow with her hand.

CONCISE RULE OF LAW: A voluntary action of a humanitarian nature will not be adequate consideration for a subsequent promise.

FACTS: Taylor (D) assaulted his wife, who sought refuge in Harrington's (P) house. Taylor (D) gained entry to the house and attempted to assault his wife again. She knocked him down and attempted to kill him with an ax. Harrington (P) intervened, deflecting the ax blow with her hand. The hand was mutilated. Taylor (D), grateful to Harrington (P) for saving his life, agreed to pay damages. After several small payments, he refused to pay anymore. Harrington (P) brought suit to enforce the promise. Taylor (D) was granted his motion to dismiss on the ground that there was inadequate consideration to support his promise.

ISSUE: Will a voluntary humanitarian act be deemed adequate consideration to support a subsequent promise?

HOLDING AND DECISION: (Per Curiam) No. The law does not recognize voluntary acts for humanitarian purposes as adequate consideration to support subsequent promises. While the court may detest Taylor's (D) actions, it has no power to enforce his promise. Judgment affirmed.

EDITOR'S ANALYSIS: Voluntary promises to settle the debts of another are generally unenforceable if the promisor is not otherwise liable for them. However, if a duty of support is owed to the debtor or a suretyship exits, such claims are enforceable. For example, suppose plaintiff cares for defendant's son who is dying. If defendant promises to repay plaintiff for his expenses and gratuitously rendered services (after they are rendered), the contract will not be enforceable if the son was an adult but may be enforceable if the son were a minor.

[For more information on donative transactions, see Casenote Law Outline on Contracts, Chapter 2, § I, Valuable Consideration: The Bargained-for Incursion of Legal Detriment.]

NOTES:

ALLEGHENY COLLEGE v. NATIONAL CHAUTAUQUA COUNTY BANK OF JAMESTOWN

246 N.Y. 369 (1927).

NATURE OF CASE: Action to enforce charitable contributions.

FACT SUMMARY: Johnston pledged $5,000 after her death to Allegheny College (P) if it would set up a memorial fund in her name.

CONCISE RULE OF LAW: When the promisor requires that the promisee do anything in exchange for the promise, there is adequate consideration present when dealing with charitable contributors.

FACTS: Johnston promised Allegheny College (P) $5,000 30 days after her death if sufficient funds remained after the payment of her specific bequests. She stated that the money should be used to fund a scholarship in her name. She gave the College (P) $1,000 as a down payment. She later attempted to revoke the bequest. After her death, the College (P) submitted a $4,000 claim to her executor, National Chautauqua County Bank of Jamestown (D). The Bank (D) refused to honor the request. At trial, the court found for the Bank (D) on the basis that no consideration for the promise was present. The College (P) appealed on the basis that their efforts to comply with Johnston's scholarship requests were adequate consideration to enforce the gift.

ISSUE: Is consideration present in charitable contributions when a donee complies with conditions imposed on a gift by the donor?

HOLDING AND DECISION: (Cardozo, C.J.) Yes. Consideration does not have to be measured in terms of its economic worth. Even a slight legal detriment or the performance of some condition may be adequate consideration. This is especially true with respect to charitable pledges. Courts are very liberal in attempting to find consideration to support the pledge. Therefore, when, as here, the contributor has imposed conditions which the donee has attempted to honor, there is sufficient consideration to support the pledge. By accepting the $1,000 down payment, the College (P) impliedly agreed to comply with Johnston's scholarship request. It is not necessary to determine whether promissory estoppel was present. The College's (P) attempt to perform its obligation under the pledge is sufficient consideration. Judgment reversed.

DISSENT: (Kellogg, J.) The pledge was a gift, not an exchange of promises. Since the College (P) has not performed the "condition," under the majority's rationale, the contract has not been accepted. The College (P), in order to accept the pledge, would have to perform. The act is the bargained-for consideration, and until it has been performed, the promise need not be kept. Here, however, there is no showing that the pledge was a unilateral contract. It was a gift not supported by consideration.

EDITOR'S ANALYSIS: Most cases enforcing gifts are based on a theory of detrimental reliance and equitable estoppel on the gift. For example, where an uncle tells his nephew to purchase a set of skis and the uncle will pay him later for them, it would be unfair to refuse enforcement if the nephew's reliance was reasonable, e.g., uncle was rich or uncle was penniless.

[For more information on "economic adequacy" of consideration, see Casenote Law Outline on Contracts, Chapter 2, § I, Valuable Consideration: The Bargained-for Incursion of Legal Detriment.]

NOTES:

FEINBERG v. PFEIFFER CO.

Mo. Ct. App., 322 S.W.2d 163 (1959).

NATURE OF CASE: Action to recover damages for breach of a promise.

FACT SUMMARY: Pfeiffer (D) promised to pay Feinberg (P) an annuity when Feinberg (P) retired, and Feinberg (P) relied on this promise to her detriment.

CONCISE RULE OF LAW: A promise which the promisor should reasonably expect to induce action or forbearance of a definite and substantial character on the part of the promisee and which does induce such action or forbearance is binding if injustice can be avoided only by enforcement of the promise.

FACTS: Feinberg (P) was a long time employee of Pfeiffer (D). In view of Feinberg's (P) ability and length of service, Pfeiffer (D) promised her that if she ever chose to retire, Pfeiffer (D) would pay her $200 per month for the rest of her life. After working another year and a half, Feinberg (P) chose to retire and began receiving the promised $200 payments. Later, the payments were stopped, and Feinberg (P), who could no longer work, sought to recover on Pfeiffer's (D) promise.

ISSUE: If an employer promises an employee, upon retirement, a stipend for the rest of his life, and if the employee retires in reliance on that promise, is the promise binding on the employer?

HOLDING AND DECISION: (Doerner, Comm'r) Yes. A promise which the promisor should reasonably expect to induce action or forbearance of a definite and substantial character on the part of the promisee and which does induce such action or forbearance is binding if injustice can be avoided only by enforcement of the promise. (Restatement of Contracts, § 90) The second illustration cited in the comments to Restatement § 90 is precisely applicable to the present case. "A promises to pay B an annuity during B's life. B thereupon resigns a profitable employment, as A expected that he might. B receives the annuity for some years, in the meantime becoming disqualified from again obtaining good employment. A's promise is binding." The fact that, in the illustration, B became "disqualified" from obtaining other employment before A discontinued the payments whereas Feinberg (P) did not discover that she had cancer and was therefore unemployable until after Pfeiffer (D) had discontinued its payments is immaterial. The reference to the disability in the illustration has to do with the prevention of injustice, and the injustice would occur regardless of when the disability occurred.

EDITOR'S ANALYSIS: Note that, in the present case, if Feinberg (P) were still healthy and able to work, the decision would have been different. In that situation, it would not be the case that injustice could be avoided only by enforcement of the promise. Note additionally that if Feinberg (P) had continued to work for Pfeiffer (D) until she became physically unable to continue and was forced to retire, she could probably not recover on Pfeiffer's (D) promise. Her retirement would not have been in reliance on Pfeiffer's (D) promise as the doctrine of promissory estoppel requires.

[For more information on promissory estoppel, see Casenote Law Outline on Contracts, Chapter 2, § II, Substitutes for Valuable Consideration as Grounds for Imparting Liability Consequences for Breaching a Promise.]

NOTES:

GROUSE v. GROUP HEALTH PLAN, INC.

Minn. Sup. Ct., 306 N.W.2d 114 (1981).

NATURE OF CASE: Appeal of dismissal of action for damages for breach of contract.

NOTES:

FACT SUMMARY: Group Health (D) withdrew an employment offer after Grouse (P) had resigned his previous employment.

CONCISE RULE OF LAW: One resigning employment in reliance on a job offer may recover damages if the offer is withdrawn.

FACTS: Grouse (P) was a pharmacist at Richter Drug. Seeking a better position, he interviewed with Group Health Plan, Inc. (D). Elliot, Group Health's (D) chief pharmacist, offered Grouse (P) a position. Grouse (P) gave Richter two weeks' notice. Shoberg, Group Health's (D) general manager, then told Elliot he wanted a reference on Grouse (P). Elliot was unable to obtain one, and the employment offer was withdrawn. It took a period of time for Grouse (P) to find new employment. Grouse (P) sued for lost wages, based on breach of contract. The trial court dismissed, and Grouse (P) appealed.

ISSUE: May one resigning employment in reliance on a job offer recover damages if the offer is withdrawn?

HOLDING AND DECISION: (Otis, J.) Yes. One resigning employment in reliance on a job offer may recover damages if the offer is withdrawn. In a situation such as this, a contract does not exist in a strict legal sense because due to the bilateral power of termination neither party is committed to performance, and, therefore, no consideration exists. However, when one party reasonably relies to his detriment on the other's promise, under the equitable doctrine of promissory estoppel a contract may be implied in law when none exists in fact. Here, Grouse (P) in good faith quit his job on the basis of what he reasonably believed to be a firm employment offer and in so doing detrimentally relied on Grop Health's (D) offer. This was sufficient to invoke promissory estoppel to supply needed consideration. Reversed.

EDITOR'S ANALYSIS: Promissory estoppel, like most equitable doctrines, is a flexible tool courts may use to fill in gaps where strict adherence to the rules of actions at law would lead to seemingly unjust results. As the court here says, it is a substitute for consideration. One changing his position in reliance on another's promise will constitute the consideration to make a nonbinding unilateral offer into a binding bilateral contract.

[For more information on promissory estoppel, see Casenote Law Outline on Contracts, Chapter 2, § II, Substitutes for Valuable Consideration as Grounds for Imparting Liability Consequences for Breaching a Promise.]

COHEN v. COWLES MEDIA CO.

Mn. Sup. Ct., 479 N.W.2d 387 (1992).

NATURE OF CASE: Remand from appeal of an award of damages for breach of contract and fraudulent misrepresentation.

FACT SUMMARY: Editors of two newspapers broke their promises to Cohen (P), the source for a story, to keep his identity confidential.

CONCISE RULE OF LAW: Under the doctrine of promissory estoppel, a court should consider all aspects of a transaction's substance in determining whether enforcement is necessary to prevent an injustice.

FACTS: Cohen (P) supplied the Minneapolis Star Tribune, published by Cowles (D), and the St. Paul Pioneer Press Dispatch with disparaging information regarding a candidate for public office. The reporter for the Tribune and the Dispatch promised Cohen (P) that he would not be revealed as the source for the information. However, editors at the Tribune and the Dispatch later decided that it was important to reveal Cohen (P) as the source for the information because he was allied with an opposing candidate. After the story was published, Cohen (P) was fired from his job. Cohen (P) filed suit against Cowles (D) and the Dispatch's publisher (D) for breach of contract and fraudulent misrepresentation. The jury awarded Cohen (P) $200,000 in compensatory damages and $250,000 in punitive damages. On appeal, the court set aside recovery on the basis of fraudulent misrepresentation but affirmed recovery of the compensatory damages on the basis of breach of contract. The Minnesota Supreme Court found that promissory estoppel could form the basis for recovery but held that First Amendment concerns precluded recovery of damages. The United States Supreme Court, concluding that the First Amendment was not implicated, overruled this decision and remanded the case to determine whether a retrial would be necessary.

ISSUE: Under the doctrine of promissory estoppel, should a court consider all aspects of a transaction substance in determining whether enforcement is necessary to prevent an injustice?

HOLDING AND DECISION: (Simonett, J.) Yes. Under the doctrine of promissory estoppel, a court should consider all aspects of a transaction's substance in determining whether enforcement is necessary to prevent an injustice. A promise that is expected to, and does, induce definite action by the promisee is binding if injustice can be avoided only by enforcing the promise. The promise must be definite, clear, and intended to induce reliance. In the instant case, the record is clear that the Dispatch's and the Tribune's reporters made unambiguous promises to treat Cohen (P) as an anonymous source, and Cohen (P) provided the information based on these promises. Thus, the only remaining issue is whether this promise must be enforced to prevent an injustice. Neither side in this case clearly holds the higher moral ground. However, even the Tribune's witnesses acknowledged the importance of protecting the confidentiality of information sources. Additionally, it does not appear that there was a compelling need to break the promises in the present case. Therefore, it would be unjust to Cohen (P) unless the promises were enforced. Accordingly, the award of compensatory damages is affirmed under a theory of promissory estoppel.

EDITOR'S ANALYSIS: The court ruled that the damages instruction the trial court provided for breach of contract was also valid for promissory estoppel recovery. A study examining the effect of this decision on publishers revealed that there was no substantial change in policies regarding confidential sources. In fact, most publishers thought the result was just and proper.

NOTES:

C.R. KLEWIN, INC. v. FLAGSHIP PROPERTIES, INC.

Conn. Sup. Ct., 220 Conn. 569, 600 A.2d 772 (1991).

NATURE OF CASE: Certified appeal in action for breach of contract.

FACT SUMMARY: Flagship (D) orally agreed to use Klewin (P) as a construction manager on a project likely to take more than one year to complete, but contracted with another contractor after becoming dissatisfied with Klewin's (P) work.

CONCISE RULE OF LAW: The Statute of Frauds, requiring a writing for an agreement that is not to be performed within one year from the making thereof, will not render unenforceable an oral contract that fails to specify explicitly the time for performance, even when performance will likely take more than one year.

FACTS: Flagship (D) representatives held a dinner with Klewin (P) representatives. During the meeting, Klewin (P) suggested what fee it would require to serve as a construction manager. At the end of the meeting, the Flagship (D) agent said that they had a deal and the agents from both parties shook hands. No other terms or conditions were conclusively established. The agreement was publicized and a press conference was held. Construction began on May 4, 1987, on the first phase of the project. In March 1988, Flagship (D) retained another contractor for the next phase. Klewin (P) filed suit in district court for breach of an oral contract. Flagship's (D) motion for summary judgment was granted. Klewin (P) appealed. The Second Circuit Court of Appeals certified questions to the Connecticut Supreme Court on issues not addressed in Conneticut case law.

ISSUE: Will the Statute of Frauds, requiring a writing for an agreement that is not to be performed within one year from the making thereof, render unenforceable an oral contract that fails to specify explicitly the time for performance when performance of that contract within one year of its making is very unlikely?

HOLDING AND DECISION: (Peter, J.) No. The Statute of Frauds, requiring a writing for an agreement that is not to be performed within one year from the making thereof, will not render unenforceable an oral contract that fails to specify explicitly the time for performance, even when performance will likely take more than one year. The Statute of Frauds excludes contracts except those whose performance cannot possibly be completed within one year. Connecticut case law has narrowly construed the statute of frauds in this area. In this case, the oral agreement did not specify a time for completion. When an oral contract does not expressly dictate that performance will last beyond one year, the contract will be construed as a matter of law to be a contract of indefinite duration for purposes of the Statute of Frauds. Given this narrow interpretation of the Statute of Frauds, it is enough that the agreement left open the possibility of completion within one year. The contract is enforceable.

EDITOR'S ANALYSIS: Historians are unclear as to the reason for including the one-year category in the Statute of Frauds. Commentators, however, agree in that the Statute does not accomplish any of its possible purposes very well. Most jurisdictions construe the one-year provision as narrowly as possible to minimize the number of contracts voided by its operation.

[For more information on the Statute of Frauds, see Casenote Law Outline on Contracts, Chapter 3, § V, Defenses Arising from the Form of the Bargain.]

NOTES:

NORTH SHORE BOTTLING CO. v. C. SCHMIDT & SONS, INC.

22 N.Y.2d 171 (1968).

NATURE OF CASE: Action for breach of exclusive distributorship contract.

FACT SUMMARY: Schmidt & Sons (D) agreed that North Shore Bottling (P) would be its exclusive distributor in the New York, Queens County area.

CONCISE RULE OF LAW: An oral agreement which may, by its terms, be performed within one year is not within the Statute of Frauds.

FACTS: Schmidt & Sons (D) entered into an exclusive distributorship contract with North Shore Bottling (P). The agreement provided that North Shore (P) would be the exclusive distributor of Schmidt's (D) beer in the Queens County area of New York so long as Schmidt (D) continued to sell beer in New York. The contract was oral. North Shore (P) expended its best efforts in promoting the beer and increased its sale 100 percent. Schmidt (D) then entered into a subsequent exclusive distributorship agreement with Midway Beverages for the same area. North Shores (P) brought suit and Schmidt (D) defended based on the Statute of Frauds. The trial court dismissed the action on this basis. The appellate division reversed, claiming that the contract, based on the contingency "so long as Schmidt (D) sold its beer in New York," could be performed in one year and was therefore outside the statute.

ISSUE: Will a contingency contained in an oral contract take it outside the Statute of Frauds if the contract is capable of being performed in a year?

HOLDING AND DECISION: (Fuld, C.J.) Yes. The Statute of Frauds is a bar to protect the innocent. When, by competent evidence, a contract can be demonstrated to the court, it will liberally apply the rule that a contract which may be completed within one year is outside the statute's purview. The fact that the parties contemplated a contract lasting a number of years is not dispositive of the issue. Schmidt (D) could, unilaterally, decide at any time to cease selling its beer in New York. It was obvious from its inclusion in the oral contract that this was a possibility and that it could occur at any time. The existence of a contingency which may occur within a year is sufficient to except the contract from the Statute of Frauds. The order of the appellate division is affirmed, and the case is remanded for a new trial.

EDITOR'S ANALYSIS: Other examples of contingencies which will except a contract from the statute are to support for life; to perform until the happening of an uncertain event or the destruction of an object; to perform until an event (e.g., war) has terminated; and until a party has married or divorced. All of these factors could occur within a year, and, in appropriate cases, they would except an oral contract from the statute's operation.

[For more information on the Statute of Frauds, see Casenote Law Outline on Contracts, Chapter 3, § V, Defenses Arising from the Form of the Bargain.]

NOTES:

MASON v. ANDERSON

Vt. Sup. Ct., 146 Vt. 242, 499 A.2d 783 (1985).

NATURE OF CASE: Appeal from summary judgment awarding damages for breach of an oral loan agreement.

FACT SUMMARY: Mason (P) sued decedent's estate on an oral agreement to repay a loan.

CONCISE RULE OF LAW: The complete performance of one party to an oral agreement takes the agreement out of the one-year provision of the Statute of Frauds.

FACTS: Mason (P) alleged that he loaned $5,000 to Miner, who orally agreed to repay the sum at the rate of $200 per month. Payments on the loan were made by Miner until the time of his death, after which Mason (P) sued the decedent's administratrix, Anderson (D), for the balance. Anderson (D) defended on the ground that since the agreement could not be performed within a year of its making it must be evidenced by a writing signed by the party to be charged. The trial court granted Mason's (P) summary judgment motion. Anderson (D) appealed.

ISSUE: Does complete performance by one party to an oral agreement take the agreement out of the one-year provision of the Statute of Frauds?

HOLDING AND DECISION: (Hill, J.) Yes. The complete performance of one party to an oral agreement takes the agreement out of the one-year provision of the Statute of Frauds. This is an exception to the rule that the agreement that is not able to be performed within one year must be evidenced by a writing signed by the party to be charged. The purpose of the Statute of Frauds is to prevent a party from being compelled, by oral and perhaps false testimony, to be held responsible for an agreement he claims was never made. Application of the statute in the present case would operate to perpetrate a fraud rather than prevent one. Mason (P) fully performed his obligations under the agreement. He acted in reliance on the agreement in lending Miner $5,000 and thereby changed his position in a manner which prejudiced himself. In such a situation, to insist on a strict and mechanical operation of the statute would defeat its purpose. Mason (P) was therefore not prevented by the statute from presenting parol evidence to prove the existence of the contract. Affirmed.

EDITOR'S ANALYSIS: The fact that memories fade as to the obligations of contracting parties prompted the drafters of the one-year provision of the Statute of Frauds to require a writing signed by the party to be charged. It is logical to hold that a party who has fully performed his end of the deal should not be precluded from using parol evidence to prove the existence of the agreement. The Statute of Frauds can be analyzed in three steps. First, the student should determine which provision of the statute is involved. Second, it must be determined whether there is a writing signed by the party to be charged. This may be satisfied by a canceled check, a letter to a person not a party to the agreement, or a combination of documents. As long as the "writing" acknowledges the existence of the agreement and is signed by the party who wishes to invoke the statute, the court can take the agreement out of the statute. Some jurisdictions require that in using more than one document to satisfy the writing requirement, the documents make specific reference to one another. Third and last is the determination of whether the agreement falls within or without the statute in light of the evidence and circumstances.

[For more information on the Statute of Frauds and equitable estoppel, see Casenote Law Outline on Contracts, Chapter 3, § V, Defenses Arising from the Form of the Bargain.]

NOTES:

CRABTREE v. ELIZABETH ARDEN SALES CORPORATION

N.Y. Ct. App., 305 N.Y. 48, 110 N.E.2d 551 (1953).

NATURE OF CASE: Action for damages for breach of an employment contract.

FACT SUMMARY: Crabtree (P) was hired by Arden (D) to be the latter's sales manager. No formal contract was signed, but separate writings pieced together showed Crabtree (P) to have been hired for a two-year term with pay raises after the first and second six months. When he did not receive his second pay raise, Crabtree (P) sued for damages for breach.

CONCISE RULE OF LAW: The Statute of Frauds does not require the memorandum expressing the contract to be in one document. It may be pieced together out of separate writings, connected with one another either expressly or by the internal evidence of subject matter and occasion.

FACTS: In September 1947, Crabtree (P) began negotiating with Arden (D) for the position of the latter's sales manager. Being unfamiliar with the cosmetics business and giving up a well-paying, secure job, Crabtree (P) insisted upon an agreement for a definite term. He asked for three years at $25,000 per year. But Arden (D) offered two years, with $20,000 per year the first six months, $25,000 per year the second six months, and $30,000 per year the second year. This was written down by Arden's (D) personal secretary with the notation "2 years to make good." A few days later, Crabtree (P) telephoned to Mr. Johns, Arden's (D) executive vice - president, his acceptance. Crabtree (P) received a "welcome" wire from Miss Arden (D). When he reported for work, a "payroll change" card was made up and initialed by Mr. Johns showing the above pay arrangement with a salary increase noted "as per contractual agreement." Crabtree (P) received his first pay raise as scheduled but not his second one. Miss Arden (D) allegedly refused to approve the second increase, denying Crabtree (P) had been hired for any specific period.

ISSUE: Is there satisfactory evidence to piece together from separate documents a written contract within the Statute of Frauds, thus enforceable?

HOLDING AND DECISION: (Fuld, J.) Yes. First, as it is alleged that the contract is for a period of two years, there must be written evidence of its terms to be enforceable, as the two-year performance places it within the Statute of Frauds. The payroll cards, one initialed by Arden's (D) executive vice - president and the other by its controller, unquestionably constituted a memorandum under the statute. It is enough that they were signed with the intent to authenticate the information contained therein and that such information does evidence the terms of the contract. The cards had all essential terms except for duration. But as the memorandum can be pieced together from more than one document, all that is required between the papers is a connection established simply by reference to the same subject matter or transaction. Parol evidence is permissible in order to establish the connection. As the note prepared by Arden's (D) personal secretary shows it was made in Miss Arden's (D) presence as well as that of Johns and of Crabtree (P), the dangers of parol evidence are at a minimum. All of the terms must be set out in writing and cannot be shown by parol. That memo, the paper signed by Johns, and the paper signed by the controller all refer on their faces to the Crabtree (P) transaction. The controller's paper shows that it was prepared for the purpose of a "salary increase per contractual arrangements with Miss Arden" (D). That is a reference to more comprehensive evidence, and parol evidence can so explain. "2 years to make good" probably had no other purpose than to denote the duration of the arrangement, and parol evidence may explain its meaning.

EDITOR'S ANALYSIS: When there is more than one writing and all are signed by the party to be charged, and it is clear by their contents that they relate to the same transaction, there is little problem. When not all the documents are signed, difficulties obviously crop up. It becomes difficult to say the memorandum has been authenticated to the party to be charged. When the unsigned document is physically attached to the signed writing, the Statute of Frauds is satisfied. And, as illustrated by this case, this is true when the signed document by its terms expressly refers to the unsigned document. The cases conflict where the papers are not attached or fail to refer to the other. The minority holds that that is a failure to show sufficient authentication. The better view is that if the signed document does not expressly refer to the unsigned, it is sufficient if internal evidence refers to the same subject matter or transaction. If so, extrinsic evidence is admissible to help show the connection between the documents.

[For more information on the statute of frauds and extrinsic evidence, see Casenote Law Outline on Contracts, Chapter 3, § V, Defenses Arising from the Form of the Bargain.]

NOTES:

DF ACTIVITIES CORP. v. BROWN

851 F.2d 920 (7th Cir. 1988).

NATURE OF CASE: Appeal from dismissal of action for damages for breach of contract.

FACT SUMMARY: DF (P), which asserted that an oral contract was made with Brown (D) to buy her valuable Frank Lloyd Wright-designed chair, sought to depose Brown (D) to get an involuntary admission of the contract's existence.

CONCISE RULE OF LAW: A party asserting the statute of frauds as a defense may not be deposed for the sole purpose of eliciting an admission that a contract was made.

FACTS: DF (P), through its art director, negotiated to buy a chair which was designed by Frank Lloyd Wright. Brown (D), the owner of the chair, denied that she agreed in a November 26 phone conversation to sell it. DF (P) contended that on that date the parties agreed to a price of $60,000, payable in two equal installments, the first being due on December 3 and the second on March 26. On December 3, DF (P) sent a letter confirming the agreement along with a check for $30,000. Two weeks later, Brown (D) returned the letter and the check with a handwritten note that said, "Since I did not hear from you until December and I spoke with you the middle of November, I have made other arrangements for the chair. It is no longer available for sale to you." Brown (D) later sold the chair for $198,000, and DF (P) sued for the difference between the price at which the chair was sold and the contract price of $60,000. Attached to Brown's (D) motion to dismiss was her affidavit denying that any agreement was made for the sale of the chair. Also attached was a letter from Brown (D) to DF (P), dated September 20, withdrawing the offer to sell the chair, and a letter from DF (P) to Brown (D), dated October 29, withdrawing DF's (P) offer to buy the chair. The trial court granted Brown's (D) motion to dismiss, and this appeal followed. DF (P) sought to depose Brown (D) in order to try to extract an involuntary admission that a contract had been made.

ISSUE: May a party asserting the statute of frauds as a defense be deposed for the sole purpose of eliciting an admission that a contract was made?

HOLDING AND DECISION: (Posner, C.J.) No. A party asserting the statute of frauds as a defense to contract formation may not be deposed for the sole purpose of eliciting an admission that a contract was made. The alleged November 26 oral contract may be within the statutory exception for sales of goods for over $500, if "the party against whom enforcement is sought admits in his pleading, testimony or otherwise in court that a contract was made." U.C.C. § 2-201(3)(b). Since Brown (D) swore in her affidavit that no agreement was made for the sale of the chair, there is no reason to keep the lawsuit alive. The chance of Brown (D) changing her testimony at deposition is too remote to prolong an effort to enforce an oral contract in the teeth of the statute of frauds. Affirmed.

EDITOR'S ANALYSIS: The judge writing the dissent in this case seemed to interpret the majority's holding to mean that a sworn denial of a contract was sufficient to block further discovery. The majority is more likely recognizing that, once a party has sworn to a fact, he is not likely to change his story later in the lawsuit. If a party perjures himself by giving untruthful information in an affidavit, changing his story later would be a virtual admission that he perjured himself in the prior statement made under oath. The court can always exercise its discretion to allow further discovery in the face of a defendant's sworn denial. Here, the judge considered it a waste of time to permit further discovery.

[For more information on the statute of frauds, see Casenote Law Outline on Contracts, Chapter 3, § V, Defenses Arising from the Form of the Bargain.]

NOTES:

CHAPTER 3
THE BARGAIN RELATIONSHIP

QUICK REFERENCE RULES OF LAW

1. **Ascertainment of Assent: The "Objective" Test.** The secret feelings, intentions, or beliefs of a party will not affect the formation of a contract if their words and acts indicate that they intend to enter into a binding agreement. (Embry v. Hargadine, McKittrick Dry Goods Co.)

    [For more information on the intent to form a contract, see Casenote Law Outline on Contracts, Chapter 1, § II, The Offer.]

2. **Ascertainment of Assent: The "Objective" Test.** If a person's words and acts, judged by a reasonable standard, manifest a certain intent, it is immaterial what may be the real but unexpressed state of that person's mind. (Lucy v. Zehmer)

    [For more information on offers made in jest, see Casenote Law Outline on Contracts, Chapter 1, § II, The Offer.]

3. **Ascertainment of Assent. The "Objective" Test.** Failure to abide by a moral or ethical obligation does not give rise to an action for breach of express contract or for breach of contract implied-in-law through the doctrine of promissory estoppel. (Cohen v. Cowles Media Company)

    [For more information on promissory estoppel, see Casenote Law Outline on Contracts, Chapter 2, § II, Substitutes for Valuable Consideration as Grounds for Imparting Liability Consequences for Breaching a Promise.]

4. **Offer: Creation of Power of Acceptance.** There can be no contract unless the minds of the parties have met and mutually agreed upon some specific thing. (Lonergan v. Scolnick)

    [For more information on the elements of an offer, see Casenote Law Outline on Contracts, Chapter 1, § II, The Offer.]

5. **Offer: Creation of Power of Acceptance.** A newspaper advertisement (for the sale of an article) which is clear, definite, and explicit, and leaves nothing to negotiation is an offer, acceptance of which will create a binding contract. (Lefkowitz v. Great Minneapolis Surplus Store)

    [For more information on offers addressed to the public, see Casenote Law Outline on Contracts, Chapter 1, § II, The Offer.]

6. **Offer: Creation of Power of Acceptance.** An "offer" has been made if, under all of the facts and circumstances existing at the time, a reasonable person in the position of the alleged offeree would have been led to believe that an offer was being made. (Southworth v. Oliver)

    [For more information on the elements of an offer, see Casenote Law Outline on Contracts, Chapter 1, § II, The Offer.]

7. **Acceptance: Exercise of Power of Acceptance.** An offer may be accepted only by a person in whom the offeror intended to create a power of acceptance and in the manner specified by the offeror. (La Salle National Bank v. Vega)

    [For more information on elements of a valid acceptance, see Casenote Law Outline on Contracts, Chapter 1, § III, The Acceptance.]

8. **Acceptance: Exercise of Power of Acceptance.** No contract is formed when the offer is revoked before the acceptance is communicated to the offeror. (Hendricks v. Behee)

[For more information on life of an offer, see Casenote Law Outline on Contracts, Chapter 2, § II, Substitutes for Valuable Consideration as Grounds for Imparting Liability Consequences for Breaching a Promise.]

9. **Acceptance: Exercise of Power of Acceptance.** Where a contract does not specify a time within which it may be accepted, a "reasonable time" will be implied. (Ever-Tite Roofing Corp. v. Green)

[For more information on unilateral contracts and the life of the offer, see Casenote Law Outline on Contracts, Chapter 1, § III, The Acceptance.]

10. **Acceptance: Exercise of Power of Acceptance.** A seller's price list is not an offer to the buyer, and a subsequent partial shipment of the buyer's order is not an acceptance sufficient to form a contract. (Corinthian Pharmaceutical Systems, Inc. v. Lederle Laboratories)

[For more information on the mode of acceptance, see Casenote Law Outline on Contracts, Chapter 1, § III, The Acceptance.]

11. **Acceptance: Exercise of Power of Acceptance.** An advertised reward to anyone who performs certain conditions specified in the advertisement is an offer, and the performance of such conditions is an acceptance which creates a valid contract. (Carlill v. Carbolic Smoke Ball Co.)

[For more information on formation of unilateral contracts, see Casenote Law Outline on Contracts, Chapter 1, § III, The Acceptance.]

12. **Acceptance: Exercise of Power of Acceptance.** Questions regarding rewards offered by private individuals and groups are to be decided according to contract law, and there can be no contract unless the person claiming the reward knew about it when she gave the desired information and acted with the intention of accepting it. (Glover v. Jewish War Veterans of United States)

[For more information on acceptance, see Casenote Law Outline on Contracts, Chapter 1, § III, The Acceptance.]

13. **Acceptance: Exercise of Power of Acceptance.** If an offer invites acceptance by performance, an offeree's performance will be deemed an acceptance unless a contrary intention on his part is shown. (Industrial America, Inc. v. Fulton Industries, Inc.)

[For more information on unilateral contracts, see Casenote Law Outline on Contracts, Chapter 1, § III, The Acceptance.]

14. **Acceptance: Exercise of Power of Acceptance.** An acceptance of an offer is effective upon dispatch. (Adams v. Lindsell)

[For more information on the mailbox rule, see Casenote Law Outline on Contracts, Chapter 1, § III, The Acceptance.]

15. **Acceptance: Exercise of Power of Acceptance.** Where the offeree exercises dominion over things which are offered to him, such exercise of dominion in the absence of other circumstances showing a contrary intention is an acceptance. (Russell v. Texas Co.)

[For more information on silence as acceptance, see Casenote Law Outline on Contracts, Chapter 1, § III, The Acceptance.]

16. **Acceptance: Exercise of Power of Acceptance.** Where an offeree fails to reply to an offer, his silence and inaction operate as an acceptance where, because of previous dealings or otherwise, the offeree has given the offeror reason to understand that the silence or inaction is intended as a manifestation of assent and the offeror does so understand. (Ammons v. Wilson & Co.)

    [For more information on previous dealings, see Casenote Law Outline on Contracts, Chapter 1, § III, The Acceptance.]

17. **Acceptance: Exercise of Power of Acceptance.** A buyer is estopped from denying the existence of an oral contract when he has benefitted from the performance and business practices of the seller. (Smith-Scharff Paper Company v. P. N. Hirsch & Co. Stores, Inc.)

    [For more information on equitable estoppel, see Casenote Law Outline on Contracts, Chapter 3, § V, Defenses Arising from the Form of the Bargain.]

18. **Acceptance: Exercise of Power of Acceptance.** Only in circumstances of actual detriment should a court intrude upon the exercise of commercial free speech. (Harris v. Time, Inc.)

    [For more information on expectation interest, see Casenote Law Outline on Contracts, Chapter 7, § III, Remedies for Breach of Contract.]

19. **Nature and Effect of Counter-Offer.** An "acceptance" which does not assent to the offer as made is a rejection and counteroffer as it manifests an unwillingness of the offeree. (Minneapolis & St. Louis Railway Co. v. Columbus Rolling-Mill Co.)

    [For more information on counteroffers, see Casenote Law Outline on Contracts, Chapter 1, § III, The Acceptance.]

20. **Nature and Effect of Counter-Offer.** A confirmation letter, between merchants, containing additional or different terms from the offer is an acceptance unless the new terms materially alter the offer, the offer expressly limits the acceptance to the conditions of the offer, or one merchant has expressed his objection to the new terms. (Leonard Pevar Company v. Evans Products Co.)

    [For more information on the impact of different or additional terms, see Casenote Law Outline on Contracts, Chapter 1, § III, The Acceptance.]

21. **Termination of Offer: Destruction of Power of Acceptance.** An offer may be withdrawn by an indirect revocation where the offeree receives reliable information from a third party that the offeror has engaged in conduct indicative to a reasonable man that the offer was withdrawn. (Dickinson v. Dodds)

    [For more information on indirect revocation, see Casenote Law Outline on Contracts, Chapter 1, § II, The Offer.]

22. **Irrevocable Offer: Nondestructable Power of Acceptance.** If the original offer is irrevocable and creates in the offeree a "binding option," the rule that a counteroffer terminates the power of acceptance does not apply. (Humble Oil & Refining Co. v. Westside Investment Corp.)

    [For more information on formation of an option, see Casenote Law Outline on Contracts, Chapter 1, § II, The Offer.]

23. **Irrevocable Offer: Nondestructable Power of Acceptance.** An offer to enter into a unilateral contract may be withdrawn at any time prior to performance of the act requested to be done. (Petterson v. Pattberg)

[For more information on the unilateral contract, see Casenote Law Outline on Contracts, Chapter 1, § III, The Acceptance.]

24. **Irrevocable Offer: Nondestructable Power of Acceptance.** Where an offer invites an offeree to accept by rendering a performance, an option contract so created is conditional on the offeree's completion of performance in accordance with the terms of the offer. (Marchiondo v. Scheck)

[For more information on revocation of offer, see Casenote Law Outline on Contracts, Chapter 1, § II, The Offer.]

25. **Irrevocable Offer: Nondestructable Power of Acceptance.** The doctrine of promissory estoppel shall not be applied in cases where there is an offer for exchange as the offer is not intended to become a promise until consideration is received. (James Baird Co. v. Gimbel Brothers, Inc.)

[For more information on performance as attempted acceptance of offer to form bilateral contract, see Casenote Law Outline on Contracts, Chapter 1, § II, The Offer.]

26. **Irrevocable Offer: Nondestructable Power of Acceptance.** A promise which the promisor should reasonably expect to induce action or forbearance of a definite and substantial character on the part of a promisee and which does induce such action or forbearance is binding if injustice can be avoided only by enforcement of the promise. (Drennan v. Star Paving Co.)

[For more information on detrimental reliance as making offer irrevocable, see Casenote Law Outline on Contracts, Chapter 1, § III, The Acceptance.]

27. **Irrevocable Offer: Nondestructable Power of Acceptance.** A subcontractor's bid, made in reliance on the contractor's conditional promise of use, is sufficient consideration to bind the contractor to his promise. (Electrical Construction & Maintenance Company, Inc. v. Maeda Pacific Corporation)

[For more information on conditional promises, see Casenote Law Outline on Contracts, Chapter 2, § I, Valuable Consideration: The Bargained-for Incursion of Legal Detriment.]

28. **Defective Formulation and Expression of Agreement.** Where neither party knows or has reason to know of the ambiguity or where both know or have reason to know, the ambiguity is given the meaning that each party intended it to have. (Raffles v. Wichelhaus)

[For more information on latent ambiguity, see Casenote Law Outline on Contracts, Chapter 1, § IV, Impact of Ambiguity and Mistake on the Bargain.]

29. **Defective Formulation and Expression of Agreement.** There can be no contract when the parties give different meanings to a material term. (Konic International Corporation v. Spokane Computer Services, Inc.)

[For more information on ambiguity of language in the bargain, see Casenote Law Outline on Contracts, Chapter 1, § IV, Impact of Ambiguity and Mistake on the Bargain.]

30. **Indefinite Agreements.** In order for a contract to be valid, the promise or the agreement of the parties to it must be certain and explicit so that their full intention may be ascertained to a reasonable degree of certainty. (Varney v. Ditmars)

[For more information on implications of essential contract terms, see Casenote Law Outline on Contracts, Chapter 1, § II, The Offer.]

31. **Incomplete and Deferred Agreement.** If the parties thereto have completed their negotiations as to what they regard as the essential elements and performance has begun on the good-faith understanding that agreement on the unsettled matters will follow, the courts will find and enforce a contract if some objective method of determining the unsettled elements is available — such as resort to the contract itself, commercial practice, or other usage and custom. (Metro-Goldwyn-Mayer, Inc. v. Scheider)

    [For more information on agreements to agree in the future on content of an essential term, see Casenote Law Outline on Contracts, Chapter 1, § II, The Offer.]

32. **Incomplete and Deferred Agreement.** A real estate lease provision calling for the renewal of the lease at a rental to be agreed upon is unenforceable due to its omission of a material term. (Joseph Martin, Jr., Delicatessen, Inc. v. Schumacher)

    [For more information on agreements to agree in the future on the content of an essential term, see Casenote Law Outline on Contracts, Chapter 1, § II, The Offer.]

33. **Incomplete and Deferred Agreement.** The court can look to the parties' course of dealing to determine their intent to be bound. (Oglebay Norton Company v. Armco, Inc.)

    [For more information on the course of dealing between parties, see Casenote Law Outline on Contracts, Chapter 3, § V, Defenses Arising from the Form of the Bargain.]

34. **Incomplete and Deferred Agreement.** Parties who have made their pact "subject to" a later definitive agreement have manifested an intent not to be bound. (Empro Manufacturing Co., Inc. v. Ball-Co Manufacturing, Inc.)

    [For more information on the formation of a contract, see Casenote Law Outline on Contracts, Chapter 1, § II, The Offer.]

35. **Remedies Where Agreement Incomplete or Indefinite.** Under the doctrine of promissory estoppel, as stated in Section 90 of Restatement, First, Contracts, "a promise which the promisor should reasonably expect to induce action or forbearance of a definite and substantial character on the part of the promisee and which does induce such action or forbearance is binding if injustice can be avoided only by enforcement of the promise." (Hoffman v. Red Owl Stores, Inc.)

    [For more information on the doctrine of promissory estoppel, see Casenote Law Outline on Contracts, Chapter 2, § II, Substitutes for Valuable Consideration as Grounds for Imparting Liability Consequences for Breaching a Promise.]

EMBRY v. HARGADINE-McKITTRICK DRY GOODS CO.

127 Missouri App. 383 (1907).

NATURE OF CASE: Action to enforce renewal of employment contract.

FACT SUMMARY: Embry (P) was allegedly rehired by Hargadine-McKittrick (D) after his employment contract had expired. Hargadine-McKittrick (D) denied the rehiring.

CONCISE RULE OF LAW: The secret feelings, intentions, or beliefs of a party will not affect the formation of a contract if their words and acts indicate that they intend to enter into a binding agreement.

FACTS: Embry (P) was working for Hargadine-McKittrick (D) under a written employment contract. After its expiration, Embry (P) approached McKittrick (D) and demanded a new contract or he would immediately quit. According to Embry (P), McKittrick (D) agreed to rehire him. Embry (P) was terminated in February of the next year. He brought suit to recover the amount due him under the contract. McKittrick (D) swore that the conversation never took place and that Embry (P) had not been rehired. The judge instructed the jury that even if the conversation occurred as related by Embry (P), to form a contract both parties must have intended to enter into a binding agreement. The jury found against Embry (P). He appealed an the basis that the judge's instruction was incorrect, that if McKittrick (D) conveyed by word and deed his intent to rehire Embry (P), a binding contract was formed regardless of McKittrick's (D) secret intention.

ISSUE: Will a hidden, undisclosed intention affect the formation of a contract?

HOLDING AND DECISION: (Goode, J.) No. If the other party reasonably relies on the promise, an undisclosed intention will not affect the formation of a binding contract. Therefore, the trial judge's instructions were erroneous. If the jury reasonably believed that McKittrick (D) had promised to rehire Embry (P), it is immaterial whether McKittrick (D) meant his promise or not. It is obvious that Embry (P) believed a valid contract had been formed because he remained on the job. His reliance was reasonable since McKittrick (D) was the president of the company and had the authority to rehire him. Therefore, the case must be remanded for a new trial since it cannot be determined on what basis the jury found for McKittrick (D). The same holding applies where a reasonable person would interpret the meaning of a conversation as the formation of a binding contract. The fact that McKittrick (D) did not intend to rehire Embry (P) is immaterial if the natural interpretation of the conversation is that he was being rehired. Again, McKittrick's (D) undisclosed intent is immaterial.

EDITOR'S ANALYSIS: In order to analyze the manifest intentions of the parties, there are several standards of interpretation which may be applied to their words. First, there is the general accepted meaning of the terms used. Then, there is the meaning of the term according to trade or custom. Finally, there is the meaning the parties may have assigned to the term in the course of past dealings. By utilizing these methods, a court attempts to determine what the parties thought they were doing and to give effect to their legitimate expectations.

[For more information on the intent to form a contract, see Casenote Law Outline on Contracts, Chapter 1, § II, The Offer.]

NOTES:

LUCY v. ZEHMER

Va. Sup. Ct. App., 196 Va. 493, 84 S.E.2d 516 (1954).

NATURE OF CASE: Action for specific performance of a land sale contract.

NOTES:

FACT SUMMARY: Zehmer (D) claimed his offer to sell his farm to Lucy (P) was made in jest.

CONCISE RULE OF LAW: If a person's words and acts, judged by a reasonable standard, manifest a certain intent, it is immaterial what may be the real but unexpressed state of that person's mind.

FACTS: Zehmer (D) and his wife (D) contracted to sell their 471-acre farm to Lucy (P) for $50,000. Zehmer (D) contended that his offer was made in jest while the three of them were drinking and that Zehmer (D) only desired to bluff Lucy (P) into admitting he did not have $50,000. Lucy (P) appeared to have taken the offer seriously by discussing its terms with Zehmer (D), rewriting it to enable Mrs. Zehmer (D) to sign also, by providing for title examination, and by taking possession of the agreement. Lucy (P) offered $5 to bind the deal and the next day sold a one-half interest to his brother (P) in order to raise money.

ISSUE: Does the law impute to a person an intention corresponding to the reasonable meaning of his words and acts?

HOLDING AND DECISION: (Buchanan, J.) Yes. The existence of an offer depends upon the reasonable meaning to be given the offeror's acts and words. For the formation of a contract, the mental assent of the parties is not required. If the words and acts of one of the parties have but one reasonable meaning, his undisclosed intention is immaterial except when an unreasonable meaning which he attaches to his manifestations is known to the other party. Accordingly, one cannot say he was merely jesting when his conduct and words would warrant reasonable belief that a real agreement was intended.

EDITOR'S ANALYSIS: Note that it is not what is said but how it is heard and reasonably understood. Mutual assent of the parties is required for the formation of a contract, but mental assent is not. Where one party can reasonably believe from the other party's acts and words that a real agreement is intended, the other party's real but unexpressed intention is immaterial. Mutual assent is an objective determination based upon what a reasonable man would believe. An offer is an expression of will or intention creating a power of acceptance upon the offeree. If the offer to sell the farm had been for a price of $50, the court could judge the ridiculousness of the offer in determining whether a reasonable man would believe it to be serious.

[For more information on offers made in jest, see Casenote Law Outline on Contracts, Chapter 1, § II, The Offer.]

COHEN v. COWLES MEDIA COMPANY

Minn. Sup. Ct., 457 N.W.2d 199 (1990).

NATURE OF CASE: Appeal from reversal of award of damages for fraudulent misrepresentation and affirmation of award of damages for breach of contract claim.

FACT SUMMARY: Even though a reporter for the Minneapolis Star Tribune, published by Cowles Media (D), promised confidentiality to Cohen (P), the source of embarrassing information about a political candidate, the editors of the Star Tribune published Cohen's (P) name anyway in connection with a story based on the information.

CONCISE RULE OF LAW: Failure to abide by a moral or ethical obligation does not give rise to an action for breach of express contract or for breach of contract implied-in-law through the doctrine of promissory estoppel.

FACTS: Cohen (P), an active political operative, possessed information about a candidate for lieutenant governor, who had previous arrests for unlawful assembly and petit theft. He offered this information, in return for a promise of confidentiality and treatment as an anonymous source, to a reporter for the Minneapolis Star Tribune, owned by Cowles Media (D). The Star Tribune reporter promised to keep Cohen's (P) identity anonymous, and Cohen (P) released the information to him. However, the editors of the Star Tribune decided after much debate to publish the story about the political candidate and to attribute the information on which the story was based to Cohen (P). On the day the story was published, Cohen (P) was fired by his employer. Cohen (P) sued Cowles Media (D) for fraudulent misrepresentation and breach of contract; the trial court ruled that the First Amendment did not bar Cohen's (P) claims and left the matter to the jury, which awarded Cohen (P) both compensatory and punitive damages. However, the court of appeals reversed the lower verdict on the misrepresentation claim and set aside the punitive damages award; it, nevertheless, upheld the award of compensatory damages on the contract claim. Both Cohen (P) and Cowles Media (D) appealed.

ISSUE: Does failure to abide by a moral or ethical obligation give rise to an action for breach of express contract or for breach of contract implied-in-law through the doctrine of promissory estoppel?

HOLDING AND DECISION: (Simonett, J.) No. The failure to abide by a moral or ethical obligation does not give rise to an action for breach of express contract or for breach of contract implied-in-law through the doctrine of promissory estoppel. Although protection of a confidential source may be a matter of honor, morality, professional ethics, and tradition in the business of news reporting, and the failure to protect such sources may have the result of drying them up, in the special milieu of newsgathering a source and a reporter do not ordinarily believe they are engaged in making a legally binding contract. They are not thinking in terms of offers and acceptances in any commercial or business sense. To impose contract law on news-source confidentiality arrangements would be inappropriate because it would result in unwarranted rigidity in relationships which are largely ethical. Nor may Cohen's (P) reliance to his detriment on the promises of the Star Tribune reporter not to reveal his name in connection with the story give rise to an implied-in-law contract under the doctrine of promissory estoppel because it would not necessarily be unjust to refuse to enforce the promise. If news publishers such as Cowles Media (D) faced the potential for civil damages if promises of confidentiality are breached, a "chilling effect" on free speech and public debate would result, and their First Amendment rights would be abridged. Affirmed as to the fraudulent misrepresentation claim; reversed as to the breach of contract claim.

DISSENT: (Yetka, J.) Cohen (P) should be allowed to recover under either a contract or promissory estoppel theory. Cowles Media (D) promised confidentiality to Cohen (P) in consideration for information it considered newsworthy. When the promise was broken, Cohen (P) lost his job. Newspapers should be required to keep their promises like everybody else.

DISSENT: (Kelly, J.) All of the elements of a legal contract and its breach were present here. The parties intended to enter into a contract, and that contract should be enforced.

EDITOR'S ANALYSIS: Moral consideration lacks the element of a bargain and therefore is not considered "valuable." The most commonly cited factual example of moral consideration is a father's promise to reimburse a Good Samaritan for the cost of care and burial of his dying adult child. Because the father did not request the services and the parent was without legal responsibility for the affairs of adult offspring, there was no element of conscious or implied bargain. See, e.g., Mills v. Wyman, 20 Mass. (3 Pick.) 207 (1825).

[For more information on promissory estoppel, see Casenote Law Outline on Contracts, Chapter 2, § II, Substitutes for Valuable Consideration as Grounds for Imparting Liability Consequences for Breaching a Promise.]

NOTES:

LONERGAN v. SCOLNICK

Cal. Ct. App., 129 Cal. App. 2d 179, 276 P.2d 8 (1954).

NATURE OF CASE: Specific performance or damages.

FACT SUMMARY: Lonergan (P) made inquiries concerning property which Scolnick (D) had advertised in a newspaper. He received a form letter describing the land and a second letter which responded to questions he had asked. Scolnick (D) sold the property to someone else.

CONCISE RULE OF LAW: There can be no contract unless the minds of the parties have met and mutually agreed upon some specific thing.

FACTS: Lonergan (P) made inquiries concerning property which Scolnick (D) had advertised in a newspaper. Scolnick (D) sent him a form letter describing the property. On April 7, 1952, Lonergan (P) wrote Scolnick (D), asking him for a legal description of the property and whether a certain bank would be a satisfactory escrow agent. Scolnick (D) wrote back on April 8, stating that Lonergan (P) would have to act fast, inasmuch as Scolnick (D) expected to have a buyer in the next week. Lonergan (P) responded on April 14 that he would proceed immediately to have escrow opened. On April 12, Scolnick (D) sold the property to someone else.

ISSUE: Can there be a contract where the minds of the parties have not met and mutually agreed upon some specific thing?

HOLDING AND DECISION: (Barnard, J.) No. There can be no contract unless the minds of the parties have met and mutually agreed upon some specific thing. This agreement is usually evidenced by one party making an offer which is accepted by the other. However, if from a promise or manifestation of intention or from existing circumstances the person to whom the promise or manifestation is addressed knows or has reason to know that the person making it does not intend it to constitute an expression of fixed purpose until he has given a further expression of assent, no offer has been made. Such was the case here. The newspaper ad was merely a request for an offer. The form letter sent by Scolnick (D) contained no definitive offer, and his letter of April 8 added nothing which caused previous communications to ripen into an offer. In fact, it stated that he expected a buyer within the week, indicating that he intended to sell to the first comer. Lonergan's (P) letter of April 15, stating that he was opening escrow, therefore could not have created a contract between the parties since there had been no offer.

EDITOR'S ANALYSIS: In Fairmount Glass Works, 51 S.W. 196, the plaintiff inquired as to the defendant's lowest price on 10 loads of Mason jars. The reply was "$4.50 and $5.00 for immediate acceptance." The defendant refused to fill plaintiff's subsequent order. The court held that defendant's reply "was not a quotation of prices but a definite offer to sell." In Harvey v. Facey, A.C. 552 (1893), plaintiff telegraphed defendant, "Will you sell us Bumper Hall Pen? Telegraph lowest price." The defendant replied, "Lowest price for Bumper Hall Pen £900." Plaintiff responded, "We agree to buy Bumper Hall Pen for £900." The court held that there was no contract.

[For more information on the elements of an offer, see Casenote Law Outline on Contracts, Chapter 1, § II, The Offer.]

NOTES:

LEFKOWITZ v. GREAT MINNEAPOLIS SURPLUS STORE

251 Minn. 188, 86 N.W.2d 689 (1957).

NATURE OF CASE: Action to recover damages for breach of contract.

FACT SUMMARY: Surplus Store (D) advertised one fur stole on a "first-come-first-served" basis but would not sell the stole to Lefkowitz (P), who accepted the alleged offer.

CONCISE RULE OF LAW: A newspaper advertisement (for the sale of an article) which is clear, definite, and explicit, and leaves nothing to negotiation is an offer, acceptance of which will create a binding contract.

FACTS: Surplus Store (D) published the following advertisement in a Minneapolis newspaper: "SATURDAY 9 A.M. 2 BRAND NEW PASTEL MINK 3-SKIN SCARFS Selling for $89.50 Out they go Saturday. Each ... $1.00 BLACK LAPIN STOLE Beautiful, worth $139.50 ... $1.00. FIRST COME FIRST SERVED." Lefkowitz (P) was the first to present himself on Saturday and demanded the Lapin Stole for one dollar. The Surplus Store (D) refused to sell to him because of a "house rule" that the offer was intended for women only. Lefkowitz (P) sued the Surplus Store (D) and was awarded $138.50 as damages. Surplus Store (D) appealed.

ISSUE: May a newspaper advertisement constitute an offer such that acceptance will complete a contract?

HOLDING AND DECISION: (Murphy, J.) Yes. The test of whether a binding obligation may originate in advertisements addressed to the public is "whether the facts show that some performance was promised in positive terms in return for something requested." Whether an advertisement is an offer or merely an invitation for offers depends on the legal intention of the parties and the surrounding circumstances. Where an offer is clear, definite, and explicit, and leaves nothing open for negotiation, it constitutes an offer such that acceptance of it will create a contract. With respect to the Lapin fur, Surplus Store's (D) advertisement was such an offer. As to Surplus Store's (D) alleged "house rule," while an advertiser has the right at any time before acceptance to modify his offer, he does not have the right, after acceptance, to impose new or arbitrary conditions not contained in the published offer.

EDITOR'S ANALYSIS: Although most advertisements for goods at a certain price are held not to be offers, the present case presents an interesting exception to that rule. Restatement Second, § 25 (Illustration No. 1) indicates that the basis of the court's decision is that the words "First come first served" create language of promise which is ordinarily lacking in advertisement for the sale of goods. Probably it was this factor in conjunction with the statement of a quantity (to wit, one) which motivated the court. Caveat: The Uniform Commercial Code has dealt a blow to the present court's insistence that nothing be left open for negotiation [See U.C.C. § 2-204(3).].

[For more information on offers addressed to the public, see Casenote Law Outline on Contracts, Chapter 1, § II, The Offer.]

SOUTHWORTH v. OLIVER

Or. Sup. Ct., 284 Or. 361, 587 P.2d 994 (1978).

NATURE OF CASE: Action for a declaratory judgment.

FACT SUMMARY: Southworth (P) claimed that a certain "writing" mailed by Oliver (D) constituted an "offer" to sell 2,933 acres of ranch land and that his acceptance thereof resulted in a specifically enforceable contract.

CONCISE RULE OF LAW: An "offer" has been made if, under all of the facts and circumstances existing at the time, a reasonable person in the position of the alleged offeree would have been led to believe that an offer was being made.

FACTS: Southworth (P) obtained a decree of specific performance that required Oliver (D) to proceed with the sale of ranch lands that Southworth (P) claimed had been the subject of an "offer" to sell by Oliver (D). Having decided to sell some of his property, Oliver (D) had inquired if Southworth (P) would be interested in buying it. According to Southworth (P) Oliver (D) agreed to determine the value and price of the land, and Southworth (P) would look into obtaining the money to purchase it. Later, Oliver (D) sent letters to Southworth (P) and three other neighbors setting forth the terms of sale and price of the land and stating that he was also selling allotment permits at a specified price per head. Southworth (P) treated this as an offer and sent a letter back indicating his acceptance. When Oliver (D) refused to go through with the sale, saying his own letter had not been an offer, Southworth (P) brought this action suit in equity for a declaratory judgment.

ISSUE: Does an "offer" exist if, under the facts and circumstances existing at the time, a reasonable person would have been led to believe that an offer was being made?

HOLDING AND DECISION: (Tongue, J.) Yes. In attempting to determine if an offer has been made, the question is whether, under all the facts and circumstances existing at the time, a reasonable person would have understood that an offer was being made or would have been led to believe such. A price quotation, standing alone, is not an offer. However, there may be circumstances under which a price quotation, when considered together with facts and circumstances, may constitute an offer which, if accepted, will result in a binding contract. Furthermore, such an offer may be made to more than one person. This proposal was definite. It was addressed to particular persons, and a reasonable person would have been led to believe an offer to sell was being made. Affirmed.

EDITOR'S ANALYSIS: Restatement of Contracts, § 25, Comment (a) (1932) notes the difficulty in drawing an exact line between offers and negotiations preliminary thereto. It suggests that particular attention must be given to whether or not there was any direct language indicating an intent to defer formation of a contract, to the usages of business, and to all accompanying circumstances.

[For more information on the elements of an offer, see Casenote Law Outline on Contracts, Chapter 1, § II, The Offer.]

LA SALLE NATIONAL BANK v. VEGA

167 Ill. App. 3d 154, 520 N.E.2d 1129 (1988).

NATURE OF CASE: Appeal from partial summary judgment denying existence of a contract.

FACT SUMMARY: After Vega's (D) offer to sell his property to La Salle National Bank (P) was not accepted in the manner specified, he later contracted with a subsequent purchaser, and La Salle (P) sought to enforce the specific performance of the contract.

CONCISE RULE OF LAW: An offer may be accepted only by a person in whom the offeror intended to create a power of acceptance and in the manner specified by the offeror.

FACTS: Vega (D) agreed to sell his property to the beneficiaries of a trust held by La Salle National Bank (P), as trustee. The agreement specifically required the contract be presented to the trust for execution. The contract was signed by Vega (D) and the purchasing agent but not by the trustee. When the contract was not presented to the trust, Vega (D) later entered into a contract with Borg for the sale of the property. The trial court, in an action to determine the validity of the contracts, granted partial summary judgment on the ground that the first contract was void for lack of proper acceptance, and La Salle National Bank (P) appealed.

ISSUE: Can an offer be accepted by someone other than the person to whom it was made?

HOLDING AND DECISION: (Lindberg, J.) No. An offer may be accepted only by a person in whom the offeror intended to create a power of acceptance. Thus, the offer is considered personal to the offeree, and the power to accept it cannot be transferred to a third party. Furthermore, no contract is formed when the acceptance does not satisfy the mode indicated in the offer. Here, the agreement specified that the contract would not be effective until it was presented to and executed by the trust. Since the trust never executed the sale contract, there was no acceptance, and, thus, there was no contract between La Salle National Bank (P) and Vega (D). Affirmed.

EDITOR'S ANALYSIS: When an offer does not specify the mode of acceptance, the acceptance may be given in any manner and medium reasonable under the circumstances. It is no longer required for the acceptance to match the offer. U.C.C. § 2-207 provides that a document may contain additional or different terms from the offer and still constitute an acceptance.

[For more information on elements of a valid acceptance, see Casenote Law Outline on Contracts, Chapter 1, § III, The Acceptance.]

HENDRICKS v. BEHEE

Mo. Ct. App., 786 S.W.2d 610 (1990).

NATURE OF CASE: Appeal from denial of specific performance and/or damages in interpleader action.

FACT SUMMARY: Hendricks (P), escrowee, instituted an interpleader action to have the court decide whether a contract was formed between the seller and the buyer of real estate and to whom the deposit money, held by Hendricks (P) in escrow, was to be paid.

CONCISE RULE OF LAW: No contract is formed when the offer is revoked before the acceptance is communicated to the offeror.

FACTS: Behee (D) engaged in negotiations with Mr. & Mrs. Smith for the purchase of their property. On March 2, Behee (D) made a written offer which was mailed to the Smiths the next day by their agents. Unbeknownst to Behee (D), the offer was accepted and signed. Shortly after, Behee (D) notified the agents that he was withdrawing his offer of purchase. Believing the offer to have been revoked, Behee (D) demanded the refund of the escrow money held by Hendricks (P). On the other hand, the Smiths, believing that a contract was formed when they signed the mailed offer, requested the escrow money to be paid to them. The Hendricks (P) instituted an interpleader action asking the court to resolve the dispute over the escrow money. Hendricks (P) was awarded $997 out of the deposit for his services, and the remainder was returned to Behee (D). The Smiths appealed.

ISSUE: Does a contract exist when the offer is revoked prior to the communication and notice of the acceptance of the offeror?

HOLDING AND DECISION: (Flanigan, J.) An offer can be revoked at any time prior to the receipt or notification of acceptance, unless it is supported by an adequate consideration. Behee (D) notified the Smiths' agents of his withdrawal of the offer before the acceptance was communicated to him. Thus, the offer was properly revoked since the agents' notification and knowledge of the withdrawal was imputed to the Smiths. Therefore, no contract was formed, and the escrow money was properly returned to Behee (D). Affirmed.

EDITOR'S ANALYSIS: Generally, in a unilateral contract, where acceptance is by performance, the offer is considered temporarily irrevocable when the offeree partially performs. However, when the offer requests the shipment of the goods, UCC allows the offeree to accept either by shipping or by promising to ship. See §§ 1-102, 1-201, 2-102, 2-105, 2-204, 2-205, 2-206, and 2-207 for further discussion of the words "offer" and "agreement."

[For more information on life of an offer, see Casenote Law Outline on Contracts, Chapter 2, § II, Substitutes for Valuable Consideration as Grounds for Imparting Liability Consequences for Breaching a Promise.]

EVER-TITE ROOFING CORPORATION v. GREEN

La. Ct. App., 83 So. 2d 449 (1955).

NATURE OF CASE: Action for damages for breach of contract.

FACT SUMMARY: The Greens (D) attempted to withdraw from a roofing contract after the Ever-Tite (P) workmen had arrived to perform the work.

CONCISE RULE OF LAW: Where a contract does not specify a time within which it may be accepted, a "reasonable time" will be implied.

FACTS: The Greens (D) signed a document setting out work to be done and price to be paid to Ever-Tite (P) for reroofing their residence. A provision in the agreement stated that it would become binding upon either written acceptance or commencement of performance by Ever-Tite (P), after credit approval was obtained. Nine days later, Ever-Tite (P) loaded its trucks and sent its workmen and material to the Greens' (D) residence, where they were not permitted to work. The Greens (D) contend they had given Ever-Tite (P) timely notice of their withdrawal from the contract, before Ever-Tite (P) commenced actual performance of the work. Ever-Tite (P) sued the Greens (D) for breach of contract.

ISSUES: (1) Did Ever-Tite (P) accept the agreement by commencing performance? (2) Were the Greens (D) justified in withdrawing from the contract because Ever-Tite (P) waited too long before accepting?

HOLDING AND DECISION: (Ayres, J.) (1) Contrary to the lower court, this court held that Ever-Tite (P) did commence performance by the loading of its trucks and transporting of its materials and workmen to the Greens' (D) residence. Thus, Ever-Tite (P) did accept the offer before withdrawal of the Greens (D), even though actual work was not begun. (2) Since the contract specified no time period within which it was to be accepted, "a reasonable time must be allowed therefor in accordance with the facts and circumstances and the evident intention of the parties." Since the Greens (D) knew a delay was necessary for credit approval, and since Ever-Tite (P) proceeded with due diligence, the court held that Ever-Tite (P) had accepted by commencing performance within a reasonable time.

EDITOR'S ANALYSIS: The problem here is somewhat different from that of White v. Corlies and Tift, where the manner of acceptance was simply omitted from the contract. The court there held with the original Restatement in its assumption that the offer looked toward a bilateral contract. The modern view, however, as stated in U.C.C. § 2-206, is that the offeree may choose either manner of acceptance when not explicitly restricted to a certain type of acceptance. Where an acceptance is contingent upon credit approval, as in this case, it is especially important that the manner of acceptance be clearly set out in the offer so that the parties will know exactly when the contract is formed. The provision of the offer requiring "written acceptance" or "commencing performance of the work" as alternate terms of acceptance could have been made more explicit by stating: (1) a specific time period allowed for acceptance and (2) what acts would constitute commencement of performance.

[For more information on unilateral contracts and the life of the offer, see Casenote Law Outline on Contracts, Chapter 1, § III, The Acceptance.]

NOTES:

CORINTHIAN PHARMACEUTICAL SYSTEMS, INC. v. LEDERLE LABORATORIES

724 F.Supp. 605 (1989).

NATURE OF CASE: Motion for specific performance of sales contract.

FACT SUMMARY: Corinthian (P), distributor of DTP vaccine, placed an order with Lederle (D), manufacturer, for 1,000 vials of vaccine, but when only part of the order was delivered and the remainder was to be shipped later at a higher price, Corinthian (P) brought an action for breach of contract.

CONCISE RULE OF LAW: A seller's price list is not an offer to the buyer, and a subsequent partial shipment of the buyer's order is not an acceptance sufficient to form a contract.

FACTS: Corinthian (P) distributed DTP vaccines, which were purchased from Lederle (D) on a regular basis. As a routine business practice, Lederle (D) issued price lists to its customers. The list stated that the prices were subject to change without notice and that any changes take effect at the time of shipment. In an internal memo to its representatives, Lederle (D) indicated that the price for the vaccine would be increased to $171 per vial due to the high cost of insurance and product liability lawsuits. The content of the memo was leaked to Corinthian (P) before the price increase was to be announced to the other customers. Corinthian (P) immediately placed an order for 1,000 vials through Lederle's (D) computer ordering system. The order stated that $64.32 would be the payable price for each vial. Lederle (D) made a partial shipment of 50 vials at the price indicated in Corinthian's (P) order, which was accepted. At the same time, Lederle (D) sent a letter to Corinthian (P) indicating that the partial shipment was to accommodate him and the remainder would be shipped for the price of $171 per vial. Subsequently, Corinthian (P) brought an action for breach of contract, seeking specific performance of the order. Lederle (D) moved for summary judgment.

ISSUE: Is a seller's price quote and a partial shipment of the buyer's order a valid offer and acceptance to form an enforceable contract?

HOLDING AND DECISION: (McKinney, J.) No. A contract is formed when the offer is properly accepted and supported by consideration. An offer is a manifestation of one's willingness to enter into a bargain. Thus, price quotations are not offers but only invitations for the recipient to make an offer. As a result, Lederle's (D) price lists sent to Corinthian (P) did not constitute an offer. The offer was actually made by Corinthian (P) when it placed an order via the computer ordering system. Since the parties were merchants and the offer was for a sale of goods, U.C.C. §2-206 governed the mode of acceptance. The Code allows for acceptance to be in any reasonable form and manner. In addition, it provides that shipment of non-conforming goods by the seller who gives notice that the shipment is merely an accommodation is not an acceptance but a counteroffer. Here, Lederle's (D) partial shipment, although non-conforming, was a counteroffer, since it was followed by a notification that the shipment is only an accommodation. Thus, there was no contract formed between the parties. Motion for summary judgment granted.

EDITOR'S ANALYSIS: This case involved the manner by which the offeree must indicate his commitment or promise. U.C.C. §2-206 no longer requires that an acceptance be the mirror image of the offer, which was required by common law. Furthermore, the commitment may either be demonstrated by promissory language or a promissory act.

[For more information on the mode of acceptance, see Casenote Law Outline on Contracts, Chapter 1, § III, The Acceptance.]

NOTES:

CARLILL v. CARBOLIC SMOKE BALL CO.

Ct. App., 1 Q.B. 256 (1893).

NATURE OF CASE: Action for breach of contract.

FACT SUMMARY: The Carbolic Smoke Ball Co. (D) advertised a reward to any person contracting influenza after using the Smoke Ball but refused to pay such reward to Carlill (P) when she caught influenza after using the ball.

CONCISE RULE OF LAW: An advertised reward to anyone who performs certain conditions specified in the advertisement is an offer, and the performance of such conditions is an acceptance which creates a valid contract.

FACTS: The Carbolic Smoke Ball Co. (D) advertised a reward to any person who caught the influenza after having used the Carbolic Smoke Ball three times daily for two weeks. Carlill (P) used the Ball as directed and still caught the influenza. Thereafter, Carlill (P) brought an action against the Carbolic Smoke Ball Co. (D) to recover damages for breach of contract. After Carlill (P) was awarded damages in the amount of the advertised reward, the Smoke Ball Co. (D) appealed.

ISSUE: When a company advertises a reward to anyone who performs certain conditions and someone performs such conditions, has a valid contract been formed?

HOLDING AND DECISION: (Lindley, J.) Yes. An advertised reward to anyone who performs certain conditions specified in the advertisement is an offer, and the performance of such conditions is an acceptance which creates a valid contract. Here, the Smoke Ball Co. (D) advertised a reward to anyone who caught the influenza after using the Smoke Ball for three weeks. The Smoke Ball Co. (D), though, contends that such advertisement was too "vague" to create an enforceable offer since it did not specify any time limit to the guarantee. Such contention, however, is without merit. The advertisement could be reasonably construed as offering a reward only to those persons who caught the influenza within a "reasonable time" after having used the Smoke Ball. Therefore, the advertisement was a valid offer which Carlill (P) accepted by performance of the specified conditions. Affirmed.

CONCURRENCE: (Bowen, J.) Here, the advertised offer requested deeds, not words, and, therefore, Carlill (P) did not need to give notice that she was going to perform such deeds to accept it. Furthermore, the contract so formed was supported by ample consideration since it operated to the Smoke Ball Co.'s (D) benefit by stimulating sales and to Carlill's (P) detriment by causing her to use the ball.

CONCURRENCE: (Smith, J.) Here, the Smoke Ball Co.'s (D) offer was supported by valid consideration, and it was accepted by Carlill's (P) deeds.

EDITOR'S ANALYSIS: This case illustrates a situation in which an advertisement is considered an offer (i.e., when there is no problem as to quantity because the ad specifies a reward to anyone who uses the product). The ordinary advertisement, though, which states that an item has been reduced in price, is not considered an offer because no quantity of the item is specified. Instead, such advertisements are generally held to represent only an intention to sell or a preliminary proposal inviting offers.

[For more information on formation of unilateral contracts, see Casenote Law Outline on Contracts, Chapter 1, § III, The Acceptance.]

NOTES:

GLOVER v. JEWISH WAR VETERANS OF U.S.

D.C. Ct. App., 68 A.2d 233 (1949).

NATURE OF CASE: Action to recover an award.

NOTES:

FACT SUMMARY: Glover (P) gave information leading to the arrest of a murderer without any knowledge that a reward had been offered for such information by the Jewish War Veterans (D), a nongovernmental group.

CONCISE RULE OF LAW: Questions regarding rewards offered by private individuals and groups are to be decided according to contract law, and there can be no contract unless the person claiming the reward knew about it when she gave the desired information and acted with the intention of accepting it.

FACTS: In response to questioning by police officers, Glover (P) gave information leading to the arrest of a murderer. At the time she did so, she had no knowledge that a reward had been offered for such information by the Jewish War Veterans (D), a nongovernmental organization. She found out about the reward a few days later.

ISSUE: Is a person who gives information leading to the arrest of a murderer without any knowledge that a reward has been offered for such information by a nongovernmental organization entitled to collect the reward?

HOLDING AND DECISION: (Clagett, J.) No. Questions regarding rewards offered by private individuals and groups are to be decided according to contract law. There can be no contract in such cases unless the person claiming the reward knew about it when she gave the desired information and acted with the intention of accepting it. An offeree cannot accept an offer unless she knows of its existence. Hence, Glover (P) cannot recover since she did not know of the reward when she gave the information to the police.

EDITOR'S ANALYSIS: There are cases in which the courts have enforced a promise even though the person rendering the required service did so in ignorance of the promise. Most, but not all, of these have been cases in which the promise was made by some public corporation, such as a state or a city. These cases are usually based on the theory that the government has benefited equally whether or not the claimant knew of the reward when she gave the information or upon the theory that the published promise of a reward was a public grant and not within the field of contract.

[For more information on acceptance, see Casenote Law Outline on Contracts, Chapter 1, § III, The Acceptance.]

INDUSTRIAL AMERICA, INC. v. FULTON IND., INC.

Del. Sup. Ct., 285 A.2d 412 (1971).

NATURE OF CASE: Suit to recover a brokerage commission.

FACT SUMMARY: Industrial America (P), a business brokerage firm, responded on behalf of one of its clients to an advertisement in which Fulton (D) had expressed a desire to acquire other businesses.

CONCISE RULE OF LAW: If an offer invites acceptance by performance, an offeree's performance will be deemed an acceptance unless a contrary intention on his part is shown.

FACTS: Industrial America, Inc. (P) was a brokerage firm, headed by Deutsch, which specialized in sales and mergers of businesses. The company (P) was contacted by Bush Hog, Inc., a farm machinery company which sought a merger with another corporation. Deutsch made several unsuccessful efforts to negotiate a merger agreement on behalf of Bush Hog but engaged in no discussions after early 1965. In the fall of that year, Deutsch was informed by a friend that Fulton Industries, Inc. (D) was seeking other companies to acquire, either by sale or by merger. Deutsch then located a Wall Street Journal advertisement in which Fulton (D) had expressed its desire to acquire other companies. The advertisement concluded with the words "Brokers fully protected." Deutsch immediately responded to the advertisement, and Fulton (D) eventually asked Deutsch to arrange a meeting between representatives of Bush Hog and Fulton (D). Deutsch then contacted Bush Hog, but the two companies ultimately arranged their meeting without using Deutsch as an intermediary. Neither company made further use of Deutsch's services, although a merger between the companies eventually occurred. Deutsch later sued to recover his brokerage commission, and Bush Hog was ordered to pay $125,000 to Industrial America (P). However, an action against Fulton (D) resulted in no recovery because the trial jury found that Deutsch had never accepted Fulton's (D) newspaper "offer."

ISSUE: Where an offer apparently invites acceptance by performance, must a party who performs nevertheless demonstrate that he subjectively intended to accept the offer?

HOLDING AND DECISION: (Hermann, J.) No. If an offer invites acceptance by performance, an offeree's performance will be deemed an acceptance unless a contrary intention on his part is shown. It is the manifestation of assent, and not the subjective intent or the motivations of the parties, which is relevant to the formation of a contract. In effect, a rebuttable presumption is created that the offeree's performance was to operate as an acceptance. Thus, Deutsch must be deemed to have accepted Fulton's (D) offer, and his letter to Fulton (D) served as notice of his acceptance, to the extent that such notice was necessary. It follows that Industrial America (P) is entitled to a judgment against Fulton (D) and its successor, Allied Products Corporation (D).

EDITOR'S ANALYSIS: Some contracts may be accepted only by performance. Others may be accepted only by a promise. Still others may be accepted by either performance or by promise. It has traditionally been assumed that a bilateral contract invites promissory acceptance, while a unilateral contract is to be accepted by performance. However, § 2-206(1) of the U.C.C., without distinguishing between bilateral and unilateral contracts, provides that an offer ordinarily "shall be construed as inviting acceptance, in any manner and by any medium reasonable in the circumstances." Section 2-206 is consistent with a developing trend toward permitting any offer to be accepted either by a promise or by performance, unless the offeror has specified the mode of acceptance which will be recognized.

[For more information on unilateral contracts, see Casenote Law Outline on Contracts, Chapter 1, § III, The Acceptance.]

NOTES:

ADAMS v. LINDSELL

King's Bench, 1 Barn & Ald. 681 (1818).

NATURE OF CASE: Action for breach of contract.

FACT SUMMARY: One day after Adams (P) had mailed his acceptance of Lindsell's (D) offer to sell wool, Lindsell (D) sold the wool to another.

CONCISE RULE OF LAW: An acceptance of an offer is effective upon dispatch.

FACTS: On September 2, 1817, Lindsell (D), a wool dealer, mailed a letter to Adams (P) in which he offered to sell Adams (P) some wool. Because Lindsell (D) had misaddressed the letter, Adams (P) did not receive it until September 5. On that same day, Adams (P) mailed his acceptance of Lindsell's (D) offer, which did not reach Lindsell (D) until September 9. On September 8, Lindsell (D), unaware that Adams (P) had accepted his offer, sold the wool to another person. In an action by Adams (P) for nondelivery of the wool, Lindsell (D) claimed that, in the usual course of the mails, the acceptance should have reached him on September 7.

ISSUE: Is an acceptance of an offer effective upon its being posted?

HOLDING AND DECISION: (Burrough, J.) Yes. An acceptance is immediately effective upon its being put out of the offeree's possession. If an offeror is not to be considered bound by his offer until he has received notice of the offeror's acceptance, then the offeree likewise should not be bound until he has received notification that the offeror has received his answer and agreed to it. There is no end to this line of reasoning. If an acceptance is only effective upon receipt, no contract could ever be completed by the mails. To give some stability and sense of finality to bargaining, an offeror must be considered in law as making, during every instant of the time his letter is en route, the same identical offer: a contract is formed by the offeree's acceptance, which is communicated upon dispatch. In the present case, the delay was caused by Lindsell's (D) neglect in properly addressing his offer. Hence, he is liable for any loss that has been sustained.

EDITOR'S ANALYSIS: Although Adams v. Lindsell states the generally adopted rule, it has met with substantial criticism. Longdell has summarized the opposing view in terms of allocating the hardship between the offeror or offeree: "the hardship consists in making one liable on a contract which he is ignorant of having made; adopting the other view, it consists in depriving one of the benefit of a contract which he supposes he has made. Between these two evils, the latter must be favored since it leaves everything in status quo." Summary of the Law of Contracts, 2d ed., 1880, pp. 20-21.

[For more information on the mailbox rule, see Casenote Law Outline on Contracts, Chapter 1, § III, The Acceptance.]

RUSSELL v. TEXAS CO.

238 F.2d 636 (9th Cir. 1956).

NATURE OF CASE: Action to quiet title to real property.

FACT SUMMARY: Russell (P), the surface owner of certain land, sent an offer of a revocable license to use the surface to Texas Co. (D), the occupier of the land. The offer stated that Texas' (D) continued use would constitute an acceptance. Texas (D) did continue to use the land.

CONCISE RULE OF LAW: Where the offeree exercises dominion over things which are offered to him, such exercise of dominion in the absence of other circumstances showing a contrary intention is an acceptance.

FACTS: Russell (P) was the surface owner of certain property. Texas Co. (D) had a mineral right lease on the land but was operating in excess of the rights granted to it by its lease. Russell (P) sent Texas (D) an offer of a revocable license for use of surface rights at a daily rental. The offer stated that Texas' (D) continued use would constitute an acceptance of the offer. Texas (D) continued to use the land but claimed that there was no contract because it did not intend to accept Russell's (P) offer.

ISSUE: Can an offeree who has accepted and retained the benefits offered by the offeror vitiate a contract which provides that acceptance of the benefits will, in and of itself, constitute acceptance by claiming that he did not intend to accept the offer?

HOLDING AND DECISION: No. Where the offeree exercises dominion over things which are offered to him, such exercise of dominion in the absence of other circumstances showing a contrary intention is an acceptance. Here, Russell's (P) offer stated that continued use would constitute an acceptance. Texas (D) did continue its use of the land and, hence, came unequivocally within the terms specified for acceptance. The true test is whether or not the offeror was reasonably led to believe that the offeree's act was an acceptance. This test is met by the facts here.

EDITOR'S ANALYSIS: There is a legal acceptance where silence is accompanied by acts of the offeree which warrant an inference of assent. Such acts may include the offeree's exercise of dominion over things offered to him or his taking the benefit of the offered services under circumstances which would indicate to a reasonable person that they were offered with the expectation of compensation. The duty imposed on the offeree by this rule is not a quasi- contractual duty to pay a fair value but a duty to pay or perform according to the terms of the offer.

[For more information on silence as acceptance, see Casenote Law Outline on Contracts, Chapter 1, § III, The Acceptance.]

AMMONS v. WILSON & CO.

Miss. Sup. Ct., 176 Miss. 645, 170 So. 227 (1936).

NATURE OF CASE: Action to recover for breach of contract.

FACT SUMMARY: Ammons (P) gave Wilson's (D) traveling salesperson an order. In previous dealings between them, Wilson (D) had always shipped Ammons' (P) orders within a week, but this time he was silent for 12 days before rejecting Ammons' (P) offer.

CONCISE RULE OF LAW: Where an offeree fails to reply to an offer, his silence and inaction operate as an acceptance where, because of previous dealings or otherwise, the offeree has given the offeror reason to understand that the silence or inaction is intended as a manifestation of assent and the offeror does so understand.

FACTS: Ammons (P) gave Wilson's (D) traveling salesperson an order. Ammons (P) heard nothing from Wilson (D) until 12 days later when he was advised by Wilson (D), in response to his inquiry as to when the shipment would be made, that the orders had been declined. Ammons (P) had previously placed several orders with Wilson (D) through its traveling salesperson. All of these orders had been accepted and shipped within a week.

ISSUE: Are there circumstances under which an offeree's silence and inaction can operate as an acceptance?

HOLDING AND DECISION: (Anderson, J.) Yes. Where an offeree fails to reply to an offer, his silence and inaction operate as an acceptance where, because of previous dealings or otherwise, the offeree has given the offeror reason to understand that the silence or inaction is intended as a manifestation of assent and the offeror does so understand. Here, it was a question for the jury whether or not Wilson's (D) delay of 12 days before rejecting the order, in view of the past history of such transactions between the parties, constituted an implied acceptance.

EDITOR'S ANALYSIS: There are many cases in which, because of the past relations of the parties or of accompanying circum-stances, the silence of the offeree after receipt of an offer has been held to constitute acceptance and create a contract. These are all cases in which the conduct of the party denying a contract has been such as to lead the other reasonably to believe that silence, without communication, constituted an acceptance. However, circumstances which will impose a contractual obligation by mere silence (not coupled with additional circumstances) are rare.

[For more information on previous dealings, see Casenote Law Outline on Contracts, Chapter 1, § III, The Acceptance.]

SMITH-SCHARFF PAPER COMPANY v. P.N. HIRSCH & CO. STORES, INC.

Miss. Ct. of App., 754 S.W.2d 328, Miss. App. (1988).

NATURE OF CASE: Appeal from award of damages for breach of contract.

FACT SUMMARY: Paper Company (P), which had agreed to sell specially marked paper bags for Hirsch (D), brought a breach of a contract action when Hirsch (D) did not buy the inventory stock of the specially made bags.

CONCISE RULE OF LAW: A buyer is estopped from denying the existence of an oral contract when he has benefitted from the performance and business practices of the seller.

FACTS: For almost 36 years, Paper Company (P) had provided Hirsch (D) with paper bags bearing Hirsch's (D) logo on it. The relationship was continuous except for a one-year interruption when Hirsch (D) sought another supplier. During the interruption, Hirsch (D) purchased Paper Company's (P) entire stock of the bags bearing its logo on it. When Hirsch Co. (D) was sold as a result of a liquidation sale, Paper Company (P) wrote a letter to Hirsch's (D) president seeking assurance that the inventory stock of the bags with the Hirsch logo on it would be purchased. Upon an oral assurance by Hirsch's (D) president, Paper Company (P) sent a bill for $65,000 for the inventory stock of the bags. When only $45,00 worth of bags was purchased, Paper Company (P) brought this action for breach of contract. Paper Company (P) was awarded the remaining value of the bags plus interest. Hirsch (D) appealed.

ISSUE: Can a buyer deny the existence of an oral contract when he has benefitted from the seller's performance and business practices?

HOLDING AND DECISION: (Stephan, J.) No. A buyer is estopped from denying the existence of an oral contract when he has accepted the benefits of the seller's performance and business practices. Hirsch (D) was aware of Paper Company's (P) business practice to pre-order bags to avoid possible delays involved in ordering the bags from the manufacturer. Furthermore, Hirsch (D) benefitted from this practice when it received its order in timely fashion. Thus, Hirsch (D) was not only estopped from denying the existence of the contract but also from denying its responsibility to pay for them. In addition, Paper Company's (P) request for assurance when it was notified of Hirsch's (D) liquidation was reasonable, and thus it was not an anticipatory repudiation of their agreement. Affirmed.

EDITOR'S ANALYSIS: Although the statute of frauds ordinarily requires the type of contract seen in this case to be in writing, the fact that the bags were specially made for Hirsch (D) and were not suitable for sale to others, allowed for the court to imply the existence of a contract as a matter of fact. Thus, the exception was made for enforcement of the oral contract here.

[For more information on equitable estoppel, see Casenote Law Outline on Contracts, Chapter 3, § V, Defenses Arising from the Form of the Bargain.]

HARRIS v. TIME, INC.

Cal. Ct. App., 191 Cal. App. 3d 465 (1987).

NATURE OF CASE: Appeal from dismissal of class action for breach of contract.

FACT SUMMARY: In Harris' (P) class action suit against Time, Inc. (D) for breach of contract, Time (D) argued that there was no contract between Harris (P) and Time (D) because the text of the mailer which Harris (P) received from Time (D) amounted to a mere advertisement, an invitation to bargain.

CONCISE RULE OF LAW: Only in circumstances of actual detriment should a court intrude upon the exercise of commercial free speech.

FACTS: Harris (P) received an advertisement through the mail from Time, Inc. (D), which stated, on the outside of the envelope, that the recipient of the advertisement would receive a calculator watch free just for opening the envelope before February 15, 1985. When Harris (P) opened the envelope, he discovered that he would not receive the watch unless he also purchased a subscription to Fortune magazine. Harris (P) then brought an action against Time (D) for breach of contract. Time (D) argued that there was no contract between Harris (P) and Time (D) because the text of the mailed advertisement which Harris (P) received from Time (D) amounted to a mere advertisement, an invitation to bargain. The lower court found for Time (D) and dismissed Harris' (P) action. Harris (P) appealed.

ISSUE: Should a court intrude upon the exercise of commercial free speech only in circumstances of actual detriment?

HOLDING AND DECISION: (King, J.) Yes. Only in circumstances of actual detriment should a court intrude upon the exercise of commercial free speech. The courts cannot solve every complaint or right every technical wrong, particularly one which causes no actual damage beyond the loss of the few seconds it takes to open an envelope and examine its contents. Here, despite the technical correctness of Harris' (P) claim for breach of contract, the decision of the lower court must be upheld. Time (D) did make Harris (P) an offer proposing a unilateral contract because the advertisement called for performance of a specific act without further communication. Harris (P) supplied adequate consideration for the contract by opening the envelope. However, Harris (P) suffered no damage from Time's (D) failure to perform according to the advertisement. The present action is de minimis in the extreme and an absurd waste of the resources of this court. It is not a use for which our legal system is designed. Affirmed.

EDITOR'S ANALYSIS: Contract damages are ordinarily based on the injured party's expectation interests. They are intended to give the party the benefit of his bargain by awarding him a sum of money that will put him in as good a position as he would have been in had the contract been performed. Expectation interest can be measured by the loss in the value to a party of the other party's performance caused by its failure or deficiency.

[For more information on expectation interest, see Casenote Law Outline on Contracts, Chapter 7, § III, Remedies for Breach of Contract.]

NOTES:

MINNEAPOLIS & ST. LOUIS R.R. CO. v. COLUMBUS ROLLING-MILL CO.

119 U.S. 149 (1886).

NATURE OF CASE: Action from specific performance of a contract for the sale of goods.

FACT SUMMARY: Columbus (D) offered to sell between 2,000 to 5,000 tons of 50 lb. rails for $54 per gross ton. Minneapolis (P) placed an order for 1,200 tons, which Columbus (D) refused to fill. Minneapolis (P) then placed a second order for 2,000 tons, which Columbus (D) also refused to fill.

CONCISE RULE OF LAW: An "acceptance" which does not assent to the offer as made is a rejection and counteroffer as it manifests an unwillingness of the offeree.

FACTS: On December 5, 1879, Minneapolis (P) inquired as to prices of 500 to 3,000 tons of 50 lb. steel rails and 2,000 to 5,000 tons of iron rails, for a March 1880 delivery. On December 8, 1879, Columbus (D) replied by letter, stating that it did not produce steel rails but would sell 2,000 to 5,000 50 lb. iron rails for $54 per gross ton. Columbus (D) would permit notification by Minneapolis (P) of its acceptance to Columbus' (D) offer until December 20, 1879. On December 16, 1879, Minneapolis (P) telegraphed Columbus (D) of its acceptance and placed an order for 1,200 tons of 50 lb. iron rails at $54 per gross ton and sent a letter the same day confirming the telegraphed acceptance and terms and requested a contract. On December 18, 1879, Columbus (D) telegraphed its refusal to book this order. On December 19, 1879, Minneapolis (P) telegraphed an order for 2,000 tons of 50 lb. iron rails and requested a contract for this. Columbus (D) refused and denied the existence of a contract.

ISSUE: Is an "acceptance" of an offer which does not assent to the offer as made a rejection by the offeree and a counteroffer to the offeror, who then acquires the right to accept or reject?

HOLDING AND DECISION: Yes. Minneapolis' (P) failure to place an order within the terms of the offer is a rejection of the offer. By so doing, Minneapolis (P) put an end to negotiations, unless the party making the original offer, Columbus (D), offered to renew negotiations or assented to the offeree's modification. Columbus (D) never assented to Minneapolis' (P) modification of 1,200 tons to Columbus' (D) offer of a minimum 2,000 tons to a maximum 5,000 tons. Neither did Columbus (D) reopen negotiations. Accordingly, Minneapolis' (P) second acceptance within the terms, and referral back to the date of the original offer, was ineffectual in creating any rights in Minneapolis (P) against Columbus (D).

EDITOR'S ANALYSIS: Under Restatement of Contracts, § 38, while a counteroffer is a rejection as it manifests the offeree's unwillingness to assent to the offer as made, there are two exceptions. A counteroffer will not have the effect of a rejection where (1) the offeror expressly invites a counteroffer or (2) the offeree in making the counteroffer states he still has the original offer under consideration. Neither exception has effect in this case. Minneapolis' (P) referral in its second acceptance to the original offer is not enough to meet the second exception above, as Minneapolis (P) never stated its continued consideration of the original offer in its first acceptance.

[For more information on counteroffers, see Casenote Law Outline on Contracts, Chapter 1, § III, The Acceptance.]

NOTES:

LEONARD PEVAR COMPANY v. EVANS PRODUCTS CO.

524 F.Supp. 546 (1981).

NATURE OF THE CASE: Diversity action for breach of express and implied contractual warranties.

FACT SUMMARY: Pevar (P) subcontracted with Evans (D) to provide plywood for his project, but when the delivered plywood was determined to be defective and Evans (D) disclaimed any warranties, Pevar (P) filed suit.

CONCISE RULE OF LAW: A confirmation letter, between merchants, containing additional or different terms from the offer is an acceptance unless the new terms materially alter the offer, the offer expressly limits the acceptance to the conditions of the offer, or one merchant has expressed his objection to the new terms.

FACTS: Evans (D), a manufacturer of plywood, quoted a price for plywood to Pevar (P) in a telephone conversation. Two days later, Pevar (P) called Evans (D) and ordered the plywood. Pevar (P) claimed that an oral contract was formed once the order was placed, but Evans (D) denied ever accepting the order. Pevar (P) followed its phone order with a written purchase order specifying the price, quantity, and shipping instructions. In response, Evans (D) sent an acknowledgment letter containing boilerplate provisions which disclaimed any warranties and limited the buyer's possible remedies. Pevar (P) filed suit when he received defective plywood. Both parties moved for summary judgment.

ISSUE: Does a confirmation letter, between merchants, containing additional or different terms from the offer, constitute an acceptance?

HOLDING AND DECISION: (Latchum, J.) Yes. A written confirmation is an acceptance, even if it states different or additional terms. U.C.C. § 2-207 recognizes that between merchants the new terms stated in a confirmation become part of the contract unless (1) the offer expressly limits acceptance to the terms of the offer; (2) the new terms materially alter the offer; and (3) notice of objection to the new terms has been given. Furthermore, U.C.C. § 2-207 states three methods by which the parties may enter into a contract. The first is when an oral agreement is followed by a written confirmation. Here, Evans' (D) confirmation letter contained a disclaimer of warranties which were not included in the telephone agreement. These terms can be added to the contract only if it does not materially alter the agreement. However, the question of material alteration is a question for the trier of facts after it is established that an oral agreement was formed via the telephone conversation. The second method is when parties have exchanged writings enclosing different terms. In this case, Pevar's (P) written order form was an offer to purchase. Evans (D) claimed that his confirmation was not an acceptance but a counteroffer containing the new terms. Evans (D) relying on Roto-Lith, Ltd. v. F.P. Bartlett & Co., argued that his counteroffer was accepted by Pevar (P) when he paid for the goods. The court rejected the Roto-Lith analysis and held that the counter offeree must expressly consent to the new terms. Thus, without the express consent of Pevar (P) there was no contract. The third method is when parties act as though there is a contract. Here, the conduct of the parties showed that they believed a contract existed. Thus, in fact, a contract was formed between Evans (D) and Pevar (P) with its terms consisting of the common provisions of the purchase order and the confirmation letter. The standard "gap fillers" can be applied to the disputable terms. Summary judgment denied; case set for trial.

EDITOR'S ANALYSIS: U.C.C. § 2-207 makes two major changes in the common law approach. First, it states that a document can constitute an acceptance even though it is not the mirror image of the offer. Second, it modifies the common law rule preventing acceptance of a contract by silence when it states that between merchants, the additional terms become part of the contract when the offeror remains silent.

[For more information on the impact of different or additional terms, see Casenote Law Outline on Contracts, Chapter 1, § III, The Acceptance.]

NOTES:

DICKINSON v. DODDS

Ct. App., Ch. Div., 2 Ch. Div. 463 (1876).

NATURE OF CASE: Action for specific performance of a contract for the sale of real property.

FACT SUMMARY: On June 10, 1874, Dodds (D) gave a writing to Dickinson (P) giving the latter until 9 A.M., June 12, 1874, to accept Dodds' (D) offer to purchase his land and buildings upon it for £800. On the afternoon of June 11, 1874, Dodds (D) sold the same property to Allan (D) for £800 and accepted a £40 deposit.

CONCISE RULE OF LAW: An offer may be withdrawn by an indirect revocation where the offeree receives reliable information from a third party that the offeror has engaged in conduct indicative to a reasonable man that the offer was withdrawn.

FACTS: On June 10, 1874, Dodds (D) gave Dickinson (P) a writing that stated that the former agreed to sell his land and buildings upon it to the latter for £800, the offer to be left open until June 12, 1874, 9 a.m. Dickinson (P) decided to accept on the morning of June 11, 1874, but did not immediately convey his acceptance, believing he had until next morning. That afternoon, one Berry informed Dickinson (P) that Dodds (D) had decided to sell the property to Allan (D). Dickinson (P) went to Dodds' (D) mother-in-law's home, where he was staying, and left his acceptance there, but it never got to Dodds (D). The next morning at 7 a.m., Berry, as Dickinson's (P) agent, attempted to give a copy of the acceptance to Dodds (D), who said it was too late. On June 11, 1874, the day before, Dodds (D) had sold the property to Allan (D) for £800 and had accepted a £40 deposit.

ISSUE: Was there adequate revocation of the offer?

OLDING AND DECISION: (James, J.) Yes. The writing was not an 'eement to sell but an offer. Both parties had not yet agreed to go ugh with the deal. There was no consideration given for the ise. The promise was not binding, so Dodds (D) was free to do ver he wanted before receiving all acceptance from Dickinson 'ere did not have to be an express and actual withdrawal of the om the circumstances, Dickinson (P) knew that Dodds (D) had his mind. It was clear from his statements and actions. ly, there was no meeting of the minds between the two no contract.

NCE: (Mellish, J.) The mere offer to sell property can be time, so it would be absurd to hold an offeror liable to has knowledge that an offer has been revoked. That writing makes no difference.

YSIS: As seen, an indirect revocation may arise y or by the circumstances. The first Restatement ne of indirect revocation should be limited to the 'els, but Restatement Second, § 42, now holds always a concern as to what information is reliable. The information must be true and put a reasonable man acting in good faith to inquiry. But what if the offeree hears reliably that the offeror has made the same offer to a second person? Grismore believes that a reasonable man would conclude that since he was given no notice of revocation, the offeror is willing to run the risk of two open offers.

[For more information on indirect revocation, see Casenote Law Outline on Contracts, Chapter 1, § II, The Offer.]

NOTES:

HUMBLE OIL & REFINING v. WESTSIDE INVEST. CORP.
Tex. Sup. Ct., 428 S.W.2d 92 (1968).

NATURE OF CASE: Action for specific performance.

FACT SUMMARY: Westside (D) granted Humble (P) an irrevocable option to purchase certain property. Humble (P) requested that Westside (D) agree to an additional term and then communicated its unqualified exercise of the option.

CONCISE RULE OF LAW: If the original offer is irrevocable and creates in the offeree a "binding option," the rule that a counteroffer terminates the power of acceptance does not apply.

FACTS: Humble (P) paid Westside (D) $50 for an irrevocable option to purchase certain property. Humble (P) then wrote Westside (D) that it sought to amend the sales contract to provide that Westside (D) would extend all utility lines to the property prior to the closing date. Before the option expired, Humble (P) wrote a second letter to Westside (D), in which it stated that it was exercising its option, that this exercise was not qualified in any way, and that Westside (D) could disregard the proposed amendment in the previous letter.

ISSUE: Does the rule that a counteroffer terminates the power of acceptance apply where the original offer was irrevocable?

HOLDING AND DECISION: (Smith, J.) No. If the original offer is irrevocable and creates in the offeree a "binding option," the rule that a counteroffer terminates the power of acceptance does not apply. In such a case, neither a counteroffer by the offeree nor the conduct of further negotiations not resulting in a contract will terminate the power of acceptance. Hence, Humble's (P) first letter did not terminate the option contract. It did not surrender or reject the option. Considered as an independent agreement, the option gave Humble (P) the right to purchase within the specified time and bound Westside (D) to keep the option open during that time. The offer of an option was still binding when Humble (P) exercised the option. Hence, Humble (P) is entitled to specific performance.

EDITOR'S ANALYSIS: One view is that an option consists of two separate elements: one, the offer to perform a certain act (such as to sell property), which is an incomplete contract until it is accepted, and the other, the agreement to give the optionee a certain time within which to exercise his option of accepting. A second view is that an option is a unilateral writing which lacks the mutual elements of a contract but which, upon acceptance by the optionee, ripens into an executory contract which is binding upon both parties. Other authorities hold that a binding option is a contract and also an offer which, when accepted, will create another contract. The Restatement, Second, provides that the power to accept an option is not terminated by revocation, counteroffer, or the death of the offeror.

[For more information on formation of an option, see Casenote Law Outline on Contracts, Chapter 1, § II, The Offer.]

NOTES:

PETTERSON v. PATTBERG

N.Y. Ct. App., 248 N.Y. 86, 161 N.E. 428 (1928).

NATURE OF CASE: Action for breach of contract.

FACT SUMMARY: Pattberg (D) offered to discount the mortgage on J. Petterson's estate on the condition that it be paid on a certain date. Pattberg (D) then sold the mortgage before Petterson (P), as executor of the estate, had paid him.

CONCISE RULE OF LAW: An offer to enter into a unilateral contract may be withdrawn at any time prior to performance of the act requested to be done.

FACTS: Pattberg (D) held a mortgage on property belonging to J. Petterson's estate. Petterson (P) was executor of that estate. Pattberg (D) offered to discount the amount of the mortgage on the condition that it be paid on a certain date. Before that date, Petterson (P) went to Pattberg's (D) home and offered to pay him the amount of the mortgage. Pattberg (D) told Petterson (P) that he had already sold the mortgage to a third person.

ISSUE: Can an offer to enter into a unilateral contract be withdrawn prior to performance of the act requested to be done?

HOLDING AND DECISION: (Kellogg, J.) Yes. An offer to enter into a unilateral contract may be withdrawn at any time prior to performance of the act requested to be done. Here, Pattberg's (D) offer proposed to Petterson (P) the making of a unilateral contract, the gift of a promise (to discount the mortgage) in exchange for the performance of an act (payment by a certain date). Pattberg (D) was free to revoke his offer any time before Petterson (P) accepted by performing the act. He revoked the offer by informing Petterson (P) that he had sold the mortgage. An offer to sell property may be withdrawn before acceptance without any formal notice to the person to whom the offer is made. It is sufficient if that person has actual knowledge that the person who made the offer has done some act inconsistent with the continuance of the offer, such as selling the property to a third person.

DISSENT: (Lehman, J.) Until the act requested was performed, Pattberg (D) had the right to revoke his offer. However, he could not revoke it after Petterson (P) had offered to make the payment.

EDITOR'S ANALYSIS: Other facts in Petterson which do not appear in the opinion may have influenced the court. The trial record shows that Pattberg (D) was prevented from testifying as to a letter sent to J. Petterson (P), in which the offer was revoked. The record also suggests that Petterson (P) knew of the sale of the mortgage. Note, 1928, 14 Cornell L.O. 81. The Restatement (Second) of Contracts provides, "Where an offer invites an offeree to accept by rendering performance, an option contract is created when the offeree begins performance." Actual performance is necessary. Preparations to perform, though they may be essential to performance, are not enough. However, they may constitute justifiable reliance sufficient to make the offeror's promise binding under § 90.

[For more information on the unilateral contract, see Casenote Law Outline on Contracts, Chapter 1, § III, The Acceptance.]

NOTES:

MARCHIONDO v. SCHECK

N.M. Sup. Ct., 78 N.M. 440, 432 P.2d 405 (1967).

NATURE OF CASE: Action to recover real estate commission.

FACT SUMMARY: Scheck (D) offered to sell realty to a specified prospective buyer and agreed to pay Marchiondo (P) a broker's commission. Later Scheck (D) revoked the offer. Shortly after the revocation and within the time limit set by the offer, Marchiondo (P) obtained the offeree's acceptance.

CONCISE RULE OF LAW: Where an offer invites an offeree to accept by rendering a performance, an option contract so created is conditional on the offeree's completion of performance in accordance with the terms of the offer.

FACTS: Scheck (D) offered to sell real estate to a specified prospective buyer and agreed to pay Marchiondo (P) a percentage of the sales price as a commission. The offer set a six-day time limit for acceptance, and Marchiondo (P) received Scheck's (D) revocation of the offer on the sixth day. Later that day, Marchiondo (P) obtained the offeree's acceptance.

ISSUE: Does partial performance by the offeree of an offer of a unilateral contract result in a binding contract which is conditional upon the offeree's full performance?

HOLDING AND DECISION: (Wood, J.) Yes. Where an offer invites an offeree to accept by rendering a performance, an option contract is created when the offeree begins to partially perform. The offeror's duty of performance under an option contract so created is conditional on the offeree's completion of performance in accordance with the terms of the offer. In such a case, the offeree's part performance furnishes the acceptance and consideration for a binding contract conditional upon the offeree's full performance. Hence, here Scheck's (D) right to revoke his offer depends upon whether Marchiondo (P) had partially performed before he received Scheck's (D) revocation. What constitutes partial performance will vary from case to case since what can be done toward performance is determined by what is authorized to be done. Hence, it is a question of fact to be determined at the trial. This case is remanded to the trial court so that it can make a finding on the issue of Marchiondo's (P) partial performance prior to the revocation.

EDITOR'S ANALYSIS: In many cases involving real estate brokers, it has been held that the owner is no longer privileged to revoke after the broker has taken substantial steps toward rendering performance by advertising the property, soliciting prospective sellers, showing the property, or otherwise. Where notice of revocation is given when the broker's services have proceeded to the point where success is probable, the court may be convinced it was given for the purpose of avoiding payment of the commission while at the same time enjoying the benefit of the services. Such a revocation is in bad faith, and the broker may be held entitled to the commission on the ground that the owner has wrongfully prevented fulfillment of the condition precedent to the right to payment.

[For more information on revocation of offer, see Casenote Law Outline on Contracts, Chapter 1, § II, The Offer.]

NOTES:

JAMES BAIRD CO. v. GIMBEL BROS.

64 F.2d 344 (2d Cir. 1933).

NATURE OF CASE: Action for breach of a contract for the sale of goods.

FACT SUMMARY: Gimbel (D) offered to supply linoleum to various contractors who were bidding on a public construction contract. Baird (P), relying on Gimbel's (D) quoted prices, submitted a bid and later the same day received a telegraphed message from Gimbel (D) that its quoted prices were in error. Baird's (P) bid was accepted.

CONCISE RULE OF LAW: The doctrine of promissory estoppel shall not be applied in cases where there is an offer for exchange as the offer is not intended to become a promise until consideration is received.

FACTS: Gimbel (D), having heard that bids were being taken for a public building, had an employee obtain the specifications for linoleum required for the building and submitted offers to various possible contractors, including Baird (P), of two prices for linoleum depending upon the quality used. The offer was made in ignorance of a mistake as to the actual amount of linoleum needed, causing Gimbel's (D) prices to be about half the actual cost. The offer concluded as follows: "If successful in being awarded this contract, it will be absolutely guaranteed . . . and . . . we are offering these prices for reasonable (sic) prompt acceptance after the general contract has been awarded." Baird (P) received this on the 28th, the same day on which Gimbel (D) discovered its mistake, and telegraphed all contractors of the error, but the communication was received by Baird (P) just after Baird (P) submitted its lump-sum bid relying on Gimbel's (D) erroneous prices. Baird's (P) bid was accepted on the 30th. Baird (P) received Gimbel's (D) written confirmation of the error on the 31st but sent an acceptance despite this two days later. Gimbel (D) refused to recognize a contract.

ISSUES: What was the intention of parties? Did Gimbel (D) intend to be bound upon a contractor's (offeree's) mere reliance on its quoted prices? If not, may the doctrine of promissory estoppel be used by the offeree to bind the offeror?

HOLDING AND DECISION: (Hand, J.) No to both questions. First, looking at the language of Gimbel's (D) offer, Gimbel's (D) use of the phrase "if successful in being awarded this contract" clearly shows Gimbel's (D) intent of not being bound simply by a contractor relying or acting upon the quoted prices. This is reinforced by the phrase "prompt acceptance after the general contract has been awarded." No award had been made at the time, and reliance on the prices cannot be said to be an award of the contract. Had a relying contractor been awarded the contract and then repudiated it, Gimbel (D) would not have had any right to sue for breach, nor could Gimbel (D) have gone against his estate had the relying contractor gone bankrupt. The contractors could have protected themselves by insisting on a contract guaranteeing the prices before relying upon them. The court will not strain to find a contract in aid of one who fails to protect himself. The theory of promissory estoppel is not available, as it is appropriate in donative or charitable cases where harsh results to the promisee arising from the promisor's breaking his relied-upon promise are to be protected against. However, an offer for an exchange, either being an act or another promise, is not meant to become a promise until consideration is received. Here, the linoleum was to be delivered for the contractor's acceptance, not his bid. An option contract has not arisen, as it is clear from the language of the offer that Gimbel (D) had no intention of assuming a one-sided obligation.

EDITOR'S ANALYSIS: Later cases have held the doctrine of promissory estoppel not to be as narrow. The majority of courts which have considered the issue hold that justifiable detrimental reliance on an offer renders it irrevocable. Naturally, the contractor must have something upon which to justifiably rely. The court in its decision notes that Restatement (Second) § 90 follows its view. However, Restatement (Second) § 90 has expanded the section so as to enlarge its scope according to the more modern viewpoint. It must be shown that the offeror foresaw that his promise would reasonably induce forbearance or action. The first inkling of this doctrine probably arose in the well-known Hamer v. Sidway, 27 N.E. 256 (1891), where an uncle promised to pay his nephew $5,000 for refraining from the use of liquor, swearing, and other activities until his 21st birthday and reached full maturity in Justice Traynor's decision in Drennan v. Star Paving Company, 51 Cal. 2d 409, 333 P. 2d 757 (1958). Generally, this case is a good example of the manner in which the court will examine the words and actions of the parties in order to determine their intent and, hence, the existence of a contract. It appears that Gimbel (D) could have used the defense of unilateral mistake based upon a clerical error, as seen in M. F. Kemper Construction Co. v. City of Los Angeles, 235 P. 2d 7 (1951).

[For more information on performance as attempted acceptance of offer to form bilateral contract, see Casenote Law Outline on Contracts, Chapter 1, § II, The Offer.]

NOTES:

DRENNAN v. STAR PAVING CO.

Cal. Sup. Ct., en banc, 51 Cal. 2d 409 (1958).

NATURE OF CASE: Appeal from denial of damages for failure to perform according to a bid.

FACT SUMMARY: Drennan (P), a contractor, in preparing his bid on a public construction project, used the bid for paving work by subcontractor Star (D), but after Drennan (P) was awarded the contract, Star (D) informed Drennan (P) that its paving bid was in error.

CONCISE RULE OF LAW: A promise which the promisor should reasonably expect to induce action or forbearance of a definite and substantial character on the part of a promisee and which does induce such action or forbearance is binding if injustice can be avoided only by enforcement of the promise.

FACTS: Drennan (P) was preparing a bid on a public school construction project. On the day the bid was to be submitted, Star (D) phoned in its bid of $7,131.60 for paving. That bid was recorded and posted on a master sheet by Drennan (P). It was customary in the area for bids to be phoned in on the day set for bidding and for general contractors to rely on them in computing their own bids. Star's (D) bid for paving was low and used by Drennan (P) in preparing his bid, which was low. The contract was awarded to Drennan (P) that same evening. The next day, Star (D) informed Drennan (P) of an error in its paving bid and refused to do the paving for less than $15,000. Drennan (P), after several months of searching, engaged another company to do the paving for $10,948.66 and sued for the cost difference. From adverse judgment in the lower courts, Drennan (P) appealed.

ISSUE: Is a promise which the promisor should reasonably expect to induce action or forbearance of a definite and substantial character on the part of a promisee and which does induce such action or forebearance binding if injustice can only be avoided by enforcement of the promise?

HOLDING AND DECISION: (Traynor, J.) Yes. A promise which the promisor should reasonably expect to induce action or forbearance of a definite and substantial character on the part of a promisee and which does induce such action or forbearance is binding if injustice can be avoided only by enforcement of the promise. Star (D) had reason to expect that if its bid was low it would be used by Drennan (P) and so induced "action . . . of a definite and substantial character on the part of the promisee." Star's (D) bid did not state nor clearly imply revocability at any time before acceptance. Where there is an offer for a unilateral contract, the theory that the offer is revocable at any time before complete performance is obsolete. When any part of the consideration requested in the offer is given or tendered by the offeree, the offeror is bound. That is, the main offer includes a subsidiary promise, which is implied, that if part of the requested performance is given, the offeror will not revoke his offer, and if tender is made, it will be accepted. Restatement § 45. In more extreme cases, merely acting in justifiable reliance of an offer may serve as sufficient reason to make the promise binding. Restatement § 90. Section 90's purpose is to make a promise binding even though consideration is lacking; its absence is not fatal to the enforcement of the subsidiary promise. Reasonable reliance acts in lieu of ordinary consideration. Star (D) had a stake in Drennan's (P) reliance on its bid. This interest plus Drennan's (P) being bound by his own bid make it only fair that Drennan (P) should have the chance to accept Star's (D) bid after the general contract was awarded Drennan (P). While Star's (D) bid was the result of mistake, it was not such a mistake that Drennan (P) knew or should have known was in error. A 160% variance in paving bids was not unusual in the area. Because the mistake misled Drennan (P) as to the paving cost under the circumstances, Star's (D) bid should be enforced.

EDITOR'S ANALYSIS: The case greatly broadened the view of promissory estoppel. Restatement § 90, as interpreted by Hand in James Baird Co. v. Gimbel Bros., 64 F. 2d 344 (1933), goes beyond the area of charitable or donative promises to general business use. This view was adopted in Restatement (Second) § 90 written after this case. Note that a subcontractor's bid must be more than a mere estimate, and, of course, if it reasonably appears to be based upon a mistake, reliance cannot be justified. The cases which apply promissory estoppel show the subcontractor to be bound by his bid, but the general contractor is not bound to accept the bid. Note that Traynor works into Restatement § 90 through § 45 (the Brooklyn Bridge hypothetical), expanding the view that giving or tendering consideration will bind the promise to include justifiable reliance to have the same effect. In the Drennan case, circumstances and business practices peculiar to the area were important. Telephoned bids were a common practice. Wide variances in paving costs were expected, thereby adding strength to Drennan's (P) position, as an error in a paving bid would not be reasonably noticed. Also see Restatement (Second) § 89B(2) for this viewpoint as extended to option contracts.

[For more information on detrimental reliance as making offer irrevocable, see Casenote Law Outline on Contracts, Chapter 1, § III, The Acceptance.]

NOTES:

ELECTRICAL CONSTRUCTION & MAINTENANCE COMPANY v. MAEDA PACIFIC CORPORATION

764 F.2d 619 (9th Cir. 1985).

NATURE OF CASE: Appeal from dismissal of action for breach of contract.

NOTES:

FACT SUMMARY: Maeda (D) orally agreed to subcontract with ECM (P) upon the acceptance of its bid on a project if ECM was the lowest bidder on the subcontract, but Maeda (D) breached the agreement when it did not subcontract with ECM after its bid was accepted.

CONCISE RULE OF LAW: A subcontractor's bid, made in reliance on the contractor's conditional promise of use, is sufficient consideration to bind the contractor to his promise.

FACTS: Maeda (D), solicited bids from various subcontractors for the electrical needs of the project for which he was bidding. ECM (P) was one of the subcontractors that was solicited by Maeda (D). The parties orally agreed that if Maeda's (D) bid was accepted, ECM would be the subcontractor as long as its bid was the lowest. Although Maeda (D) was awarded the project, it refused to subcontract with ECM (P), claiming that there was no contract obligating it to contract with ECM (P). The court dismissed the case for failure to state a claim, concluding that there was no consideration for ECM's (P) promise to bid on the condition that its bid be accepted if it were the lowest bid. ECM (P) appealed.

ISSUE: Is a subcontractor's bid, made in reliance on the contractor's conditional promise of use, sufficient consideration to bind the contractor to its promise?

HOLDING AND DECISION: (Pregerson, J.) Yes. A contractor's mere use of the subcontractor's bid is not the acceptance of the bid. However, when a subcontractor agrees to bid only after the contractor's conditional promise to accept its bid upon winning the project, and if its bid was the lowest, the contractor is bound by his promise. Since a subcontractor does not owe a legal duty to the contractor to bid, its bid becomes consideration for the contractor's promise. Here, ECM (P) bargained for Maeda's (D) conditional promise to accept its bid by submitting its own bid on the electrical work. Reversed and remanded for hearing on this issue of damages.

EDITOR'S ANALYSIS: This was a case of first impression. Recognizing the potential abuses by the contractors, the California legislature adopted the Subletting and Subcontracting Fair Practices Act. This statute provides that a subcontractor listed in a contractor's bid cannot be replaced by another unless he refuses to execute a written contract, becomes insolvent, or fails to satisfy the bonding requirements.

[For more information on conditional promises, see Casenote Law Outline on Contracts, Chapter 2, § I, Valuable Consideration: The Bargained-for Incursion of Legal Detriment.]

RAFFLES v. WICHELHAUS

Ct. of Exchequer, 159 Eng. Rep. 375 (1864).

NATURE OF CASE: Action for damages for breach of a contract for the sale of goods.

FACT SUMMARY: Raffles (P) contracted to sell cotton to Wichelhaus (D) to be delivered from Bombay at Liverpool on the ship "Peerless." Unknown to the parties was the existence of two different ships carrying cotton, each named "Peerless" arriving at Liverpool from Bombay, but at different times.

CONCISE RULE OF LAW: Where neither party knows or has reason to know of the ambiguity or where both know or have reason to know, the ambiguity is given the meaning that each party intended it to have.

FACTS: Raffles (P) contracted to sell Wichelhaus (D) 125 bales of Surrat cotton to arrive from Bombay at Liverpool on the ship "Peerless." Wichelhaus (D) was to pay 17% pence per pound of cotton within an agreed upon time after the arrival of the goods in England. Unknown to the parties, there were two ships called "Peerless" each of which was carrying cotton from Bombay to Liverpool. One ship was to sail in October by Wichelhaus (D) for delivery of the goods while Raffles (P) had expected the cotton to be shipped on the "Peerless" set to sail in December. As Wichelhaus (D) could not have the delivery he expected, he refused to accept the later delivery.

ISSUE: Did a latent ambiguity arise showing that there had been no meeting of the minds, hence, no contract?

HOLDING AND DECISION: (Per Curiam) Yes. While the contract did not show which particular "Peerless" was intended, the moment it appeared two ships called "Peerless" were sailing from Bombay to Liverpool with a load of cotton, a latent ambiguity arose, and parol evidence was admissible for the purpose of determining that both parties had intended a different "Peerless" to be subject in the contract. When there is an ambiguity, it is given the meaning that each party intended it to have. However, if different meanings were intended there is no contract if the ambiguity relates to a material term. Consequently, there was no meeting of the minds and no binding contract.

EDITOR'S ANALYSIS: When there is no integration of the contract, the standard for its interpretation is the meaning that the party making the manifestation should reasonably expect the other party to give it, i.e., a standard of reasonable expectation. This case illustrates an exception to this rule. Where there is an ambiguity, if both parties give the same meaning to it, there is a contract. If the parties each give a different meaning to the ambiguity, then there is no contract, as occurred here. The ambiguity struck at a material term, as payment was to be made within an agreed upon time after delivery. The parties could not even agree on the time of delivery. The other exception occurs when one party has reason to know of the ambiguity and the other does not, so it will bear the meaning given to it by the latter, that is the party who is without fault. Note that under U.C.C. § 2-322, delivery ex ship, it would make no difference which ship would be carrier of the goods and the case would have gone the other way. However, Restatement, First, §71 would appear to follow the general rule of the present case.

[For more information on latent ambiguity, see Casenote Law Outline on Contracts, Chapter 1, § IV, Impact of Ambiguity and Mistake on the Bargain.]

NOTES:

KONIC INTERNATIONAL CORPORATION v. SPOKANE COMPUTER SERVICES, INC.
Idaho Ct. of App., 109 Idaho 527, 708 P.2d 932 (1985).

NATURE OF CASE: Appeal from order of rescission of contract.

FACT SUMMARY: Both purchaser and seller of an electronic device attached different meanings to the seller's price quote of "fifty-six twenty."

CONCISE RULE OF LAW: There can be no contract when the parties give different meanings to a material term.

FACTS: Young, and employee of Spokane (D), was instructed to shop for a surge protector, which is a device which protects computers from damaging surges of electrical current. Young's investigation turned up several models priced between $50 and $200, but none of these met his employer's needs. Young then decided on a unit made by Konic (P) and asked Konic's (D) salesman what the unit's price was. The salesman responded, "fifty-six twenty." The salesman meant $5,620. Young thought the quoted price was $56.20. Young ordered the unit, which was then shipped to and installed by Spokane (D). Two weeks later, when Spokane (D) was processing its purchase order and Konic's (P) invoice, the discrepancy between the purchase order amount and the invoice amount was discovered. Spokane (D) immediately tried to disaffirm the purchase, saying that Young had no authority to make that large a purchase. Konic (P) responded that Spokane (D) owned the device, Spokane (D) refused to pay, and this lawsuit ensued. The trial magistrate found that their was no contract because of Young's lack of authority to make the purchase. On appeal, the district court affirmed the magistrate's decision, and this appeal followed.

ISSUE: Can there be a contract when the parties give different meanings to a material term?

HOLDING AND DECISION: (Walters, C.J.) No. There can be no contract when the parties give different meanings to a material term. Since Young interpreted the words "fifty-six twenty" to mean $56.20, and Konic's (P) salesman actually meant $5,620, it cannot be said that the minds of the parties met regarding the price term. Affirmed.

EDITOR'S ANALYSIS: While it is true that if the parties fail to agree to the price term in a contract, the court can "fill in" one which is reasonable, once an attempt is made to set a price, as here, the court cannot impose its idea of what is reasonable. Note the there is a difference between a material term and one that is essential to contract formation. In the sale of goods, the only truly essential term is the quantity, and the court will never attempt to substitute a reasonable quantity. Any other terms, while considered material, can be "filled in," if the parties have not attempted to supply them.

[For more information on ambiguity of language in the bargain, see Casenote Law Outline on Contracts, Chapter 1, § IV, Impact of Ambiguity and Mistake on the Bargain.]

NOTES:

VARNEY v. DITMARS

N.Y. Ct. App., 217 N.Y. 223, 111 N.E. 822 (1916).

NATURE OF CASE: Action brought for an alleged wrongful discharge of an employee.

FACT SUMMARY: Ditmars (D) told Varney (P) that if the latter would continue working for him until the first of the year, he would close his books and give Varney (P) a fair share of his profits.

CONCISE RULE OF LAW: In order for a contract to be valid, the promise or the agreement of the parties to it must be certain and explicit so that their full intention may be ascertained to a reasonable degree of certainty.

FACTS: Ditmars (D) told Varney (P) that if the latter would continue working for him until the first of the year, he would close his books and give Varney (P) a fair share of his profits. Varney (P) told Ditmars (D) that he intended to stay home on Election Day which was November 6. That day, Varney (P) became ill and was unable to return to work until December 1. Ditmars (D) informed Varney (P) that because Varney (P) did not come to work on Election Day, he was being discharged.

ISSUE: Is the question whether the words "fair" and "reasonable" have a definite and enforceable meaning when used in business transactions dependent upon the intention of the parties in using such words and upon the subject matter to which they refer?

HOLDING AND DECISION: (Chase, J.) Yes. In the case of a contract for the sale of goods or for hire without a fixed price or consideration being named, it will be presumed that a reasonable price or consideration is intended. However, in order for a contract to be valid, the promise or agreement of the parties to it must be certain and explicit so that their full intention may be ascertained to a reasonable degree of certainty. The contract here, so far as it relates to a share of Ditmars' (D) profits is not only uncertain, but it is necessarily affected by so many other facts that are in themselves indefinite and uncertain that the intention of the parties is pure conjecture. Such an executory contract must rest for performance upon the honor and good faith of the parties making it. The courts cannot aid parties when they are unable or unwilling to agree upon the terms of their own proposed contract.

DISSENT: (Cardozo, J.) It is not true that a promise to pay an employee a fair share of the profits is always and of necessity too vague to be enforced. Here, since Varney (P) failed to supply the data essential to computation, profits were properly not included in the damages. However, he was entitled to his loss of salary since he was to work until the end of the year.

EDITOR'S ANALYSIS: As indicated by Varney v. Ditmars, where an agreement makes no statement as to the price to be paid, the law invokes the standard of reasonableness, and a promise to pay the fair value of the services or property is implied. Likewise, a promise to pay a reasonable sum for goods or services is generally held valid. As to promises to pay a fair share of profits, like the one in Varney, agreements specifying the maximum percentage of profits to be paid have been upheld.

[For more information on implications of essential contract terms, see Casenote Law Outline on Contracts, Chapter 1, § II, The Offer.]

NOTES:

METRO-GOLDWYN-MAYER, INC. v. SCHEIDER

N.Y. Ct. App., 40 N.Y.2d 1069, 392 N.Y.S.2d 252, 360 N.E.2d 930 (1976).

NATURE OF CASE: Action for breach of contract.

FACT SUMMARY: Scheider (D), who refused to perform in a television series for MGM (P), maintained that there had not been a complete contract between the parties, but the court found otherwise.

CONCISE RULE OF LAW: If the parties thereto have completed their negotiations as to what they regard as the essential elements and performance has begun on the good-faith understanding that agreement on the unsettled matters will follow, the courts will find and enforce a contract if some objective method of determining the unsettled elements is available — such as resort to the contract itself, commercial practice, or other usage and custom.

FACTS: MGM (P) brought suit against Scheider (D) when he refused to perform in a television series. The court found that the parties had entered into an oral contract that called for Scheider (D) to appear in both a pilot film and the television series that might develop therefrom. Initially, the parties negotiated for a period of several weeks, reaching agreement on the broad outlines of the contract and its financial dimensions, and both having explicit expectations that further agreements were to follow. Additional important provisions were negotiated over the following weeks; the only essential term without an articulated understanding was the starting date for filming the television series. The trial court supplied this term by a finding based on proof of established custom and practice in the industry, of which both parties were found to be aware, set in the context of the other understandings reached by them. Scheider (D) appealed, challenging the court's determination that there was a complete contract between the parties.

ISSUE: Can there be a complete contract absent agreement on all elements?

HOLDING AND DECISION: (Per curiam) Yes. In many instances, parties complete their negotiations on what they regard as the essential elements of a contract and begin performance on the good-faith understanding that agreement on the unsettled matters will follow. In such instances, the courts will find and enforce a contract if some objective method of determining the unsettled elements or terms is available. Such objective criteria may be found in the agreement itself, commercial practice, or other usage and custom. If the contract can be rendered certain and complete, by reference to something certain, the court will fill in the gaps. That is precisely what was done here. Affirmed.

EDITOR'S ANALYSIS: Section 204 of Restatement (Second) of Contracts looks to the court to supply "a term which is reasonable in the circumstances" in those instances "when the parties to a bargain sufficiently defined to be a contract have not agreed with respect to a term which is essential to a determination of their rights and duties."

[For more information on agreements to agree in the future on content of an essential term, see Casenote Law Outline on Contracts, Chapter 1, § II, The Offer.]

NOTES:

JOSEPH MARTIN, JR. DELICATESSEN v. SCHUMACHER

52 N.Y.2d 105, 417 N.E.2d 541 (1981).

NATURE OF CASE: Appeal from denial of specific enforce-ment.

FACT SUMMARY: Schumacher (D) sought to enforce a lease provision which stated that the lease may be renewed at a rental "to be agreed upon."

CONCISE RULE OF LAW: A real estate lease provision calling for the renewal of the lease at a rental to be agreed upon is unenforceable due to its omission of a material term.

FACTS: Schumacher (D) leased a store from Martin (P) for a five-year term at a specified rental. A clause in the lease provided that Schumacher (D), as tenant, was entitled to renew the lease for an additional five-year term at a rental "to be agreed upon." Schumacher (D) gave timely notice of his desire to exercise his privilege of renewal, and Martin (P) responded that the price would be $900 a month, almost double the current rent. Schumacher (D) hired an appraiser, who placed the fair market value of the store at $545 a month. Schumacher (D) then filed suit for specific performance. Martin (P) brought a separate eviction action, and the trial court ruled in his favor, holding that the lease provision was only an agreement to agree and therefore unenforceable. On appeal, the court expressly overruled an established line of precedents and held that Schumacher (D) should be able to prove whether a binding agreement by the parties was intended. Martin (P) appealed.

ISSUE: May a real estate lease provision calling for the renewal of the lease at a rental to be agreed upon be specifically enforced?

HOLDING AND DECISION: (Fuchsberg, J.) No. It is a well-settled principle of law that a court may enforce a contract only where the terms of that contract are sufficiently certain and specific. Otherwise, a court would be forced to impose its own conception of what the parties should or might have agreed upon, rather than attempting to implement the bargain actually made. Accordingly, definiteness and specificity as to material matters is the essence of contract law. For that reason, a mere agreement to agree on a material term in the future without any details as to the methods of ascertaining that term cannot be enforced since the court, rather than the parties, would be creating the agreement. A real estate lease which provides for a renewal term at a rental to be agreed upon is nothing more than an agreement to agree and, hence, cannot be enforced due to its omission of a material term. Reversed.

CONCURRENCE: (Meyer, J.) While the majority was correct in its decision in the instant case, it goes too far in suggesting that such a lease provision would never be enforceable.

CONCURRENCE AND DISSENT: (Jasen, J.) Although the renewal clause was unenforceable due to its uncertainty, Schumacher (D) should have been able to prove his entitlement to renewal of the lease on other grounds.

EDITOR'S ANALYSIS: The difficulty courts have in enforcing contracts which are left incomplete by the parties is illustrated by the case of Ansorge v. Kane, 244 N.Y. 395 (1927). The parties had agreed on a sale of land and had specified the price and the amount which was to be paid in cash up front. The manner of the deferred payments was "to be agreed upon." When the seller reneged, the buyer sought specific performance. In denying the remedy, the court held that an agreement to agree upon such a material term as contract payments rendered the contract unenforceable. However, the court stated that had the contract been absolutely silent regarding the payments, rather than saying they would be as agreed upon, the contract could have been enforced using reasonable and customary payment terms.

[For more information on agreements to agree in the future on the content of an essential term, see Casenote Law Outline on Contracts, Chapter 1, § II, The Offer.]

NOTES:

OLGEBAY NORTON COMPANY v. ARMCO, INC.

Ohio Sup. Ct., 52 Ohio St. 3d 232, 556 N.E.2d 515 (1990).

NATURE OF CASE: Appeal from declaratory judgment setting contract price.

FACT SUMMARY: After the parties' contract-pricing mechanisms failed, the trial court determined that it could set the price of shipments.

CONCISE RULE OF LAW: The court can look to the parties' course of dealing to determine their intent to be bound.

FACTS: In 1957, Olgebay Norton Company (Olgebay) (P) and Armco, Inc. (Armco) (D) entered into a long-term contract for the shipment of Armco's (D) iron ore by Olgebay (P). The parties had a long history of a close business relationship, including joint ventures, Armco's (D) ownership of Olgebay (P) stock, and interlocking directorates. Both parties recognized that Armco's (D) ever-increasing capacity requirements would require that Olgebay (P) invest substantial capital to maintain, upgrade, and purchase iron ore carrier vessels. The agreement provided for primary and secondary price rate mechanisms tied to those prices recognized by leading iron ore shippers in the industry. After many years and several extensions of the contract, the parties were unable to agree upon a shipping rate for the 1985 season after the pricing mechanisms had broken down. Olgebay (P) billed Armco (D) $7.66 per gross ton, and Armco (D) reduced the invoice amount to $5 per gross ton and paid the $5 per ton figure, indicating payment in full language on the check to Olgebay (P) and explaining its position in an accompanying letter. In late 1985, the parties again tried to agree on a rate, this time for the 1986 season, but failed to reach a mutually satisfactory price. On April 11, 1986, Olgebay (P) sought declaratory relief requesting the court declare a reasonable rate for the shipments. Armco (D) counterclaimed, asserting that the contract was unenforceable because the parties did not intend to be bound in the event that their agreed-upon pricing mechanisms broke down. The trial court held that the parties intended to be bound by the 1957 agreement, established $6.25 as a reasonable rate for Armco (D) to pay for Olgebay's (P) services, and ordered the parties to utilize a mediator if they were unable to agree on a shipping rate for each annual shipping season.

ISSUE: Can the court look to the parties' course of dealing to determine their intent to be bound?

HOLDING AND DECISION: (Per Curiam) Yes. The court can look to the parties' course of dealing to determine their intent to be bound. The evidence demonstrated the longstanding and close business relationship, including (D) ownership of Olgebay (P) stock, and a seat for Armco (D) on Olgebay's (P) board of directors. The parties continued this business relationship despite the fact that the pricing mechanisms had failed, which further showed their intent to be bound in the face of such a failure. Olgebay's (P) dedication of bulk vessels to Armco's (D) service was a major and ongoing investment in reliance on the 1957 agreement. Affirmed.

EDITOR'S ANALYSIS: Consider a lease agreement where the lessor and lessee provide that the latter, at the end of the lease term, can extend his lease at a rental fee to be determined at the time he exercises his option. The common law view would hold that such an "agreement to agree" prevents the exercise of the option. The modern and better view is that the parties intend to be bound, and they are merely exercising their right to agree on a rate when the reasonable value based on current market conditions can be determined.

[For more information on the course of dealing between parties, see Casenote Law Outline on Contracts, Chapter 3, § V, Defenses Arising from the Form of the Bargain.]

NOTES:

EMPRO MANUFACTURING CO., INC. v. BALL-CO MANUFACTURING, INC.

870 F.2d 423 (7th Cir. 1989).

NATURE OF CASE: Appeal of dismissal of action for breach of contract.

FACT SUMMARY: Empro (P) contended that a letter of intent had the effect of binding Ball-Co (D).

CONCISE RULE OF LAW: Parties who have made their pact "subject to" a later definitive agreement have manifested an intent not to be bound.

FACTS: Empro (P) and Ball-Co (D) signed a letter of intent containing the general provisions of the sale of Ball-Co's (D) assets to Empro (P), which proposed to pay $2.4 million, with $650,000 to be paid on closing and a 10-year promissory note for the remainder. The letter stated, "Empro's purchase shall be subject to the satisfaction of certain conditions precedent to closing including, but not limited to" the definitive Asset Purchase Agreement and, among five other conditions, "[t]he approval of the shareholders and board of directors of Empro." The sticking point for the deal turned out to be the security for Empro's (P) promissory note. When Ball-Co (D) started negotiating with someone else, Empro (P) sued, contending that the letter of intent bound Ball-Co (D) to sell only to Empro (P). The trial court dismissed, and Empro (P) appealed.

ISSUE: Have parties who have made their pact "subject to" a later definitive agreement manifested an intent not to be bound?

HOLDING AND DECISION: (Easterbrook, C.J.) Yes. Parties who have made their pact "subject to" a later agreement have manifested an intent not to be bound. Contract law gives effect to parties' wishes, but these must be expressed openly. Intent in contract law is measured objectively rather than subjectively and must be determined solely from the language used when no ambiguity in its terms exists. Parties may decide for themselves whether the results of preliminary negotiations bind them, but they do this through their words. "Subject to a definitive agreement" appears twice in the letter. The letter also recites, twice, that it contains the "general terms and conditions," implying that each side retained the right to make additional demands. The fact that Empro (P) listed as a condition that its own shareholders and board of directors had to approve the deal showed an intent not to be bound. Letters of intent and agreements in principle often, as here, do no more than set the stage for negotiations on details which may or may not be ironed out. Approaching agreement by stages is a valuable method of doing business because it allows parties to agree on the basics without bargaining away their privilege to disagree on specifics. Ball-Co (D) did not intend to be bound by its letter of intent. Affirmed.

EDITOR'S ANALYSIS: Compare this situation with one where the parties have agreed that their agreement is to be reduced to writing and signed by both of them. If the agreement is sufficient to be deemed to be a contract and one party withdraws before the signing, there can be no contract if the parties have clearly stated that they do not intend to be bound until the writing is signed. The Second Circuit, in Winston v. Mediafare Entertainment Corporation, 777 F.2d 78, 80 (2d Cir., 1985), has set forth the following factors to determine whether the parties intend to be bound before the document is fully executed: "(1) whether there has been an express reservation of the right not to be bound in the absence of a writing; (2) whether there has been partial performance of the contract; (3) whether all of the terms of the alleged contract have been agreed upon; and (4) whether the agreement at issue is the type of contract that is usually committed to writing."

[For more information on the formation of a contract, see Casenote Law Outline on Contracts, Chapter 1, § II, The Offer.]

NOTES:

HOFFMAN v. RED OWL STORES, INC.

Wis. Sup. Ct., 133 N.W.2d 267, 26 Wis.2d 683 (1965).

NATURE OF CASE: Appeal from award of damages.

FACT SUMMARY: Hoffman (P) was assured by an agent of the Red Owl Stores, Inc. (D) that if he took certain steps he would obtain a supermarket franchise, but after taking these steps at great expense, Hoffman (P) did not receive the franchise.

CONCISE RULE OF LAW: Under the doctrine of promissory estoppel, as stated in Section 90 of Restatement, First, Contracts, "a promise which the promisor should reasonably expect to induce action or forbearance of a definite and substantial character on the part of the promisee and which does induce such action or forbearance is binding if injustice can be avoided only by enforcement of the promise."

FACTS: An agent of the Red Owl Stores, Inc. (D) promised Hoffman (P) that Red Owl (D) would establish him in a supermarket store for the sum of $18,000. In reliance upon this promise, and upon the recommendations of the agent, Hoffman (P) purchased a grocery store to gain experience. Thereafter, upon further recommendations of the agent, Hoffman (D) sold his grocery store fixtures and inventory to Red Owl (D), before the profitable summer months started, and paid $1,000 for an option on land for building a franchise outlet. After moving near this outlet, Hoffman (P) was told that he needed $24,100 for the promised franchise. After Hoffman (P) acquired this amount, most of it through a loan from his father-in-law, he was told that he needed an additional $2,000 for the deal to go through. Finally, after acquiring the additional $2,000, Hoffman (P) was told he would be established in his new store as soon as he sold a bakery store which he owned. After doing this, though, Red Owl (D) told Hoffman (P) that in order to enhance his credit rating he must procure from his father-in-law a statement that the funds acquired from him were an outright gift and not a loan. In response, Hoffman (P) sued for damages to recover income which he lost and expenses which he incurred in reliance upon the promises of Red Owl (D). After an award of damages for Hoffman (P), Red Owl (D) appealed.

ISSUE: When a promisor makes a promise which he should reasonably expect to induce action on the part of the promisee and which does induce such action, can he be estopped from denying the enforceability of that promise?

HOLDING AND DECISION: Yes. Under the doctrine of promissory estoppel, as stated in Section 90 of Restatement, First, Contracts, "a promise which the promisor should reasonably expect to induce action for forbearance of a definite and substantial character on the part of the promisee and which does induce such action or forbearance is binding if injustice can be avoided only by enforcement of the promise." Of course, such damages as are necessary to prevent injustice can be awarded under the doctrine of promissory estoppel instead of specific performance. Furthermore, an action based upon promissory estoppel is not equivalent to a breach of contract action, and therefore, the promise does not have to "embrace all essential details of a proposed transaction between promisor and promisee so as to be the equivalent of an offer that would result in a binding contract between the parties if the promisee were to accept the same." Here, therefore, it is not important that no final construction plans, etc. were ever completed. It is instead important that Hoffman (P) substantially relied to his detriment on Red Owl's (D) promise and that Red Owl (D) should have reasonably foreseen such reliance. Therefore, Hoffman (P) is entitled to those damages which are necessary to prevent injustice. He is entitled to losses resulting from selling his bakery, from purchasing the option on land for a franchise, from moving near the franchise outlet, and from selling his grocery store fixtures and inventory. Hoffman's (P) reasonable damages from selling his grocery store fixtures and inventory, though, do not include any future lost profits, since he purchased the grocery store only temporarily to gain experience (i.e., he is only entitled to any loss measured by the difference between the sales price and fair market value).

EDITOR'S ANALYSIS: This case illustrates the doctrine of promissory estoppel. At common law, such doctrine afforded protection to any party threatened with "substantial economic loss" after taking "reasonable steps in foreseeable reliance upon a gratuitous promise." The Restatement, Second, though, does not require that the promise be gratuitous or that the reliance be "substantial." It requires only reasonable, foreseeable reliance upon any promise. Note that an action under the doctrine of promissory estoppel is not equivalent to an action for breach of contract, and, therefore, no consideration is necessary to make the promise binding. Furthermore, the promise upon which a person reasonably relies will be enforced specifically or by damages whenever the court decides that the interests of justice would be served by such enforcement.

[For more information on the doctrine of promissory estoppel, see Casenote Law Outline on Contracts, Chapter 2, § II, Substitutes for Valuable Consideration as Grounds for Imparting Liability Consequences for Breaching a Promise.]

NOTES:

CHAPTER 4
AVOIDANCE OF CONTRACT

QUICK REFERENCE RULES OF LAW

1. **Capacity to Contract: Infancy.** A minor may disaffirm a contract, except for necessaries, during his minority regardless of whether the other party is returned to the status quo. (Bowling v. Sperry)

   [For more information on contract promises of minors, see Casenote Law Outline on Contracts, Chapter 3, § II, Defenses Related to the Capacity of One of the Parties.]

2. **Capacity to Contract: Mental Incompetence.** The party asserting lack of capacity must rebut the presumption of competency by clear and convincing proof. (Heights Realty, Ltd. v. Phillips)

   [For more information on contract promises of the mentally infirm, see Casenote Law Outline on Contracts, Chapter 3, § II, Defenses Related to the Capacity of One of the Parties.]

3. **Unilateral and Mutual Mistake.** One who errs in preparing a bid for a public works contract is entitled to rescission if he can establish that the mistake is material, enforcement of a contract pursuant to terms of the erroneous bid would be unconscionable, the mistake did not result from violation of a positive legal duty or from culpable negligence, the party to whom the bid was submitted will not be prejudiced except by loss of the bargain matters, and prompt notice of error was given. (Boise Junior College District v. Mattefs Construction Co.)

   [For more information on material mistake, see Casenote Law Outline on Contracts, Chapter 1, § IV, Impact of Ambiguity and Mistake on the Bargain.]

4. **Unilateral and Mutual Mistake.** A mutual mistake as to a basic assumption on which the contract was made provides a basis for rescission of the contract for mutual mistake of fact. (Beachcomber Coins, Inc. v. Boskett)

   [For more information on mutual mistake, see Casenote Law Outline on Contracts, Chapter 1, § IV, Impact of Ambiguity and Mistake on the Bargain.]

5. **Unilateral and Mutual Mistake.** A court need not grant rescission in every case in which there was a mutual mistake that relates to a basic assumption of the parties upon which the contract was made and which materially affects the agreed performances of the parties. (Lenawee County Board of Health v. Messerly)

   [For more information on mutual mistake, see Casenote Law Outline on Contracts, Chapter 1, § IV, Impact of Ambiguity and Mistake on the Bargain.]

6. **Unilateral and Mutual Mistake.** As between the sender and receiver, the party who selects the telegraph as the means of communication shall bear the loss caused by the errors of the telegraph. (Ayer v. Western Union Telegraph Co.)

   [For more information on mistakes made by third parties, see Casenote Law Outline on Contracts, Chapter 1, § IV, Impact of Ambiguity and Mistake on the Bargain.]

7. **Fraud and the Duty to Disclose.** An agreement must be upheld absent cause in fact or law for invalidating it. (Morta v. Korea Insurance Corp.)

   [For more information on the theory of contract formation, see Casenote Law Outline on Contracts, Chapter 1, § I, The Agreement Process — Manifesting Mutual Consent.]

8. **Fraud and the Duty to Disclose.** A vendee is not obligated to communicate to the vendor information which might influence the price of the commodity being purchased, even if such information is exclusively within his (the vendee's) knowledge. (Laidlaw v. Organ)

   [For more information on misrepresentation, see Casenote Law Outline on Contracts, Chapter 3, § IV, Defenses Centered on the Deceptive or Coercive Formation Tactics of One of the Parties.]

9. **Fraud and the Duty to Disclose.** Where one party has superior knowledge, statements made within the area of such knowledge may be treated as statements of fact. (Vokes v. Arthur Murray, Inc.)

   [For more information on fraud in the inducement, see Casenote Law Outline on Contracts, Chapter 3, § IV, Defenses Centered on the Deceptive or Coercive Formation Tactics of One of the Parties.]

10. **Fraud and the Duty to Disclose.** Where the seller of a home knows of facts materially affecting the value of the property which are not readily observable and are not known to the buyer, the seller is under a duty to disclose them. (Hill v. Jones)

    [For more information on misrepresentation and nondisclosure of material facts, see Casenote Law Outline on Contracts, Chapter 3, § IV, Defenses Centered on the Deceptive or Coercive Formation Tactics of One of the Parties.]

11. **Duress.** A contract modification is voidable on the ground of duress when the party claiming duress establishes that its agreement to the modification was obtained by means of a wrongful threat from the other party which precluded the first party's exercise of free will. (Austin Instrument, Inc. v. Loral Corp.)

    [For more information on economic duress, see Casenote Law Outline on Contracts, Chapter 3, § IV, Defenses Centered on the Deceptive or Coercive Formation Tactics of One of the Parties.]

12. **Duress.** Where a party is forced into a transaction as a result of unlawful threats or wrongful, oppressive, or unconscionable conduct by the other party which leaves him no reasonable alternative but to acquiesce, he may void the transaction and recover any economic loss. (Machinery Hauling, Inc. v. Steel of West Virginia)

    [For more information on economic duress, see Casenote Law Outline on Contracts, Chapter 3, § IV, Defenses Centered on the Deceptive or Coercive Formation Tactics of One of the Parties.]

13. **Consumer Transactions.** Where an important clause is in fine print and is buried within the body of a plaintiff's form contract, it is unenforceable. (Cutler Corp. v. Latshaw)

    [For more information on unconscionable contracts, see Casenote Law Outline on Contracts, Chapter 3, § III, Defenses Rooted in Social Objection to the Content of the Bargain.]

14. **Commercial Transactions.** Where there is no showing of a voluntary, knowing, and understanding release of rights, there is unequal bargaining power, and the clause is grossly unfair, the court may find it unconscionable. (Weaver v. American Oil Co.)

    [For more information on procedural unconscionability, see Casenote Law Outline on Contracts, Chapter 3, § IV, Defenses Centered on the Deceptive or Coercive Formation Tactics of One of the Parties.]

15. **Commercial Transactions.** A contract provision that permits termination of the contract without cause is not per se unconscionable. (Zapatha v. Dairy Mart, Inc.)

[For more information on substantive unconscionability, see Casenote Law Outline on Contracts, Chapter 3, § III, Defenses Rooted in Social Objection to the Content of the Bargain.]

16. **Illegality: Agreements Unenforceable on Grounds of Public Policy.** A court will not enforce an illegal contract. (Sinnar v. Le Roy)

[For more information on illegality in a contract, see Casenote Law Outline on Contracts, Chapter 3, § III, Defenses Rooted in Social Objection to the Content of the Bargain.]

17. **Illegality: Agreements Uneforceable on Grounds of Public Policy.** A contract which has an illegal purpose is contrary to public policy and void. (Homami v. Iranzadi)

[For more information on illegality in a contract, see Casenote Law Outline on Contracts, Chapter 3, § III, Defenses Rooted in Social Objection to the Content of the Bargain.]

18. **Illegality: Agreements Unenforceable on Grounds of Public Policy.** 42 U.S.C. § 1981 prohibits discrimination in the formation and enforcement contracts only, but not discriminatory behavior occurring during the contractual relationship. (Patterson v. McLean Credit Union)

19. **Illegality: Agreements Unenforceable on Grounds of Public Policy.** An overbroad covenant by the employee not to compete with his employer following termination will be reasonably modified to render it enforceable unless the employer did not draft the covenant in good faith. (Data Management, Inc. v. Greene)

[For more information on covenants not to compete, see Casenote Law Outline on Contracts, Chapter 5, § II, The Assignment of Contract Rights.]

20. **Illegality: Agreement Unenforceable on Grounds of Public Polisy.** An unmarried cohabitant may assert contract and property claims against the other party to the cohabitation. (Watts v. Watts)

[For more information on quasi-contracts, see Casenote Law Outline on Contracts, Chapter 1, § I, The Agreement Process — Manifesting Mutual Consent.]

BOWLING v. SPERRY

133 Ind. App. 692 (1962).

NATURE OF CASE: Action to disaffirm contract and to recover purchase price.

NOTES:

FACT SUMMARY: Bowling (P) purchased a used car from Sperry (D) and subsequently attempted to disaffirm the contract and recover the purchase price.

CONCISE RULE OF LAW: A minor may disaffirm a contract, except for necessaries, during his minority regardless of whether the other party is returned to the status quo.

FACTS: Bowling (P), a minor, his aunt, and grandmother went to Sperry's (D) used car lot to purchase a car. The aunt lent Bowling (P) $90 to pay partially for the car. Bowling (P) paid the balance shortly thereafter. The car burned out its bearings within a week and Bowling (P) was informed that it would cost between $45 and $95 to fix it. Bowling (P) left the car at Sperry's (D) lot and demanded a return of his money. Sperry (D) refused. Bowling (P) brought suit to disaffirm the contract and to recover the $140 purchase price. Sperry (D) defended on the ground that Bowling (P) had been accompanied by two adults and that his aunt had lent him $90. Sperry (D) also maintained that the damage to the car was caused by Bowling's (P) negligence and that the car was a "necessity" to take him to and from work. The court dismissed the action on these bases.

ISSUE: May a minor disaffirm a contract, except for necessaries, regardless of whether the other party is returned to the status quo?

HOLDING AND DECISION: (Myers, J.) Yes. A minor may, during his minority or upon reaching his majority, disaffirm any or all of his contracts except those for necessaries. It is not necessary for the other party to the contract to be returned to a position of status quo. The contract herein was between Bowling (P) and Sperry (D) and the presence of adults with Bowling (P) or the fact that money was lent to Bowling (P) is immaterial. As a minor he had the absolute right to disaffirm the contract. While a car is no longer a luxury, Sperry (D) did not meet his burden of showing that it was a necessity for Bowling (P). Reversed.

EDITOR'S ANALYSIS: The law requires that minors be protected from improvident bargains. For this reason it allows them to disaffirm their contracts. An exception is made for necessaries because vendors/renters would be hesitant to supply life necessities to needy minors if they could easily avoid paying for them. "Necessaries" have been deemed those items which are necessary to sustain life (e.g., food, housing, clothing, etc.) and those necessary to maintain the minor's social position. 27 Am. Jr., Infants, Section 17.

[For more information on contract promises of minors, see Casenote Law Outline on Contracts, Chapter 3, § II, Defenses Related to the Capacity of One of the Parties.]

HEIGHTS REALTY, LTD. v. PHILLIPS

N.M. Sup. Ct., 106 N.M. 692, 749 P.2d 77 (1988).

NATURE OF CASE: Appeal from denial of damages for breach of contract.

FACT SUMMARY: Heights Realty (P) sued to recover a broker's commission and lost when the trial court deemed Phillip's (D) conservatee incompetent.

CONCISE RULE OF LAW: The party asserting lack of capacity must rebut the presumption of competency by clear and convincing proof.

FACTS: On September 26, 1984, 84-year-old Mrs. Gholson listed her home for sale with Heights Realty (P). The agreement included a purchase price of $250,000, with a down payment of $75,000. On October 10, 1984, Mrs. Gholson changed her mind about the down payment and signed an addendum raising it to $100,000. In November 1984, an offer was made to purchase the property for $255,000, but Mrs. Gholson did not accept it. Heights Realty (P) then sued to recover its commission for having provided a buyer, but while the action was pending, Mrs. Gholson was adjudged incompetent, and Phillips (D) was named conservator of the estate. Following a bench trial, the district court found that Mrs. Gholson lacked the capacity to have validly executed the listing agreement and entered judgment in favor of Phillips (D). Heights Realty (P) appealed, claiming that the presumption of Mrs. Gholson's competency was not overcome by clear and convincing evidence. Heights Realty (P) presented testimonial evidence that Mrs. Gholson had sufficient command of her facilities to enter into the agreement, and Phillips (D) presented contrary testimony to the issue of competency.

ISSUE: Must the party asserting lack of capacity rebut the assumption of competency by clear and convincing proof?

HOLDING AND DECISION: (Stowers, J.) Yes. The party asserting lack of capacity must rebut the presumption of competency by clear and convincing proof. Even though some of the evidence adduced was conflicting, this goes to the question of credibility, a question solely for resolution by the trier of fact, who after hearing testimony resolved the question in favor of Mrs. Gholson. This court will not resolve conflicts or substitute its judgment where the record as a whole substantially supports the trial court's findings of fact. That the trial court found for Phillips (D) implies that the burden of proof had been sustained. Affirmed.

EDITOR'S ANALYSIS: The law presumes everyone to be competent. However, had Mrs. Gholson been adjudged incompetent prior to entering into the listing agreement, the incapacity would be presumed to have continued unless Height's Realty (P) could have presented proof of a lucid moment where Mrs. Gholson was capable of understanding in a reasonable manner the nature and affect of her actions.

[For more information on contract promises of the mentally infirm, see Casenote Law Outline on Contracts, Chapter 3, § II, Defenses Related to the Capacity of One of the Parties.]

NOTES:

BOISE JUNIOR COLLEGE DIST. v. MATTEFS CONSTRUCTION CO.

Idaho Sup. Ct., 92 Idaho 757, 450 P.2d 604 (1969).

NATURE OF CASE: Action to recover on a bid bond.

FACT SUMMARY: Mattefs's (D) erroneously omitted an item representing 14% of its total bid submitted to Boise (P). Boise (P) had expected to pay $150,000 for the work and ended up paying another contractor $149,000.

CONCISE RULE OF LAW: One who errs in preparing a bid for a public works contract is entitled to rescission if he can establish that the mistake is material, enforcement of a contract pursuant to terms of the erroneous bid would be unconscionable, the mistake did not result from violation of a positive legal duty or from culpable negligence, the party to whom the bid was submitted will not be prejudiced except by loss of the bargain matters, and prompt notice of error was given.

FACTS: Mattefs (D) erroneously omitted an item representing 14% of its total bid submitted to Boise (P). Boise (P) had expected to pay $150,000 for the work. Mattefs's (D) bid was $141,000 and Boise (P) ended up paying another contractor $149,000. It was found that if Mattefs (P) were compelled to perform he would incur a pecuniary loss of $10,000. The trial court also found that Mattefs's (D) error did not result from violation of a legal duty or from culpable negligence. Boise (P) had notice of Mattefs's (D) error prior to its attempted acceptance of Mattefs's (D) bid.

ISSUE: Is one who errs in preparing a bid for a public works contract entitled to rescission in certain circumstances?

HOLDING AND DECISION: (Spear, J.) Yes. One who errs in preparing a bid for a public works contract is entitled to rescission if he can establish that the mistake is material, the enforcement of a contract pursuant to terms of the erroneous bid would be unconscionable, the mistake did not result from violation of a positive legal duty or from culpable negligence, the party to whom the bid was submitted will not be prejudiced except by loss of his bargain, and prompt notice of error was given. Here the item omitted represented 14% of Mattefs's (D) total bid, which is a substantial and material omission; to enforce Mattefs's (D) bid would be unconscionable since he would incur a $10,000 loss. Since the trial court's finding that the error did not result from violation of a legal duty or from culpable negligence is supported by competent evidence it will not be disturbed on appeal. Since Boise (P) expected to pay $150,000 for the work and will still pay less than that ($149,000), if rescission is allowed it has not shown that it will be prejudiced except by loss of the bargain of paying Mattefs's (D) $141,000. Finally relief from mistaken bids is consistently allowed where, as was the case here, the acceptor had actual notice of the error prior to its attempted acceptance.

EDITOR'S ANALYSIS: The offeree's actual or constructive knowledge of a mistake is often an important factor in opinions granting relief to the mistaken party. As in Boise, relief typically takes the form of rescission, an equitable remedy invalidating the contract. Thus, it is evidently conceded that a voidable contract of some sort has been formed. However it has also been held that if the offeree knew or should have known of the mistake, he had no power to accept the offer at all, since a meeting of the minds does not occur.

[For more information on material mistake, see Casenote Law Outline on Contracts, Chapter 1, § IV, Impact of Ambiguity and Mistake on the Bargain.]

NOTES:

AYER v. WESTERN UNION TELEGRAPH CO.

Me. Sup. Jud. Ct., 79 Me. 493, 10 A. 495 (1887).

NATURE OF CASE: Action to recover damages for negligence.

FACT SUMMARY: Ayer (P) sent a telegram through Western Union (b) offering to sell "800 M laths two ten net." the word "ten" was omitted in the transmission of the telegram.

CONCISE RULE OF LAW: As between the sender and receiver, the party who selects the telegraph as the means of communication shall bear the loss caused by the errors of the telegraph.

FACTS: Ayer (P) sent a telegram through Western Union (D) offering to sell "800 M laths two ten net." the word "ten" was omitted in the transmission of the telegram and it read "two net" when received. The receiver immediately wired his acceptance of the offer. The mistake was discovered, but Ayer's (P) correspondent insisted he was entitled to the laths at that price, and they were shipped accordingly. Western Union (D) claims that Ayer (P) was not bound by the erroneous message and hence need not have shipped the laths at the lesser price.

ISSUE: Is the message written by the sender, and entrusted to a telegraph company for transmission, rather than the message written out and delivered by the company to the receiver at the other end of the line, the better evidence of the rights of the receiver against the sender?

HOLDING AND DECISION: (Emery, J.) No. As between the sender and receiver, the party who selects the telegraph as the means of communication shall bear the loss caused by the errors of the telegraph. The first proposer can select one of many modes of communication. The receiver has no choice except as to his answer. If he cannot safely act upon the message he received through the agency selected by the proposer, business must be seriously hampered and delayed. However this rule presupposes the innocence of the receiver and that there is nothing to cause him to suspect an error. Hence here Ayer (P) is entitled to recover the difference between the two dollars and two ten as to the laths.

EDITOR'S ANALYSIS: There is a difference of opinion upon the question whether one who makes an offer by telegram, which is negligently altered during the transmission, is bound by the offer as it reaches the person to whom it is made. The question is often determined according to the view the court takes as to whether the telegraph company is or is not the agent of the sender. Some courts have held that in view of the character of the service rendered by a telegraph company and the fact that the sender is powerless to control the conduct of the company, the telegraph company should be considered an independent contractor rather than the sender's agent. Other courts have accepted the English rule that a telegraph company is not the agent of either party, and so a sender is not bound by an error in transmission.

[For more information on mistakes made by third parties, see Casenote Law Outline on Contracts, Chapter 1, § IV, Impact of Ambiguity and Mistake on the Bargain.]

NOTES:

MORTA v. KOREA INSURANCE CORP.

840 F.2d 1452 (9th Cir. 1988).

NATURE OF CASE: Appeal from award of damages for fraud.

FACT SUMMARY: Morta (P) sought to have a release he signed held invalid.

CONCISE RULE OF LAW: An agreement must be upheld absent cause in fact or law for invalidating it.

FACTS: Morta (P), who was injured in an automobile accident, was treated twice during the week following the accident, both times being assured by the attending physician that he was fine and could go home. Morta (P) then sought compensation for his losses from Korea Insurance Corp. (KIC) (D), which in acknowledging the liability of its insured, made Morta (P) an offer which covered his medical bills, damage to his car, pain and suffering, and loss of compensation from work. Morta (P) then took the offer to a lawyer who advised him that the offer was about as much as he could expect to receive, and that demanding more would just delay payment. Morta (P) accepted the settlement and signed a standard release. A week after the settlement, Morta (P) was hospitalized and required surgery for a blood clot in his brain. The medical bills incurred by Morta (P) after signing the release totalled about $11,000, and he sought to have the release invalidated on the grounds of fraud. The release clearly stated that it released KIC (D) of all claims "growing out of any and all known and unknown, foreseen and unforeseen bodily and personal injuries and property damage" arising out of the accident in question. The trial court held in favor of Morta (P), and KIC (D) appealed.

ISSUE: Must an agreement be upheld absent cause in fact or law for invalidating it?

HOLDING AND DECISION: (Kowzinski, C.J.) Yes. An agreement must be upheld absent cause in fact or law for invalidating it. Written instruments, fixing the parties' rights and responsibilities by mutual consent, bring an important measure of order to life and greatly facilitate the adjudicatory process. Despite recent cynicism, sanctity of contract remains an important civilizing concept. A person who, without coercion or undue persuasion, executes a solemn release cannot subsequently impeach it on the grounds of his carelessness if at the time of execution he might have advised himself fully as to the nature and legal effect of the act done. It appears to be the rule that where the parties expressly and intentionally settle for unknown injuries the release given by the claimant is incontestible. Morta's (P) latent injury makes this a hard case factually but not legally. Parties can never be sure about what the future will bring; they sign contracts for the very purpose of guarding against unforeseen contingencies. Morta (P) freely entered into a settlement that specifically released unknown claims for latent or progressive personal injuries. Reversed.

EDITOR'S ANALYSIS: The trial court's decision reflects the tendency of some courts to attempt to protect people for their own bad decisions. The rules of construction in contracts are often used to eliminate document ambiguities and meanings susceptible to different interpretations. This is especially prevalent in consumer cases. Note that the appeals court cited the old legal maxim, "Hard cases make bad law." In other words, if a court finds for a party to whom it may be sympathetic, as the court was to Morta (P), but lacks a legal basis for its conclusion, the decision will create bad precedent which will be impossible to resolve in future cases.

[For more information on the theory of contract formation, see Casenote Law Outline on Contracts, Chapter 1, § I, The Agreement Process – Manifesting Mutual Consent.]

NOTES:

LAIDLAW v. ORGAN

15 U.S. (2 Wheat.) 178 (1817).

NATURE OF CASE: Appeal from award of recovery of tobacco.

FACT SUMMARY: Laidlaw (D) repossessed tobacco which Organ (P) had purchased from him while remaining silent about information affecting its price.

CONCISE RULE OF LAW: A vendee is not obligated to communicate to the vendor information which might influence the price of the commodity being purchased, even if such information is exclusively within his (the vendee's) knowledge.

FACTS: Organ (P) desired to purchase tobacco from Laidlaw (D). Before the contract of sale was completed, though, Laidlaw (D) asked Organ (P) "if there was any news which was calculated to enhance the price or value of the tobacco." Although Organ (P) had knowledge of such information (i.e., of the peace treaty of Ghent ending the war of 1812 and the end of the British blockade of New Orleans), he remained silent and purchased the tobacco at a depressed price. Subsequently, though, Laidlaw (D) learned of the treaty and repossessed the tobacco, the value of which had risen. Thereupon, Organ (P) brought an action to recover possession of the tobacco. After a directed verdict for Organ (P), Laidlaw (D) appealed.

ISSUE: Must a vendee communicate to the vendor any information exclusively within his knowledge which might influence the price of the commodity being purchased?

HOLDING AND DECISION: (Marshall, C.J.) No. A vendee is not obligated to communicate to the vendor information which might influence the price of the commodity being purchased, even if such information is exclusively within his (the vendee's) knowledge. Of course, however, either party (vendee or vendor) may not "say" or "do" anything tending to "impose" misinformation on the other (i.e., actively imparting misinformation is fraud). Here, although Organ (P) had no duty to disclose his knowledge to Laidlaw (D), the question of whether he "imposed" misinformation on Laidlaw (D) should have been submitted to the jury (i.e., a directed verdict was improper). New trial awarded.

CONCURRENCE: (Key, J.) Here, the information which was not disclosed could have been obtained by Laidlaw (D) if he had been equally diligent or equally fortunate. In such circumstances, Organ (P) had no duty to disclose the information.

DISSENT: (Ingersoll, C.J.) "Suppression of material circumstances, within the knowledge of the vendee and not accessible to the vendor, is equivalent to fraud and vitiates the contract." That is the situation here.

EDITOR'S ANALYSIS: This case illustrates the fact that fraud voids a contract, but it also restricts the definition of fraud (to actively giving misinformation) in order to preserve the concept of freedom of contract. Today, though, many courts are more inclined to require disclosure of material facts. Note that there are two types of contractual fraud: (1) "fraud in executing the agreement" (i.e., one party does not know that the paper he signs is a contract), and (2) "fraud in the inducement" (i.e., misrepresentation of material facts).

[For more information on misrepresentation, see Casenote Law Outline on Contracts, Chapter 3, § IV, Defenses Centered on the Deceptive or Coercive Formation Tactics of One of the Parties.]

NOTES:

VOKES v. ARTHUR MURRAY, INC.

212 So. 2d 906 (1968).

NATURE OF CASE: Action for cancellation of contracts.

NOTES:

FACT SUMMARY: Vokes (P) was continually cajoled into purchasing thousands of hours of dancing lessons at Arthur Murray (D).

CONCISE RULE OF LAW: Where one party has superior knowledge, statements made within the area of such knowledge may be treated as statements of fact.

FACTS: Vokes (P), at age 51, decided she wished to become an accomplished dancer. Over a period of years, by flattery, cajolery, awards, etc., Vokes (P) was convinced to sign up under a number of contracts for $31,000 worth of dancing lessons from Arthur Murray (D). Vokes (P) was repeatedly informed that she was a promising student who was quickly becoming sufficiently skilled to pursue a career as a professional dancer. Vokes(P) subsequently brought an action to cancel the unused portion of approximately 2,302 hours of lessons to which she had subscribed. Vokes (P) alleged that she had attained little or no skill as a dancer and obviously had no such aptitude. Vokes (P) alleged that Arthur Murray (D) employees had purposefully misrepresented her skills and had taken unconscionable advantage of her. Vokes (P) alleged that she had relied on Arthur Murray (D) employees' superior knowledge as to her ability and the skills necessary to become a professional dancer.

ISSUE: May a party reasonably rely on opinions as assertions of fact when given by a party of superior knowledge on the subject?

HOLDING AND DECISION: (Pierce, J.) Yes. Normally, the party to a contract has no reasonable right to rely on opinions expressed by the other party to the contract. Misrepresentations of opinion are normally not actionable. However, a statement made by a party having superior knowledge may be regarded as a statement of fact even though it would be regarded as opinion if the parties were dealing on the basis of equal knowledge. Where a party undertakes to make representations based on its superior knowledge, it is under a duty to act honestly and to disclose the entire truth. Vokes (P) has stated a valid cause of action.

EDITOR'S ANALYSIS: Basically, Vokes is concerned with reliance and credibility. One has a right to rely on opinions of attorneys, doctors, etc. Vokes extends such reasonable reliance to experts or those highly knowledgeable in a field in which plaintiff is generally unfamiliar. Ramel v. Chasebrook Construction Company, 135 So. 2d 876 (1961). To be actionable, the misrepresentation must be material, and there must be some overreaching in cases such as Vokes.

[For more information on fruad in the inducement, see Casenote Law Outline on Contracts, Chapter 3, § IV, Defenses Centered on the Deceptive or Coercive Formation Tactics of One of the Parties.]

HILL v. JONES

Ariz. Ct. of App., 151 Ariz. 81, 725 P.2d 1115 (1986).

NATURE OF CASE: Appeal from summary dismissal of action for rescission of real estate purchase contract.

FACT SUMMARY: Before buying Jones' (D) home, Hill (P) asked whether it had been infested with termites, and Jones (D) denied that there had been previous infestations, despite firsthand knowledge of them.

CONCISE RULE OF LAW: Where the seller of a home knows of facts materially affecting the value of the property which are not readily observable and are not known to the buyer, the seller is under a duty to disclose them.

FACTS: During escrow for the purchase of Jones' (D) home, Hill (P) expressed concern about a "ripple" in a parquet floor. Jones (D) claimed that the problem was due to flooding from a broken water heater, when in fact it demonstrated a termite infestation. Hill (P) asked that a termite inspection report be placed in escrow. An exterminator inspected Jones' (D) home but failed to find instances of prior infestation due to strategic placement of boxes and plants. When the results of the termite report were revealed to Hill (P) by his realtor, Hill (P) closed escrow with Jones (D). After moving in, Hill (P) found termites and discovered that the previous seller of the home had paid for termite guarantees and semiannual inspections when he sold the house to Jones (D). Despite previous infestations which had been treated during Jones' (D) ownership and occupancy of the house, Jones (D) had said nothing about termites to either Hill (P) or the exterminator. Hill (P) sued to rescind the purchase contract on grounds of intentional nondisclosure of the termite damage. The trial court dismissed the action on summary judgment for failure to state a claim, and Hill (P) appealed.

ISSUE: Where the seller of a home knows of facts materially affecting the value of the property which are not readily observable and are not known to the buyer, is the seller under a duty to disclose them?

HOLDING AND DECISION: (Meyerson, J.) Yes. Where the seller of a home knows of facts materially affecting the value of the property which are not readily observable and are not known to the buyer, the seller is under a duty to disclose them to the buyer. Such a disclosure is necessary to correct mistakes of the purchaser as to a basic assumption on which he is making the contract and to protect him from misplaced trust in the vendor. The existence of termite damage in a residential dwelling is the type of material fact which gives rise to the duty to disclose because it is a matter to which a reasonable person would attach importance in deciding whether or not to purchase such a dwelling. Here, Jones (D) failed to reveal the home's prior history of termite infestation, despite knowledge of such infestation and previous attempts to treat it. Allegations to this effect raise triable issues of material fact which must be determined by the trier of fact. Whether Hill (P) was put on reasonable notice of the termite problem despite Jones' (D) nondisclosure or whether he exercised reasonable diligence in informing himself about the termite problem should also be left to the trier of fact. Reversed and remanded.

EDITOR'S ANALYSIS: This case is somewhat exceptional in that the court recognized a duty of disclosure between parties in an ordinary arm's-length, commercial transaction. More typically, courts will recognize a "duty to speak up" only in the presence of a confidential or fiduciary relationship. See, e.g., Vai v. Bank of America Trust & Savings Association, 15 Cal. Rptr. 71, 364 P.2d 247 (1961) (community property settlement set aside on grounds that husband had failed to disclose value of property involved to his wife). Beyond the existence of a confidential or fiduciary relationship, courts traditionally have imposed a duty of disclosure between businessmen only when necessary to correct a previous misstatement or mistaken impression.

[For more information on misrepresentation and nondisclosure of material facts, see Casenote Law Outline on Contracts, Chapter 3, § IV, Defenses Centered on the Deceptive or Coercive Formation Tactics of One of the Parties.]

NOTES:

AUSTIN INSTRUMENT, INC. v. LORAL CORP.
N.Y. Ct. App., 29 N.Y.2d 124, 272 N.E.2d 533 (1971).

NATURE OF CASE: Action to recover damages for breach of contract.

FACT SUMMARY: Austin (P) threatened to withhold delivery of precision parts unless Loral (D) would raise the contract price.

CONCISE RULE OF LAW: A contract modification is voidable on the ground of duress when the party claiming duress establishes that its agreement to the modification was obtained by means of a wrongful threat from the other party which precluded the first party's exercise of free will.

FACTS: Loral (D) was under contract to produce radar sets for the government. The contract contained a liquidated damage clause for late delivery and a cancellation clause in case of default by Loral (D). Loral (D), who did a substantial portion of its business with the government, awarded Austin (P) a subcontract to supply some of the precision parts. Subsequently, Austin (P) threatened to cease delivery of the parts unless Loral (D) consented to substantial increases in the subcontract price. After contacting 10 manufacturers of precision gears and finding none who could produce the parts in time to meet its commitment to the government, Loral (D) acceded to Austin's (P) demand.

ISSUE: Is a contract modification acceded to by one party under circumstances amounting to economic duress enforceable against that party?

HOLDING AND DECISION: (Fuld, C.J.) No. A contract modification "is voidable on the ground of duress when it is established that the party making the claim was forced to agree to it by means of a wrongful threat precluding the exercise of his free will." Loral (D) has made out a classic case of economic duress in that: (1) Austin (P) threatened to withhold delivery of "needful goods" unless Loral (D) agreed, (2) Loral (D) could not obtain the goods from another source of supply, and (3) the ordinary remedy of an action for breach of the original subcontract would not be adequate [since so much was riding on Loral's (D) own general contract with the government] . Thus it is "manifest" that Austin's (P) threat deprived Loral (D) of his free will. "Loral (D) actually had no choice."

DISSENT: Three dissenting judges felt that in applying the law of duress, the majority necessarily overturned crucial findings of fact by the lower courts.

EDITOR'S ANALYSIS: Although it has generally been held that a threat to breach a contract does not constitute economic duress, courts have recently begun to hold that various kinds of unethical business compulsion do constitute duress. The present case is an example of this trend. Note that even under the U.C.C. (which recognizes modification without consideration — § 2-209) the requirement of good faith is ever present.

[For more information on economic duress, see Casenote Law Outline on Contracts, Chapter 3, § IV, Defenses Centered on the Deceptive or Coercive Formation Tactics of One of the Parties.]

NOTES:

MACHINERY HAULING, INC. v. STEEL OF WEST VIRGINIA

W. Va. Sup. Ct. App., 384 S.E.2d 139 (1989).

NATURE OF CASE: Question certified for appeal in action for economic loss due to business compulsion.

FACT SUMMARY: After Steel of West Virginia (D) hired Machinery Hauling (P) to transport steel to a third party, the third party rejected the delivered goods as unmerchantable, and Steel (D) demanded that Machinery Hauling (P) pay it the value of the rejected goods or else lose its business.

CONCISE RULE OF LAW: Where a party is forced into a transaction as a result of unlawful threats or wrongful, oppressive, or unconscionable conduct by the other party which leaves him no reasonable alternative but to acquiesce, he may void the transaction and recover any economic loss.

FACTS: Steel of West Virginia (D) hired Machinery Hauling (P) to transport steel product to a third party. The third party rejected the goods as unmerchantable. Steel (D) demanded that Machinery Hauling (P) pay the price of the undelivered loads "or else [it] would cease to do business with" it. Machinery Hauling (P) refused to pay and sued Steel (D) for the loss of business that resulted from this severance of business relations, which amounted to over $1 million per year. The lower court concluded that although under the proper facts a claim could be stated for threats against business interests, Machinery Hauling (P) had not alleged facts which would support its claim for "extortionate demands." Machinery Hauling (P) appealed, and the lower court certified the question whether threats made by one party for the purpose of inducing contract concessions from the other are actionable.

ISSUE: Where a party is forced into a transaction as a result of unlawful threats or wrongful, oppressive, or unconscionable conduct by the other party which leaves him no reasonable alternative but to acquiesce, may he void the transaction and recover any consequent economic loss?

HOLDING AND DECISION: (Miller, J.) Yes. Where a party is forced into a transaction as a result of unlawful threats or wrongful, oppressive, or unconscionable conduct by the other party which leaves him no reasonable alternative but to acquiesce, he may void the transaction and recover any consequent economic loss. This concept is known as business compulsion or economic duress and often consists of a threat which deprives the victim of his unfettered will. Between Machinery Hauling (P) and Steel (D), however, there was no such duress. They did not have a continuing contract between them; Steel's (D) demand that Machinery Hauling (P) pay it the value of the undelivered goods was not coupled with a threat to terminate an existing contract. Further, Machinery Hauling's (P) mere prospect of doing future business with Steel (D) amounted only to an expectancy, which is not a legal right upon which Machinery Hauling (P) can premise a claim of economic duress. Certified question answered and dismissed.

EDITOR'S ANALYSIS: This case is unusual in that it appears to recognize duress as an independent tort, whereas typically duress is pled as an affirmative defense so that the transaction in question may be voided and restitution made. Further, a distinction should be made between duress by physical compulsion, which renders a contract void at its formation, and duress by threats, which merely makes a contract voidable at the election of the "threatened" party. See Restatement (Second) of Contracts § 174. Duress often takes the form of threats of criminal prosecution or civil process; in the former case, the threat is almost always considered improper and a basis for avoiding the contract, but in the latter, it is considered improper only if made in bad faith. See Restatement (Second) § 176, comments c and d.

[For more information on economic duress, see Casenote Law Outline on Contracts, Chapter 3, § IV, Defenses Centered on the Deceptive or Coercive Formation Tactics of One of the Parties.]

NOTES:

CUTLER CORP. v. LATSHAW

374 Pa. 1 (1953).

NATURE OF CASE: Action to set aside a confession of judgment contained in a contract clause.

FACT SUMMARY: On the back of Cutler Corporation's (P) form contract, in fine print, was a confession of judgment in the event of the buyer's default.

CONCISE RULE OF LAW: Where an important clause is in fine print and is buried within the body of a plaintiff's form contract, it is unenforceable.

FACTS: Latshaw (D) authorized Cutler Corporation (P) to perform construction work for her. She became dissatisfied with the work and ordered Cutler (P) employees to stop further work until the defects were corrected. Cutler (P) entered a confession of judgment against Latshaw (D) for $5,238. The attorney's confession of judgment was contained on the reverse side of Cutler's (P) form contract. It was in very fine print and was buried in numerous other conditions. Latshaw (D) had signed only a separate document called "Owner's Consent," which stated she assented to the contract terms.

ISSUE: Are material contract provisions, written in fine print and inconspicuously located in the contract, binding?

HOLDING AND DECISION: (Musmanno, J.) No. An attorney's confession of judgment is one of the most potent clauses a contract can contain. It must be conspicuously placed in the contract using, at a minimum, normal print size. The normal homeowner would not expect such a provision in a simple remodeling contract, and it would be unjust and inequitable to enforce it where diminutive type is used and it is well hidden in a mass of verbiage on the reverse of a contract. The confession of judgment is reversed.

EDITOR'S ANALYSIS: In some circumstances, either the courts or the legislature have held that certain contractual provisions are per se unconscionable. Cross-collateral agreements, confessions of judgment, etc., have been set aside, even when conspicuously placed in large type, where there is a gross disparity of bargaining power. Where a certain contractual provision is used by all automobile manufacturers (e.g., release from all warranty liability), such provisions are deemed invalid as unconscionable.

[For more information on unconscionable contracts, see Casenote Law Outline on Contracts, Chapter 3, § III, Defenses Rooted in Social Objection to the Content of the Bargain.]

WEAVER v. AMERICAN OIL CO.

257 Ind. 458 (1971).

NATURE OF CASE: Personal injury action.

FACT SUMMARY: Weaver signed an indemnification agreement holding the lessor, American Oil (P), harmless for its negligence.

CONCISE RULE OF LAW: Where there is no showing of a voluntary, knowing, and understanding release of rights, there is unequal bargaining power, and the clause is grossly unfair, the court may find it unconscionable.

FACTS: Weaver (D) leased an American Oil (P) station. As part of the standardized contract, in small print and without a heading, there was a clause under which Weaver (D) agreed to indemnify American (P) for its negligent acts. The clause was never explained to Weaver (D), and it was never even established that he had read the contract or was otherwise aware of the clause. An American (P) employee negligently sprayed Weaver (D) and an assistant with gasoline, causing them to be burned and injured on the leased premises. American (P) sought a declaratory judgment to determine Weaver's (D) liability for the injuries under the clause. Weaver (D) alleged that the clause was unconscionable.

ISSUE: Where there is no showing of a valid waiver of normal rights, is a highly unreasonable contract clause imposed by a party with superior bargaining power unconscionable?

HOLDING AND DECISION: (Arterburn, C.J.) Yes. Unconscionability may be found where a party with superior bargaining power exploits the unequal position to impose highly unfair and unreasonable terms on the other party. A court may find that such a grossly unfair use of bargaining power is unconscionable. This is not to say that parties may not voluntarily, knowingly, and intelligently accept such clauses. However, it is the burden of the party attempting to enforce the clause to show such a waiver. Here, Weaver (D) had little formal education, the clause was in fine print, and it was not titled. No one ever explained the clause to him, and there is no showing that he even read the contract. In such cases, a lessor in a dominant position such as American (P) cannot be allowed to enforce such an unfair clause to produce an unconscionable result.

EDITOR'S ANALYSIS: While the law will not normally relieve a party from a business mistake, where one party has taken advantage of another's necessities and disadvantage to obtain an unfair advantage, and the other party has, owing to his condition, encumbered himself with a heavy liability or an onerous obligation for the sake of a small or inadequate present gain, the courts are prone to grant relief. Stiefler v. McCullough, 97 Ind. App. 123.

[For more information on procedural unconscionability, see Casenote Law Outline on Contracts, Chapter 3, § IV, Defenses Centered on the Deceptive or Coercive Formation Tactics of One of the Parties.]

ZAPATHA v. DAIRY MART, INC.

Mass. Sup. Jud. Ct., 381 Mass. 284, 408 N.E. 2d 1370 (1980).

NATURE OF CASE: Action to enjoin termination of an agreement.

FACT SUMMARY: Dairy Mart (D) appealed a judgment that the termination provision in its contract with Zapatha (P) was unconscionable and that its conduct in terminating the agreement had amounted to an unfair and deceptive act or practice.

CONCISE RULE OF LAW: A contract provision that permits termination of the contract without cause is not per se unconscionable.

FACTS: The Zapathas (P) signed a franchise agreement with Dairy Mart (D), which operated a chain of franchise "convenience" stores. It provided that Dairy Mart (D) would furnish the store and equipment, pay the rent, utility bills, and other costs of doing business, and receive a percentage of the store's gross sales as a franchise fee. The Zapathas (P) were responsible for paying for a starting inventory, maintaining a minimum inventory thereafter, paying employees and taxes, and operating the store on a daily basis. There was a termination provision permitting Dairy Mart (D) to terminate without cause on 90 days' written notice after 12 months. Termination thereunder and without cause later occurred, and the Zapathas (P) sought an injunction. The court held that the termination provision was unconscionable and that termination had been an unfair and deceptive act or practice. Dairy Mart (D) appealed.

ISSUE: Is a contract provision allowing termination without cause per se unconscionable?

HOLDING AND DECISION: (Wilkins, J.) No. Even the Uniform Commercial Code implies that a contract provision allowing termination without cause is not per se unconscionable. Since there is no clear, all-purpose definition of "unconscionable," unconscionability is something that must be determined on a case-by-case basis. In each instance, the focus should be on whether, at the time of the execution of the agreement, the contract provision could result in unfair surprise and was oppressive to the allegedly disadvantaged party. There was no potential for unfair surprise to the Zapathas (P), nor was there any oppression in its inclusion in the agreement. Oppression is direct to the substantive fairness to the parties of permitting the termination provision to operate as written. Under the circumstances, there was no unfairness in permitting it to operate. Furthermore, there was no violation of the general duty of good faith and fair dealing. Reversed.

EDITOR'S ANALYSIS: It is clear that a party can meet the obligation to deal in "good faith" in entering into a contract which contains an unconscionable provision. Section 208 of Restatement (Second) provides that a court can refuse to enforce the entire contract if one term thereof is unconscionable or enforce the remainder of the contract without the unconscionable term or "so limit the application" of the unconscionable term "as to avoid any unconscionable result."

[For more information on substantive unconscionability, see Casenote Law Outline on Contracts, Chapter 3, § III, Defenses Rooted in Social Objection to the Content of the Bargain.]

NOTES:

SINNAR v. LEROY

44 Wash. 2d 728 (1954).

NATURE OF CASE: Action to recover money obtained by fraud.

NOTES:

FACT SUMMARY: Sinnar (P) attempted to bribe Lewis in order to obtain a beer license for his store.

CONCISE RULE OF LAW: A court will not enforce an illegal contract.

FACTS: Sinnar (P) applied for a liquor license from the state in order to sell beer in his store. He was denied the permit. LeRoy (D), Sinnar's (P) friend, suggested that a Mr. Lewis might help him obtain a permit. Sinnar (P) paid Lewis $450 to help him obtain a $60 license. Lewis kept the money but never delivered the license. Sinnar (P) sued LeRoy (D) for the $450. The trial court found for Sinnar (P). LeRoy (D) appealed on the basis that the contract was illegal. Sinnar (P) claimed that since this was never raised at trial, the defense of illegality had been waived.

ISSUE: Where the evidence supports a finding that the contract was illegal, will the courts enforce it?

HOLDING AND DECISION: (Weaver, J.) No. Serious illegality renders the contract void and unenforceable. To prevent the formation of such contracts, the courts will refuse to enforce them, leaving the parties as the court found them. Here, a license could be obtained only from the state. To prevent bribery, which is illegal, violative of public policy, and immoral, such contracts will not be enforced. Sinnar (P) must have realized that $450 for a $60 permit involved some form of illegality. Such serious illegality need not be pleaded. If it appears on the record, the court itself should deny recovery. The defense cannot be waived. The court, if it suspects illegality, should examine witnesses in order to determine the true nature of the contract. A finding of such serious illegality acts as a bar to plaintiff's recovery. The evidence adduced here sustains such a finding. The judgment is reversed.

EDITOR'S ANALYSIS: Bribery of corporate officers, while not a crime, is violative of public policy. Therefore, recovery will be denied even though the contract is not illegal. When a legal contract subsequently becomes illegal (e.g., a trade embargo passed after the contract was entered into), it becomes void and unenforceable. However, either party may maintain an action for restitution.

[For more information on illegality in a contract, see Casenote Law Outline on Contracts, Chapter 3, § III, Defenses Rooted in Social Objection to the Content of the Bargain.]

HOMAMI v. IRANZADI

Cal. Ct. of App., 211 Cal.App.3d 1104 (1989).

NATURE OF CASE: Appeal from award of damages for breach of contract.

FACT SUMMARY: Homami (P) made a loan to Iranzadi (D), and they agreed not to report any interest.

CONCISE RULE OF LAW: A contract which has an illegal purpose is contrary to public policy and void.

FACTS: Homami (P) loaned $250,000 to his brother-in-law Iranzadi (D) for a real estate transaction. The loan was evidenced by two identical promissory notes dated March 22, 1984, in the amount of $125,000 each. Each note recited that all monies were due and payable in two years, and that they would bear no interest. Each note was secured by real property belonging to Iranzadi (D). A later modification agreement between the parties provided for the commencement of interest payments. When Iranzadi (D) stopped making the agreed-upon payments, Homami (P) commenced foreclosure proceedings on the properties that Iranzadi (D) had put up for collateral. On October 15, 1986, Homami (P) sued for all unpaid monies, and Iranzadi (D) claimed a credit for almost $40,000 that he had paid. At trial, Homami (P) testified that the parties had orally agreed that interest would be paid on the loan, and that the income received by Homami (P) would not be reported. The trial court awarded $39, 324.68 to Homami (P), finding that this amount which Iranzadi (D) had paid represented interest only, and no principal reduction. Iranzadi (D) appealed.

ISSUE: Is a contract which has an illegal purpose contrary to public policy and void?

HOLDING AND DECISION: (Brauer, J.) Yes. A contract which has an illegal purpose is contrary to public policy and void. The contract must have a lawful object. The general principle is well established that a contract founded on an illegal consideration, or which is made for the purpose of furthering any matter or thing prohibited by statute, is void. This rule applies to every contract which is founded on a transaction malum in se, or which is prohibited by a statute on the ground of public policy. In order to state his claim to the funds from the property used as collateral, Homami (P) was obliged to testify and did testify that he collected interest secretly in order to circumvent tax laws. Homami (P) was not entitled to the $39,624.86 he collected as unreported interest. Reversed and remanded.

EDITOR'S ANALYSIS: A common situation involves the unlicensed contractor, or other unlicensed professional, who seeks to collect money for services rendered. Courts have routinely refused to grant relief in such cases on the ground that the failure to comply with licensing requirements violates a law designed to protect and benefit the public. Therefore a party who has violated the law and entered into an agreement while unlicensed cannot obtain the aid of courts to enforce the agreement. Other types of cases in which courts refuse to grant relief on contracts against public policy include actions for monies arising from illegal gambling activities and cases, such as above, where parties have attempted to circumvent tax laws.

[For more information on illegality in a contract, see Casenote Law Outline on Contracts, Chapter 3, § III, Defenses Rooted in Social Objection to the Content of the Bargain.]

NOTES:

PATTERSON v. McLEAN CREDIT UNION

491 U.S. 164 (1989).

NATURE OF CASE: Review of appeal in suit alleging racial discrimination in violation of 42 U.S.C. § 1981.

NOTES:

FACT SUMMARY: A bank teller alleged that her supervisor repeatedly made racially abusive comments before eventually discharging her.

CONCISE RULE OF LAW: 42 U.S.C. § 1981 prohibits discrimination in the formation and enforcement contracts only, but not discriminatory behavior occurring during the contractual relationship.

FACTS: Patterson (P), a black woman, was employed by the McLean Credit Union (D). During her employment, her supervisor would assign her to sweep and dust, a duty not given to white employees. At one point, her supervisor told her that blacks are known to work slower than whites. Patterson (P) was eventually discharged by her supervisor. Patterson (P) filed suit, alleging discrimination based upon race in violation of 42 U.S.C. § 1981. The district court ruled that the statute did not apply to her case, and the court of appeals affirmed. Patterson (P) appealed to the Supreme Court.

ISSUE: Is racially abusive conduct during the course of a contractual relationship prohibited by 42 U.S.C. § 1981?

HOLDING AND DECISION: (Kennedy, J.) No. 42 U.S.C. § 1981 prohibits discrimination in the formation and enforcement contracts only, but not discriminatory behavior occurring during the contractual relationship. 42 U.S.C. 1981 is one of the oldest civil rights statutes in the United States. The statute protects the rights to make and enforce contracts from racial discrimination. However, racially motivated conduct during the performance of the contract is not proscribed by this particular statute. In this case, Patterson's (P) claim cites racial harassment during the course of her employment. She has not claimed that racial discrimination prevented her from contracting with her employer. Nor has she claimed that she was denied the right to enforce her employment contract on racially discriminatory grounds. While the conduct of her employer was reprehensible and may be actionable under state contract law and Title VII, it cannot be the basis for a claim under 42 U.S.C. § 1981. Affirmed.

EDITOR'S ANALYSIS: The court has suggested that racial abuse is a matter that amounts to a breach of contract under state law. However, there are better vehicles for protecting against racial discrimination than relying on implied covenants in contracts. Title VII covers conditions of employment and would likely have provided the best opportunity for Patterson (P) to recover for the wrongs she alleged.

DATA MANAGEMENT, INC. v. GREENE

Alaska Sup. Ct., 757 P.2d 62 (1988).

NATURE OF CASE: Appeal from summary denial of order enjoining competition.

FACT SUMMARY: Greene's (D) employment contract with Data Management (P) contained a covenant not to compete in the state of Alaska for five years following termination.

CONCISE RULE OF LAW: An overbroad covenant by the employee not to compete with his employer following termination will be reasonably modified to render it enforceable unless the employer did not draft the covenant in good faith.

FACTS: Greene (D) signed an employment contract drafted by Data Management (P) which provided that Greene (D) would not compete with Data Management (P) anywhere in the state of Alaska for five years following termination. Greene (D) was terminated. Shortly thereafter, Data Management (P) sued to enjoin Greene (D) from providing computer services to various individuals in Alaska. Although a preliminary injunction was granted, Greene (D) eventually won a summary judgment after the trial court found that the anticompetition clause was not severable from the employment contract and therefore was wholly unenforceable. Data Management (P) appealed.

ISSUE: Will an overbroad covenant by the employee not to compete with his employer following termination be reasonably modified to render it enforceable provided the employer drafted the covenant in good faith?

HOLDING AND DECISION: (Matthews, C.J.) Yes. An overbroad covenant not to compete will be reasonably modified to render it enforceable unless the court determines that the employer did not draft the covenant in good faith. In adopting this rule, this court rejects older rules adopted in other jurisdictions, such as the strict view implemented by the lower court here (i.e., all overbroad covenants are unconscionable and will not be enforced) and the "blue-pencil" rule (i.e., offending words may be deleted from the covenant to render it enforceable). However, the burden remains on the employer to prove the covenant was drafted in good faith. This "rule of reasonableness" test permits courts to determine, on the basis of evidence demonstrating the intent of the parties at the time of contracting, what would be reasonable between the parties. Factors courts will consider in determining reasonableness include: whether the employee has sole customer contact or possession of confidential information or trade secrets; whether the covenant stifles the inherent skill and experience of the employee or bars the employee's sole means of support; whether the forbidden employment is merely incidental to the main employment; and whether the employee's talent was developed during the period of employment. Here, because Data Management's (P) covenant was stricken in its entirety, there was no evidence received as to its good faith and the intent of the parties at the time the covenant was signed. Remanded for receipt of this evidence and determination of whether the covenant can be reasonably altered.

EDITOR'S ANALYSIS: The position taken by this court is consistent with the Restatement (Second) of Contracts § 184(2) and with the law of most states. It also accords with the Uniform Commercial Code § 2-302. Courts are more likely to uphold covenants not to compete which are ancillary to the sale of a business because in such cases the covenants protect the goodwill of the business being sold. And courts are not likely to uphold covenants which prohibit the employee from using general skills or knowledge obtained during the employment as opposed to trade secrets, confidential information, or customer lists. Compare Field v. Alexander & Alexander of Indiana, Inc., 503 N.E.2d 627 (Ind. App. 1987) (covenant of insurance salesman not to solicit customers acquired during previous employment upheld) with American Shippers Supply Co. v. Campbell, 456 N.E.2d 1040 (Ind. App. 1983) (covenant could not prohibit contacting of customers whose identity could be ascertained from trade publications or telephone directories).

[For more information on covenants not to compete, see Casenote Law Outline on Contracts, Chapter 5, § II, The Assignment of Contract Rights.]

NOTES:

WATTS v. WATTS

Wisc. Sup. Ct., 137 Wis.2d 506, 405 N.W.2d 303 (1987).

NATURE OF CASE: Appeal from dismissal of action for account and property division.

FACT SUMMARY: Sue Ann (P) sued James (D) for accounting and division of property after their 12-year nonmarital cohabitation ended.

CONCISE RULE OF LAW: An unmarried cohabitant may assert contract and property claims against the other party to the cohabitation.

FACTS: Sue Ann (P) and James (D) Watts been living together, holding themselves out to the public as husband and wife. Sue Ann (P) assumed James' (D) surname as her own, and she gave birth to two children who bore the same surname. The parties filed joint income tax returns, maintained joint bank accounts, and purchased real and personal property as husband and wife. James (D) insured Sue Ann (P) as his wife on his medical insurance policy and named her as beneficiary on his life insurance policy. In short, Sue Ann (P) contributed to the relationship as a married wife would, and when the relationship ended after 12 years, she sued James (D) for breach of an express or implied-in-fact contract to share the property that the couple had accumulated during their relationship. Sue Ann (P) claimed that James (D) was unjustly enriched by his breach. At trial, Sue Ann's (P) complaint was dismissed for not pleading facts necessary to state a cause of action. This appeal followed.

ISSUE: May an unmarried cohabitant assert contract and property claims against the other party to the cohabitation?

HOLDING AND DECISION: (Abrahamson, J.) Yes. An unmarried cohabitant may assert contract and property claims against the other party to the cohabitation. Sue Ann (P) alleged that James (D) accepted and retained the benefit of services she provided knowing that she expected to share equally in the wealth accumulated during their relationship. She argued that it was unfair for James (D) to retain all the assets they accumulated under these circumstances and that a constructive trust should be imposed on the property as a result of his unjust enrichment. Unlike claims for breach of an express or implied-in-fact contract, a claim of unjust enrichment does not arise out of an agreement entered into by the parties. Rather, an action for recovery based upon unjust enrichment is grounded on the moral principle that one who has received a benefit has a duty to make restitution where retaining such a benefit would be unjust. In this case, Sue Ann (P) alleged that she contributed both property and services to the parties' relationship. She claimed that because of these contributions the parties' assets increased, but she was never compensated for her contributions. She further alleged it would be unfair for James (D) to retain everything, knowing the Sue Ann (P) expected to share in the property accumulated. Sue Ann's (P) pleaded allegations were sufficient to state a claim for damages resulting from James' (D) breach of an express or an implied-in-fact contract to share with her the property accumulated by the efforts of both parties during their relationship. Complaint reinstated.

EDITOR'S ANALYSIS: The court did not judge the merits of Sue Ann's (P) claim but merely held that she should be given the chance to litigate her claim. In this type of case, the defendant often tries to show that the applicable family code law does not purport to offer relief to unmarried cohabitants on the ground that such a living arrangement is illegal and against the public policy that promotes marriage. However, the logical interpretation of such statutes is that they promote family life instead of the specific practice of marriage. The courts, aware of society's changing values, are recognizing that many couples live together as family units, hence this argument of illegality will not be allowed to unjustly enrich one party.

[For more information on quasi-contracts, see Casenote Law Outline on Contracts, Chapter 1, § I, The Agreement Process — Manifesting Mutual Consent.]

NOTES:

CHAPTER 5
PERFORMANCE OF THE CONTRACT

QUICK REFERENCE RULES OF LAW

1. **Integrated Writings and the Parol Evidence Rule.** An oral agreement is permitted to vary a written contract only if it is collateral in form, does not contradict express or implied conditions of the written contract, and consists of terms which the parties could not reasonably have been expected to include in the written contract. (Mitchill v. Lath)

   [For more information on collateral agreements, see Casenote Law Outline on Contracts, Chapter 3, § V, Defenses Arising from the Form of the Bargain.]

2. **Integrated Writings and the Parol Evidence Rule.** Evidence of oral collateral agreements should be excluded only when the fact finder (the court) is likely to be misled. (Masterson v. Sine)

   [For more information on the admission of parol evidence, see Casenote Law Outline on Contracts, Chapter 3, § V, Defenses Arising from the Form of the Bargain.]

3. **Integrated Writings and the Parol Evidence Rule.** Evidence that contradicts an integrated contract term is not admissible to aid in the interpretation of that term. (Alaska Northern Development, Inc. v. Alyeska Pipeline Service Co.)

   [For more information on the parol evidence rule, see Casenote Law Outline on Contracts, Chapter 3, § V, Defenses Arising from the Form of the Bargain.]

4. **Integrated Writings and the Parol Evidence Rule.** The parol evidence rule does not bar testimony of an oral agreement as a condition precedent to a final written contract. (Luther Williams, Jr., Inc. v. Johnson)

   [For more information on the parol evidence rule, see Casenote Law Outline on Contracts, Chapter 3, § V, Defenses Arising from the Form of the Bargain.]

5. **Interpretation.** The test of admissibility of extrinsic evidence to explain the meaning of a written instrument is not whether it appears to the court to be plain and unambiguous on its face but whether the offered evidence is relevant to prove a meaning to which the language of the instrument is reasonably susceptible. (Pacific Gas and Electric Co. v. G. W. Thomas Drayage & Rigging Co.)

   [For more information on the admission of parol evidence, see Casenote Law Outline on Contracts, Chapter 3, § V, Defenses Arising from the Form of the Bargain.]

6. **Interpretation.** The test of admissibility of extrinsic evidence is whether it is relevant to prove a meaning to which the contract language is reasonably susceptible. (A. Kemp Fisheries, Inc. v. Castle & Cooke, Inc.)

   [For more information on extrinsic evidence, see Casenote Law Outline on Contracts, Chapter 3, § V, Defenses Arising from the Form of the Bargain.]

7. **Interpretation.** The party who seeks to interpret the terms of the contract in a sense narrower than their everyday use bears the burden of persuasion to so show, and if that party fails to support its burden, it faces dismissal of its complaint. (Frigaliment Importing Co. v. B.N.S. International Sales Corp.)

   [For more information on ambiguity in course of dealing and usage of trade, see Casenote Law Outline on Contracts, Chapter 1, § IV, Impact of Ambiguity and Mistake on the Bargain.]

8. **Interpretation.** In an insurance contract, doubts as to meaning must be resolved against the insurer, and any exception to the performance of the obligations thereunder must be so stated as to apprise the insured of its effect. (Gray v. Zurich Insurance Co.)

[For more information on adhesion contracts, see Casenote Law Outline on Contracts, Chapter 3, § IV, Defenses Centered on the Deceptive or Coercive Formation Tactics of One of the Parties.]

9. **Nature and Effect.** A party is bound to perform all conditions knowingly accepted under a contract, and unless such conditions are met, performance by the other party is not required. (Dove v. Rose Acre Farms, Inc.)

[For more information on conditions precedent, see Casenote Law Outline on Contracts, Chapter 4, § I, Classification of Conditions According to Their Impact upon the Modified Promise.]

10. **Nature and Effect.** A lessee's compliance with a provision requiring him to give notice of any defects is a condition precedent to the lessor's performance of his obligation to make repairs. (Wal-Noon Corp. v. Hill)

[For more information on conditions precedent, see Casenote Law Outline on Contracts, Chapter 4, § I, Classification of Conditions According to Their Impact upon the Modified Promise.]

11. **Nature and Effect.** For damages in construction contracts, the owner is entitled merely to the difference between the value of the structure if built to specifications and the value it has as constructed. (Jacob & Youngs v. Kent)

[For more information on substantial performance, see Casenote Law Outline on Contracts, Chapter 4, § III, Maturing of Contract Duties: Satisfaction or Excuse of Conditions.]

12. **Nature and Effect.** An express condition precedent to a party's performance of a contract may not be treated as a warranty. (In re Carter)

[For more information on express conditions, see Casenote Law Outline on Contracts, Chapter 4, § II, Sources of Conditions in a Bargain.]

13. **Excuse of Conditions.** A condition in a contract may be waived, but no waiver is implied by mere acceptance of the proffered performance. (Clark v. West)

[For more information on waiver of a condition, see Casenote Law Outline on Contracts, Chapter 4, § III, Maturing of Contract Duties: Satisfaction or Excuse of Conditions.]

14. **Excuse of Conditions.** An insured who belatedly gives notice of an insurance claim may nonetheless recover on the insurance contract by rebutting the presumption that the delay prejudiced the insurer.(Aetna Casualty and Surety Co. v. Murphy)

[For more information on adhesion contracts, see Casenote Law Outline on Contracts, Chapter 3, § IV, Defenses Centered on the Deceptive or Coercive Formation Tactics of One of the Parties.]

15. **Historical Development.** Breach of a covenant by one party to a contract relieves the other party's obligation to perform another covenant which is dependent thereon, the performance of the first covenant being an implied condition precedent to the duty to perform the second covenant. (Kingston v. Preston)

[For more information on constructive conditions, see Casenote Law Outline on Contracts, Chapter 4, § II, Sources of Conditions in a Bargain.]

16. **Historical Development.** A plaintiff must tender his own performance before the defendant's failure to perform his reciprocal duties will be considered a breach. (Goodison v. Nunn)

[For more information on conditions concurrent, see Casenote Law Outline on Contracts, 4, § I, Classification of Conditions According to Their Impact upon the Modified Promise.]

17. **Historical Development.** Where conditions are concurrent and dependent, the failure of one party to perform exercises the other party's counterperformance. (Palmer v. Fox)

[For more information on conditions concurrent, see Casenote Law Outline on Contracts, Chapter 4, § I, Classification of Conditions According to Their Impact upon the Modified Promise.]

18. **The Avoidance of Forfeiture.** In order to establish that he has substantially performed a contract, a party must demonstrate that he intended in good faith to comply with his obligations and that any omissions or deviations which did occur were unintentional and comparatively insignificant. (O.W. Grun Roofing and Construction Co. v. Cope)

[For more information on substantial performance, see Casenote Law Outline on Contracts, 4, § III, Maturing of Contract Duties: Satisfaction or Excuse of Conditions.]

19. **The Avoidance of Forfeiture.** A contractor may recover for work actually performed under a construction contract if he has substantially performed his contractual duty in good faith. (Lowy v. United Pacific Insurance Co.)

[For more information on substantial performance, see Casenote Law Outline on Contracts, Chapter 4, § III, Maturing of Contract Duties: Satisfaction or Excuse of Conditions.]

20. **The Avoidance of Forfeiture.** A defaulting party, although unable to recover on a contract, may recover under a quasi-contractual theory the reasonable value of his services less any damages to the other party arising out of the default. (Britton v. Turner)

[For more information on substantial performance, see Casenote Law Outline on Contracts, Chapter 4, § III, Maturing of Contract Duties: Satisfaction or Excuse of Conditions.]

21. **The Avoidance of Forfeiture.** If the buyer defaults under or improperly cancels an agreement to purchase real property, the seller has the right to retain the buyer's down payment as liquidated damages. (Maxton Builders, Inc. v. Lo Galbo)

[For more information on liquidated damage, see Casenote Law Outline on Contracts, Chapter 7, § III, Remedies for Breach of Contract.]

22. **Limitations of Warranties.** An express warranty that seeks to severely limit the manufacturer's liability and that disclaims all other warranties can be voided as against public policy. (Henningsen v. Bloomfield Motors)

[For more information on disclaimer of warranties, see Casenote Law Outline on Contracts, Chapter 3, § III, Defenses Rooted in Social Objection to the Content of the Bargain.]

23. **Limitations of Warranties.** Where the remedies in a limited warranty fail to correct a seller's breach, the limitations will be disregarded in favor of ordinary U.C.C. remedies. (Murray v. Holiday Rambler, Inc.)

[For more information on disclaimer of warranties, see Casenote Law Outline on Contracts, Chapter 3, § III, Defenses Rooted in Social Objection to the Content of the Bargain.]

24. **Existing Impracticability.** A party is excused from performing under a contract where such performance is so much more expensive than contemplated that it would be impracticable to complete. (Mineral Park Land Co. v. Howard)

[For more information on commercial impracticability, see Casenote Law Outline on Contracts, Chapter 6, § I, Excusable Non-Performance under the Common Law.]

25. **Existing Impracticability.** Usually with the production of new products or use of new processes where the manufacturer has contended that compliance under existing technology is impossible, the contractor has assumed the risk that production was possible. (United States v. Wegematic Corp.)

[For more information on the failure of presupposed conditions, see Casenote Law Outline on Contracts, Chapter 6, § II, Excusable Non-Performance under the U.C.C.]

26. **Supervening Impracticability.** In contracts in which the performance depends on the continued existence of a given person or thing, a condition is implied that the impossibility of performance arising from the perishing of the person or thing shall excuse the performance. (Taylor v. Caldwell)

[For more information on impossibility of performance, see Casenote Law Outline on Contracts, Chapter 6, § I, Excusable Non-Performance under the Common Law.]

27. **Supervening Impracticability.** If the promisor is in some respects responsible for the event which makes performance of his promise impossible, justice does not dictate that he be excused. (Canadian Industrial Alcohol Co. v. Dunbar Molasses Co.)

[For more information on impossibility of performance, see Casenote Law Outline on Contracts, Chapter 6, § I, Excusable Non-Performance under the Common Law.]

28. **Supervening Impracticability.** The occurrence of a foreseeable event that was contemplated at the time of the contract does not render the obligor's performance impractical and excused. (Dills v. Town of Enfield)

[For more information on the failure of presuppposed conditions, see Casenote Law Outline on Contracts, Chapter 6, § II, Excusable Non-Performance under the U.C.C.]

29. **Supervening Impracticability.** Fluctuations in the market price or demand of the goods do not excuse the obligor's promised performance. (Kaiser-Francis Oil Co. v. Producer's Gas Co.)

[For more information on the role of foreseeability, see Casenote Law Outline on Contracts, Chapter 6, § II, Excusable Non-Performance under the U.C.C.]

30. **Frustration of Purpose.** When a party by his own contract creates a charge or duty upon himself, he is bound to make it good notwithstanding any frustration because he might have provided against it in the contract. (Paradine v. Jane)

[For more information on frustration of purpose, see Casenote Law Outline on Contracts, Chapter 6, § I, Excusable Non-Performance under the Common Law.]

31. **Frustration of Purpose.** Where the object of one of the parties is the basis upon which both parties contract, the duties of performance are constructively conditioned upon the attainment of that object. (Krell v. Henry)

[For more information on frustration of purpose, see Casenote Law Outline on Contracts, Chapter 6, § I, Excusable Non-Performance under the Common Law.]

32. **Frustration of Purpose.** A drastic decrease in market demand or price is to be considered evidence supporting the frustration of a contractual purpose which excuses the obligor's performance. (Washington State Hop Producers, Inc. v. Goschie Farms, Inc.)

[For more information on frustration of purpose, see Casenote Law Outline on Contracts, Chapter 6, § I, Excusable Non-Performance under the Common Law.]

33. **Scope and Content of Good Faith Duty.** A party to a contract is not bound by the implied obligation of good faith and fair dealing to do something not expressly required by the contract. (Centronics Corporation v. Genicom Corporation)

[For more information on breach of covenant of good faith, see Casenote Law Outline on Contracts, Chapter 7, § I, Breach — Disappointment of Reasonable Expectations.]

34. **Reserved Discretion.** U.C.C. § 2-104 requires a merchant's claim of dissatisfaction with tendered goods be made in good faith, that he judge objectively based on honesty in fact, and observance of reasonable commercial standards of fair dealing in the trade. (Neumiller Farms, Inc. v. Cornett)

[For more information on good faith dealing obligations, see Casenote Law Outline on Contracts, Chapter 2, § I, Valuable Consideration: The Bargained-for Incursion of Legal Detriment.]

35. **Reserved Discretion.** The implied covenant of good faith is measured by an objective standard. (Reid v. Key Bank of Southern Maine, Inc.)

[For more information on conditions implied-in-fact, see Casenote Law Outline on Contracts, Chapter 4, § II, Sources of Conditions in a Bargain.]

36. **Reserved Discretion.** Implicit in every output contract is the understanding that the supplier will act in good faith in determining the quantity of goods which he will produce. (Feld v. Henry S. Levy & Sons, Inc.)

[For more information on output contracts, see Casenote Law Outline on Contracts, Chapter 2, § I, Valuable Consideration: The Bargained-for Incursion of Legal Detriment.]

37. **Modification.** A court must, in determining whether a particular modification was obtained in good faith, determine whether: (1) a party's conduct was consistent with reasonable commercial standards of fair dealing in the trade and (2) the parties were in fact motivated to seek modification by an honest desire to compensate for commercial exigencies. (Roth Steel Products v. Sharon Steel Corp.)

[For more information on modification of an existing contract, see Casenote Law Outline on Contracts, Chapter 2, § I, Valuable Consideration: The Bargained-for Incursion of Legal Detriment.]

38. **Mutual Termination of Contractual Relations: Discharge.** In conditional check situations, § 1-207 of the Uniform Commercial Code supersedes the common law rule of accord and satisfaction. (AFC Interiors v. DiCello)

[For more information on accord and satisfaction, see Casenote Law Outline on Contracts, Chapter 2, § I, Valuable Consideration: The Bargained-for Incursion of Legal Detriment.]

39. **Unilateral Termination of Contractual Relations.** Covenants of good faith and fair dealing can be inferred from an at-will employment contract in order to limit the employer's power to discharge an employee. (Seubert v. McKesson Corporation)

[For more information on good faith, see Casenote Law Outline on Contracts, Chapter 4, § II, Sources of Conditions in a Bargain.]

MITCHILL v. LATH

N.Y. Ct. App., 247 N.Y. 377, 160 N.E. 646, 68 A.L.R. 239 (1928).

NATURE OF CASE: Action for specific performance.

FACT SUMMARY: Mitchill (P) bought some property from Lath (D) pursuant to a full and complete written sales contract. She sought to compel Lath (D) to perform on his parol agreement to remove an icehouse on neighboring property.

CONCISE RULE OF LAW: An oral agreement is permitted to vary a written contract only if it is collateral in form, does not contradict express or implied conditions of the written contract, and consists of terms which the parties could not reasonably have been expected to include in the written contract.

FACTS: Mitchill (P), through a contract executed by her husband, bought some property from Lath (D). The written contract of sale was completely integrated. Lath (D) then made an oral agreement with Mitchill (P) that in consideration of her purchase of the property, he would remove an icehouse which he maintained on neighboring property and which Mitchill (P) found objectionable.

ISSUE: Will an oral agreement which is not collateral, which contradicts express or implied conditions of a written contract, or which consists of terms which the parties could reasonably have been expected to embody in the original writing be permitted to vary a written contract?

HOLDING AND DECISION: (Andrews, J.) No. An oral agreement is permitted to vary a written contract only if it is collateral in form, does not contradict express or implied conditions of the written contract, and consists of terms which the parties could not reasonably have been expected to include in the original writing. Here, the parol agreement does not meet these requirements since it is closely related to the subject of the written contract. It could also be said to contradict the conditions of the written contract. The fact that the written contract was made with her husband while the oral agreement was made with Mitchill (P) herself is not determinative since the deed was given to her, and it is evident that she, and not her husband, was the principal in the transaction.

DISSENT: I agree with the general rule formulated by the majority but disagree with its application to these facts. I feel that all of the elements necessary to permit an oral agreement to vary a written one are present in this case.

EDITOR'S ANALYSIS: U.C.C. § 2-202 provides, "Terms with respect to which the writings of the parties agree or which are set forth in a writing intended by the parties as a final expression of their agreement may not be contradicted by evidence of any prior agreement or of a contemporaneous oral agreement but may be explained or supplemented by course of dealing or usage of trade, or by course of performance, and by evidence of consistent additional terms unless the court finds the writing to have been intended as a complete and exclusive statement of the terms of the agreement." The section, according to the official commentator, conclusively rejects any assumption that, because a writing is final in some respects, it is to be interpreted as including all matters agreed upon by the parties.

[For more information on collateral agreements, see Casenote Law Outline on Contracts, Chapter 3, § V, Defenses Arising from the Form of the Bargain.]

NOTES:

LUTHER WILLIAMS JR., INC. v. JOHNSON

229 A.2d 163.

NATURE OF CASE: Action for breach of contract to recover liquidated damages.

FACT SUMMARY: Johnson (D) testified that he signed a contract thinking it was merely an estimate, and there was an oral agreement between the parties that he would not be bound if he could not get the funds.

CONCISE RULE OF LAW: The parol evidence rule does not bar testimony of an oral agreement as a condition precedent to a final written contract.

FACTS: Luther Williams, Jr., Inc. (P) sued Johnson (D) to recover liquidated damages for breach of a contract for improvements. At trial the corporation testified that prior to the signing of the contract, it had offered to obtain financing but was told by Johnson (D) that he had his own. Johnson (D) testified that he signed the contract thinking it was merely an estimate and that it was orally agreed to by the parties that the contract would not be binding until he had procured the funds. Luther Williams, Jr., Inc. (P) objected to the introduction of testimony concerning the parol agreement and offered into evidence the written contract, which contained a clause that it was to be the entire understanding between the parties.

ISSUE: Does the parol evidence rule bar testimony concerning an oral agreement as a condition precedent to a final written contract?

HOLDING AND DECISION: (Quinn, J.) No. It is well settled that a written contract may be conditioned upon an oral agreement as a condition precedent. Though the contract contained a clause stating that it embodied the entire agreement between the parties, it is a question of the intent of the parties whether a particular subject is embodied within the contract. This is a preliminary question for the judge which must be sought in the conduct and language of the parties and the surrounding circumstances. Also, the testimony that the oral agreement was a condition precedent did not contradict the writing if there was nothing in the writing inconsistent therewith. Here, there was no provision made for financing in the written contract; therefore, the parol agreement as a condition precedent would not contradict the writing.

EDITOR'S ANALYSIS: The purpose of the parol evidence rule is to protect truly integrated writings embodying the terms of a contract. But, if there is no contract, the rule's operation is forestalled. Thus, evidence showing duress, failure of consideration, fraud, or illegality is admissible. However, if the contract is valid, but one party alleges the failure of an oral condition precedent, the authorities are in conflict as to whether evidence of the condition is admissible and, if so, on what grounds.

[For more information on the parol evidence rule, see Casenote Law Outline on Contracts, Chapter 3, § V, Defenses Arising from the Form of the Bargain.]

NOTES:

PACIFIC GAS & ELECTRIC CO. v. G.W. THOMAS DRAYAGE & RIGGING CO.

Cal. Sup. Ct., 442 P.2d 641 (1968).

NATURE OF CASE: Action for damages for breach of a contract.

FACT SUMMARY: Thomas (D) contracted to repair Pacific's (P) steam turbine and to perform work at its own risk and expense and to indemnify Pacific (P) against all loss and damage. Thomas (D) also agreed not to procure less than $50,000 insurance to cover liability for injury to property. But when the turbine rotor was damaged, Pacific (P) claimed it was covered under that policy, while Thomas (D) said it was only to cover injury to third persons.

CONCISE RULE OF LAW: The test of admissibility of extrinsic evidence to explain the meaning of a written instrument is not whether it appears to the court to be plain and unambiguous on its face but whether the offered evidence is relevant to prove a meaning to which the language of the instrument is reasonably susceptible.

FACTS: Thomas (D) contracted to replace the upper metal cover on Pacific's (P) steam turbine and agreed to perform all work "at [its] own risk and expense" and to "indemnify" Pacific (P) against all loss, damage, expense, and liability resulting from injury to property arising out of or in any way connected with performance of the contract. Thomas (D) agreed to obtain not less than $50,000 insurance to cover liability for injury to property. Pacific (P) was to be an additional named insured, but the policy was to contain a cross-liability clause extending the coverage of Pacific's (P) property. During the work, the cover fell, damaging the exposed rotor in the amount of $25,144.51. Thomas (D) during trial offered to prove through its conduct and under similar contracts entered into by Pacific (P) that the indemnity clause was meant to cover injury to third person's property only, not to Pacific's (P).

ISSUE: Was Thomas' (D) offered evidence relevant to proving a meaning to which the language of the instrument was susceptible?

HOLDING AND DECISION: (Quinn, J.) Yes. While the trial court admitted that the contract was "the classic language for a third-party indemnity provision," it held that the plain language of the contract would give a meaning covering Pacific's (P) damage. However, this admission by the court clearly shows the ambiguous nature of the agreement and the need for extrinsic evidence in order to clarify the intentions of the parties. Extrinsic evidence for the purpose of showing the intent of the parties could be excluded only when it is feasible to determine the meaning of the words from the instrument alone. Rational interpretation requires at least an initial consideration of all credible evidence to prove the intention of the parties.

EDITOR'S ANALYSIS: This case strongly disapproves of the "plain meaning rule," which states that if a writing appears clear and unambiguous on its face, the meaning must be determined from "the four corners" of the writing without considering any extrinsic evidence at all. The trial court applied this rule. However, the rule, while generally accepted but widely condemned, would exclude evidence of trade usage, prior dealings of the parties, and even circumstances surrounding the creation of the agreement. U.C.C. § 2-202 expressly throws out the plain meaning rule. Instead, it allows use of evidence of a course of performance or dealing to explain the writing "unless carefully negated." Here, Mr. C.J. Traynor greatly expanded the admission of extrinsic evidence to show intent. When he says it should not be admitted only when it is feasible "to determine the meaning the parties gave to the words from the instrument alone," he is saying in all practicality that extrinsic evidence to show intent should be admissible in just about any case, that rarely will the instrument be so exact as to clearly show intent.

[For more information on the admission of parol evidence, see Casenote Law Outline on Contracts, Chapter 3, § V, Defenses Arising from the Form of the Bargain.]

NOTES:

A. KEMP FISHERIES, INC. v. CASTLE & COOKE, INC.

852 F.2d 493 (9th Cir. 1988).

NATURE OF CASE: Appeal from award of damages for breach of contract.

FACT SUMMARY: Kemp (P) sued for damages resulting from the breakdown of freezer engines on the fishing vessel it had chartered from Castle & Cooke (D).

CONCISE RULE OF LAW: The test of admissibility of extrinsic evidence is whether it is relevant to prove a meaning to which the contract language is reasonably susceptible.

FACTS: Kemp (P) chartered a fishing boat from Bumble Bee, a subsidiary of Castle & Cooke (D), to be used to fish salmon and herring. When the agreement was sent to Kemp's (P) president for his signature, he found that it differed from his understanding of the agreement. Specifically, he understood that Bumble Bee has represented orally that the freezing engines would be in good working order and that the freezing system would meet Kemp's (P) specific needs. The written agreement in fact required Bumble Bee to maintain a vessel in "good" condition and to have it surveyed to show that it met insurance requirements of being "tight, staunch, and seaworthy." The writing further disclaimed all warranties upon Kemp's (P) acceptance of the vessel. Kemp (P) signed it without voicing his concerns. When the boat's freezer engines failed at sea, Kemp (P) sued for the resulting damages. The trial court awarded damages to Kemp (P), finding that Bumble Bee warranted the vessel to be seaworthy and the engines to be in good working order to meet Kemp's (P) freezing requirements. Castle & Cooke (D) appealed.

ISSUE: Is the test of admissibility of extrinsic evidence whether it is relevant to prove a meaning to which the contact language is reasonably susceptible?

HOLDING AND DECISION: (Wright, J.) Yes. The test of admissibility of extrinsic evidence is whether it is relevant to prove a meaning to which the contract is reasonably susceptible. The contract imposes on Bumble Bee an obligation to maintain the vessel in "good," not seaworthy condition, and to provide that a surveyor inspect the boat. The contract warrants neither the accuracy of the survey nor the seaworthiness of the vessel. The language releasing Bumble Bee from all liability after delivery cannot be interpreted reasonably to warrant the vessel's seaworthiness. The contract is not ambiguous, and the trial court erred in admitting parol evidence on the warranty of seaworthiness, the capacity of the engines, and freezing capacity. The agreement contains none of these warranties since Bumble Bee effectively waived all of them. Reversed.

EDITOR'S ANALYSIS: The court followed fairly closely the plain meaning of the words used in the instrument in relieving Castle & Cooke (D) from liability. Courts often charge sophisticated parties with the duty to read their contracts. If the writing does not reflect their understanding of the negotiations, they should complain before signing instead of waiting until a problem arises.

[For more information on extrinsic evidence, see Casenote Law Outline on Contracts, Chapter 3, § V, Defenses Arising from the Form of the Bargain.]

NOTES:

FRIGALIMENT IMPORTING CO. v. B.N.S. INTERNATIONAL SALES CO.

190 F. Supp. 116 (S.D.N.Y. 1960).

NATURE OF CASE: Action for breach of warranty of a contract for the sale of goods.

FACT SUMMARY: Frigaliment (P) ordered a large quantity of "chicken" from B.N.S. (D), intending to buy young chicken suitable for broiling and frying, but B.N.S. (D) believed, in considering the weights ordered at the prices fixed by the parties, that the order could be filled with older chicken, suitable for stewing only and termed "fowl" by Frigaliment (P).

CONCISE RULE OF LAW: The party who seeks to interpret the terms of the contract in a sense narrower than their everyday use bears the burden of persuasion to so show, and if that party fails to support its burden, it faces dismissal of its complaint.

FACTS: Frigaliment (P), a Swiss corporation, and B.N.S. (D), a New York corporation, made two almost identical contracts for the sale of chicken by the latter to the former as follows: U.S. fresh frozen chicken, Grade A, government inspected, eviscerated, all wrapped and boxed suitably for export, 75,000 lbs. 2˚-3 lbs. at $33 per 100 lbs., and 25,000 lbs. 1˚-2 lbs. at $36.50 per 100 lbs. The second contract was the same except for 25,000 lbs. less of the heavier chicken and a price of $37 per 100 lbs. for the lighter birds. B.N.S. (D), which was new to the poultry business, believed any kind of chicken could be used to fill the order, including stewing chickens. Most of the order for heavier birds was filled with stewers as that was the only way B.N.S. (D) could make a profit on the contract.

ISSUE: Did Frigaliment support its burden of persuasion that the word "chicken" should be used in its narrower sense so as to exclude stewing chicken?

HOLDING AND DECISION: (Friendly, C.J.) No. Frigaliment (P) failed to support its burden. While cables leading up to negotiations were predominantly in German, the use of the English word "chicken" as meaning "young chicken" rather than the German word "huhn" meaning broilers and stewers lost its force when B.N.S. (D) asked if any kind of chickens were wanted, to which an affirmative answer meaning "huhn" was given. B.N.S. (D) being new to the chicken trade, the other party must show the other's acceptance of the trade use of a term. Frigaliment (P) failed to offer such proof. There was conflicting evidence anyway as to the trade use of the word "chicken." B.N.S.'s (D) price of $33 per 100 lbs. for the larger birds was $2 to $4 less than for broilers. Frigaliment (P) could not say that the price appeared reasonable because it was closer to the $35 broiler price than the $30 stewer price. B.N.S. (D) could be expected not to sell at a loss. While the evidence is generally conflicting, overall it appeared that B.N.S. (D) believed it could comply by supplying stewing chicken. This did conform with one dictionary meaning, with the definition in the department of animal regulations to which at least there was a contractual reference, and with some trade usage. This evidence must be relied upon, as the contract language itself could not settle the question here.

EDITOR'S ANALYSIS: In determining the intent of the parties, the court will turn first to the language of the contract to see whether the meaning of the ambiguous term can be raised. If this is unsuccessful, the court must look to other evidence. Under Restatement (First) § 2235, certain guidelines aid in determining meaning. First, the ordinary meaning of language throughout the country is given to words unless circumstances show that a different meaning is applicable. Also, all circumstances surrounding the transaction may be taken into consideration. Also, if after consideration of all factors, it is still uncertain what meaning should be given, a reasonable, lawful, and effective meaning to all manifestations of intention is preferred to an interpretation which leaves a part of such unreasonable, unlawful, or ineffective, Restatement (First) § 236 (a). Even so, the principal apparent purpose of the parties should be given greater weight in determining the meaning to be given.

[For more information on ambiguity in course of dealing and usage of trade, see Casenote Law Outline on Contracts, Chapter 1, § IV, Impact of Ambiguity and Mistake on the Bargain.]

NOTES:

GRAY v. ZURICH INSURANCE COMPANY

Cal. Sup. Ct., 419 P.2d 168.

NATURE OF CASE: Action for breach of a duty to defend under an insurance contract.

FACT SUMMARY: Gray (P) was being sued for assault; he asked Zurich Insurance Company (D) to defend him. The insurance company refused to defend on the grounds that the complaint alleged an intentional tort.

CONCISE RULE OF LAW: In an insurance contract, doubts as to meaning must be resolved against the insurer, and any exception to the performance of the obligations thereunder must be so stated as to apprise the insured of its effect.

FACTS: Gray (P) was injured in an altercation with John R. Jones. He was later sued by Jones for assault and asked Zurich Insurance Company (D) to defend him under a Comprehensive Personal Liability Endorsement in an insurance policy which provided that the company would defend any suit for bodily injury even if the allegations were groundless. The insurance company refused to defend on the ground that the complaint alleged an intentional tort which fell outside the coverage of the policy as specified under an "exclusions" section in small print. Gray (P) suffered a judgment against him and then sued Zurich Insurance Company (D) for breach of its duty to defend.

ISSUE: In determining the coverage of an insurance contract, must all doubts as to meaning be resolved against the insurer and any exceptions as to coverage be clearly stated so as to appraise the insured?

HOLDING AND DECISION: (Tobriner, J.) Yes. An insurance contract is essentially an adhesion contract between two parties of unequal bargaining strength which is written by the stronger and offered to the weaker. In view of such, we ascertain the meaning of the contract which the insured would reasonably expect. An exclusion will not be enforced if it is unclear or inconspicuous. In this contract, the obligation to defend is uncertain though broadly stated. It is not conspicuously conditioned and would lead one to expect the defense of any suit for bodily injury regardless of cause. The exclusionary clause as to intentional injury is anything but clear and contains an ambiguity as to the extent the insurer must defend. Because the uncertainties are to be resolved in favor of the insured, we hold that the policy provides an obligation to defend independent of any indemnification coverage.

EDITOR'S ANALYSIS: The importance of this case can hardly be understated when one considers the "deluge" of adhesion contracts the average person is faced with on a day-to-day basis. By construing the language in the contract strictly, against its maker, the doctrine of "contra proferentum" takes on an aspect of protecting the average citizen from the ravages of big business. This rule is generally followed with respect to insurance contracts.

[For more information on adhesion contracts, see Casenote Law Outline on Contracts, Chapter 3, § IV, Defenses Centered on the Deceptive or Coercive Formation Tactics of One of the Parties.]

NOTES:

DOVE v. ROSE ACRE FARMS, INC.

Ind. Ct. App., 434 N.E.2d 931 (1962).

NATURE OF CASE: Appeal from denial of recovery of a contractual bonus.

FACT SUMMARY: Dove (P) contended that although he did not perform exactly as prescribed under the contact with Rose Acre Farms (D), his employer, he substantially performed and was entitled to payment of a bonus under the contract.

CONCISE RULE OF LAW: A party is bound to perform all conditions knowingly accepted under a contract, and unless such conditions are met, performance by the other party is not required.

FACTS: Rose Acre Farms (D) was in the business of producing eggs and was run by Rust, its president. Rust instituted many bonus programs for the employees, always insisting upon strict compliance with the conditions of the bonus and always refusing payment for the slightest breach. Of these conditions, tardiness and absenteeism were of primary importance to Rust. In 1979, Rust approached Dove (P), a construction crew leader, and offered him a $5,000 bonus if certain construction work could be completed in 12 weeks. The terms of the bonus included that Dove (P) complete the work and work at least five days a week for 10 weeks. Dove (P) knew of the requirements of strict compliance and accepted the offer. Subsequently, on Thursday of the tenth week, Dove (P) contracted strep throat and told Rust he was unable to work. Rust told him he could come in to work and sleep through the remaining days or make up his absence on the weekend and still qualify for the bonus. Dove (P) refused and sought medical attention. Thereafter, Rust refused to pay the bonus because of Dove's (P) failure to fulfill the conditions. Dove (P) sued, contending he had substantially performed and was entitled to payment. The trial court found for Rose Acre Farms (D), and Dove (P) appealed.

ISSUE: May a party who fails to perform all the conditions of a contract recover payment on the contract?

HOLDING AND DECISION: (Neal, J.) No. A party is held to perform all conditions knowingly accepted under a contract, as prerequisite to recovery under the contract. In this case, completion of the project was not the exclusive theme of the bonus offer. Absenteeism was also a central theme, and such was known by Dove (P) prior to entering into the agreement. Even though the conditions were harsh, Dove (P) knowingly accepted them, and his failure to fulfill them precludes his recovery. Affirmed.

EDITOR'S ANALYSIS: There are two types of contractual conditions: conditions precedent and conditions subsequent. A party must fulfill a condition precedent before reciprocal performance by the other party becomes due. A condition subsequent acts to extinguish a duty to perform under the contract. The condition of attending work in the present case was a condition precedent to Dove's (P) right to payment. The failure of an insured to file a timely suit could release the insurer from its contractual indemnification obligation as a condition subsequent. The distinction between conditions precedent and subsequent is important from a procedural point of view. A party to whom a duty is owed bears the burden of proving satisfaction of a condition precedent, while a party attempting to avoid performance of a contractual duty must prove the occurrence of a condition subsequent that discharged such performance.

[For more information on conditions precedent, see Casenote Law Outline on Contracts, Chapter 4, § I, Classification of Conditions According to Their Impact upon the Modified Promise.]

NOTES:

WAL-NOON CORPORATION v. HILL

45 Cal. App. 3d 605 (1975).

NATURE OF CASE: Suit seeking repair costs.

FACT SUMMARY: Wal-Noon (P) leased property from Hill (D). When the roof began to leak, Wal-Noon (P) repaired it and ultimately replaced it without prior notice to Hill (D).

CONCISE RULE OF LAW: A lessee's compliance with a provision requiring him to give notice of any defects is a condition precedent to the lessor's performance of his obligation to make repairs.

FACTS: Wal-Noon Corporation (P) leased property from Hill (D). Most of the building was used by Wal-Noon (P) as a store, but a portion of it was subleased by Wal-Noon (P) to other enterprises. Eight or nine years after the lease was executed, Wal-Noon (P) and the other tenants began noticing leakage from the roof of the building. The roof was repaired a dozen or more times, and Wal-Noon (P) was eventually told that the roof should be replaced. After obtaining competitive bids, Wal-Noon (P) paid $8,800 to have the roof replaced. Later, Wal-Noon (P) became aware of a lease provision which made Hill (D) responsible for maintenance of the roof. Hill (D) refused to reimburse Wal-Noon (P), however, arguing that there had been no compliance with a clause which required Wal-Noon (P) to give notice of defective conditions in need of repair. Wal-Noon (P) then sued to enforce the lease provision requiring Hill (D) to repair the roof. The trial court ruled that Wal-Noon's (P) failure to give notice of the leakage prevented it from recovering pursuant to the lease but awarded Wal-Noon (P) two-thirds of the replacement costs on the theory that Hill (D) had been unjustly enriched by that amount. Wal-Noon (P) appealed, claiming that the trial court should have considered the contractual basis of its claim and should have concluded that the giving of notice of the defective roof was not a condition precedent to Hill's (D) obligation to bear the cost of repairs.

ISSUE: Does a lessee's failure to give notice of a defective condition relieve the lessor of his duty to perform a covenant to make repairs?

HOLDING AND DECISION: (Puglia, J.) Yes. A lessee's compliance with a provision requiring him to give notice of any defects is a condition precedent to the lessor's performance of his obligation to make repairs. Since Wal-Noon (P) gave no notice of the defective roof, Hill (D) is not liable for any portion of the cost of replacing it. Had Hill (D) been notified of the leakage, arrangements for repairs or replacement at a lower cost might have been made. Nor may Wal-Noon (P) recover on a theory of quasi-contract since both parties acknowledge that there was, at all times, an actual agreement existing between the parties. Therefore, Wal-Noon (P) is entitled to recover nothing, while Hill (D) is entitled to recover reasonable attorney fees expended in defending the action to enforce the lease provision imposing the covenant to make repairs.

EDITOR'S ANALYSIS: Some courts adopt the Wal-Noon Corporation v. Hill approach and treat a requirement that notice be given as an express condition. Where this analysis is employed, the failure to give notice excuses the other party from whatever obligations have been imposed upon him.

[For more information on conditions precedent, see Casenote Law Outline on Contracts, Chapter 4, § I, Classification of Conditions According to Their Impact upon the Modified Promise.]

NOTES:

JACOB & YOUNGS v. KENT

N.Y. Ct. App., 230 N.Y. 239, 129 N.E. 889 (1921).

NATURE OF CASE: Action for damages for breach of a construction contract.

FACT SUMMARY: Jacob (P) was hired to build a $77,000 country home for Kent (D). When the dwelling was completed, it was discovered that through an oversight, pipe not of Reading manufacture (though of comparable quality and price), which had been specified in the contract, was used. Kent (D) refused to make final payment of $3,483.46 upon learning of this.

CONCISE RULE OF LAW: For damages in construction contracts, the owner is entitled merely to the difference between the value of the structure if built to specifications and the value it has as constructed.

FACTS: Jacob (P) built a country home for $77,000 for Kent (D) and sued for $3,483.46 which remained unpaid. Almost a year after completion, Kent (D) discovered that not all pipe in the home was of Reading manufacture, as specified in the contract. Kent (D) ordered the plumbing replaced, but as it was encased in the walls, except in those spots where it must necessarily remain exposed, Jacob (P) refused to replace the pipe, stating that the pipe used was of comparable price and quality. It appears that the omission was neither fraudulent nor willful and was due to oversight. Kent (D) refused to pay the balance of the construction cost still due.

ISSUE: For damages in construction contracts, is the owner entitled merely to the difference in value of the structure built to specifications and the value it has as constructed?

HOLDING AND DECISION: (Cardozo, J.) Yes. Where the significance of the default or omission is grievously out of proportion to the oppression of the forfeiture, the breach is considered to be trivial and innocent. A change will not be tolerated if it is so dominant and pervasive so as to frustrate the purpose of the contract. The contractor cannot install anything he believes to be just as good. It is a matter of degree judged by the purpose to be served, the desire to be gratified, the excuse for deviation from the letter, and the cruelty of enforced adherence. Under the circumstances, the measure of damages should not be the cost of replacing the pipe, which would be great. Instead, the difference in value between the dwelling as specified and the dwelling as constructed should be the measure even though it may be nominal or nothing. Usually, the owner is entitled to the cost of completion but not where it is grossly unfair and out of proportion to the good to be obtained. This simply is a rule to promote justice when there is substantial performance with trivial deviation.

DISSENT: (McLaughlin, J.) Jacob (P) failed to perform as specified. It makes no difference why Kent (D) wanted a particular kind of pipe. Failure to use the kind of pipe specified was either intentional or due to gross neglect, which amounted to the same thing.

EDITOR'S ANALYSIS: Substantial performance cannot occur where the breach is intentional, as it is the antithesis of material breach. The part unperformed must not destroy the purpose or value of the contract. Because here there is a dissatisfied landowner who stands to retain the defective structure built on his land, there arises the problem of unjust enrichment. Usually, it would appear that the owner would pocket the damages he collected rather than remedying the defect by tearing out the wrong pipe and replacing it with the specified pipe. The owner would have a home substantially in compliance and a sum of money greatly in excess of the harm suffered by him. Note that under the doctrine of de minimis not curat lex, that is, that the law is not concerned with trifles, trivial defects, even if willful, will be ignored. The party who claims substantial performance has still breached the contract and is liable for damages but in a lesser amount than for a willful breach.

[For more information on substantial performance, see Casenote Law Outline on Contracts, Chapter 4, § III, Maturing of Contract Duties: Satisfaction or Excuse of Conditions.]

NOTES:

IN RE CARTER

Pa. Sup. Ct., 390 Pa. 365, 134 A.2d 908 (1957).

NATURE OF CASE: Appeal of arbitrator's award.

FACT SUMMARY: Kardon (P) sought to purchase the Edwin J. Schoettle Co. Kardon (P) alleged a breach of a warranty provision, but the seller (D) stated that the provision was a condition precedent and that Kardon's (P) only remedy was to refuse consummation of the sale.

CONCISE RULE OF LAW: An express condition precedent to a party's performance of a contract may not be treated as a warranty.

FACTS: Kardon (P) agreed to purchase the Edwin J. Schoettle Co. and its subsidiaries in which a certain amount of the purchase price was put in an escrow fund to indemnify Kardon (P) against the seller (D) for breach of the agreement to purchase. The agreement provided, among other things, under paragraph 5, the seller (D) represented, as a "warranty," that there had been no changes in the financial condition of the company other than in the ordinary course of business that were materially adverse. Also, under paragraph 9, the seller (D) stated that as a "condition precedent" to the buyer's obligation, the financial condition of the company should not be less favorable than what had been represented to Kardon (P) in an earlier statement. Kardon (P) sought to claim against the escrow fund, alleging that the financial condition on the date of purchase was less favorable than what had been represented earlier. The seller (D) contended that such fell under paragraph 9 as a "condition precedent" and not a warranty, and because Kardon (P) did not refuse consummation of the sale, he elected to waive the condition.

ISSUE: May a party in a sales contract treat an express condition precedent to the contract as a warranty?

HOLDING AND DECISION: (Jones, J.) No. Here the agreement distinguished between "warranties" and "conditions." The conditions precedent in the agreement were to take place prior to the closing, and the buyer's obligation to perform was subject to their fulfillment. The argument that the financial condition of the company being less favorable than represented earlier constituted a breach of warranty is directly in conflict with the terms of the agreement in that it falls under the paragraph providing for "warranties." The paragraph on warranties provided for an entirely different situation where the financial condition of the company changed to be materially adverse other than in the ordinary course of business. Because Kardon (P) elected to accept the contract, the provisions of paragraph 9 on "conditions precedent" cease to be operative, and he is left with no right to recover damages.

EDITOR'S ANALYSIS: A warranty is an undertaking that a certain fact in relation to the subject of a contract is or shall be as it is stated or promised to be. Where a condition precedent is not fulfilled, the contract does not become effective as between the parties, but, where there is a breach of warranty, the contract remains binding, but damages are recoverable for its breach. A condition precedent may be waived by a party whose obligations under the contract are dependent upon fulfillment of the condition. As such, once waived, the condition becomes extinguished, and neither party can assert it as a defense to his obligations nor as a warranty for damages.

[For more information on express conditions, see Casenote Law Outline on Contracts, Chapter 4, § II, Sources of Conditions in a Bargain.]

NOTES:

CLARK v. WEST

193 N.Y. 349 (1908).

NATURE OF CASE: Action for breach of contract and an accounting.

FACT SUMMARY: West (D) paid Clark (P) only $2 per page for writing a legal treatise, and Clark (P) demanded the $6 per page he had been promised if he quit drinking, alleging that West (D) had not objected when he continued to drink.

CONCISE RULE OF LAW: A condition in a contract may be waived, but no waiver is implied by mere acceptance of the proffered performance.

FACTS: West (D) entered into a contract with Clark (P) whereby Clark (P) was to write a multivolume treatise on corporations for West (D). The contract price was $6 per page if Clark (P) totally abstained from liquor during the contract or $2 per page if he drank. West (D) became aware that Clark (P) was drinking moderately during the term of the contract but made no objection. West (D) accepted Clark's (P) work and paid him $2 per page. Clark (P) sued for the difference, claiming that he was owed $6 per page. West (D) demurred, and both the trial court and the court of appeals sustained the demurrer. Clark (P) appealed, claiming that West (D) had waived the abstinence requirement and that the waiver was effective since abstinence was a mere condition precedent to West's (D) obligation to pay $6 per page.

ISSUE: May a condition precedent to performance be waived?

HOLDING AND DECISION: (Werner, J.) Yes. A condition to a contract may be waived, but mere acceptance of performance does not constitute a waiver. While it is West's (D) contention that Clark's (P) abstinence was the consideration for the payment of $6 rather than $2, a careful analysis of the contract shows that it was the writing of the treatise, rather than abstinence, which was the bargained-for consideration. Since abstinence was not the consideration for the contract, it was a condition which could be waived without a new agreement based upon a good consideration. No formal agreement or additional consideration is required to waive a condition precedent to performance. West (D) received and accepted the bargained-for consideration, i.e., the treatise. If the condition was waived, then West (D) is liable for the $6 contract price, but mere silence and acceptance of performance will not be deemed a waiver of the condition. However, since Clark (P) alleges an express waiver of the condition, he should be allowed to prove this at trial. The demurrer is therefore overruled and the case remanded for trial.

EDITOR'S ANALYSIS: Frequently, as in Clark, it is difficult to determine whether one is dealing with a promise or a condition. Modification of a promise typically requires a new consideration, while the waiver of a condition does not. A condition may be described as qualifying a contractual duty by providing either that performance is not called for unless a stated event occurs or fails to occur or that performance may be suspended or terminated if a stated event occurs or fails to occur. Stated more simply, the condition is outside of and modifies the promised performance called for under the contract.

[For more information on waiver of a condition, see Casenote Law Outline on Contracts, Chapter 4, § III, Maturing of Contract Duties: Satisfaction or Excuse of Conditions.]

NOTES:

AETNA CASUALTY AND SURETY CO. v. MURPHY

206 Conn. 409, 538 A.2d 219.

NATURE OF CASE: Appeal from summary judgment denying payment of insurance proceeds.

FACT SUMMARY: Murphy (D) delayed over two years in notifying his insurance company of a claim against him.

CONCISE RULE OF LAW: An insured who belatedly gives notice of an insurance claim may nonetheless recover on the insurance contract by rebutting the presumption that the delay prejudiced the insurer.

FACTS: When Murphy (D) terminated a lease with Aetna's (P) insured, he damaged the premises, which gave rise to a claim for those damages. Although Murphy (D) was served with the complaint on November 21, 1983, he did not notify his insurance company of the claim until January 10, 1986. Murphy's (D) insurer, Chubb, became a third party defendant by Murphy's (D) impleading. Murphy's (D) insurance contract provided: "In the event of an occurrence, written notice . . . shall be given by or for the insured to the company . . . as soon as practible." Murphy (D) delayed over two years in notifying Chubb of the claim against him. Chubb claimed that Murphy (D) had inexcusably and unreasonably delayed in complying with the notice provision in the insurance contract and obtained summary judgment. This appeal followed.

ISSUE: Can an insured who belatedly gives notice of an insurance claim nonetheless recover on the insurance contract by rebutting the presumption that the delay prejudiced the insurer?

HOLDING AND DECISION: (Peters, C.J.) Yes. An insured who belatedly gives notice of an insurance claim may nonetheless recover on the insurance contract by rebutting the presumption that the delay prejudiced the insurer. Three considerations are key to deciding this case. First is that the contract is one of adhesion. Because the contract is drawn up by the insurer, the insured, who merely "adheres" to it, has little choice as to its terms. Clearly, Murphy (D), like any other insured, had no opportunity to bargain as to the consequences of delayed notice of a claim. Second, is that the insured's noncompliance with the notice provision will cause a forfeiture. Because he will lose his insurance coverage despite dutiful payment of insurance premiums, Murphy's (D) failure to comply with the notice provision operates as a forfeiture. Third, the insurer's legitimate purpose of assuring itself a fair opportunity to investigate accidents and claims can be protected by demanding strict compliance with regard to the notice requirement in the contract. A proper balance between the interests of the insurer and the insured requires a factual inquiry into whether, in the circumstances of a case, the insurer has been prejudiced by its insured's delay in providing notice of a claim. Here, Chubb (D) was not automatically discharged of its contract duties because of Murphy's (D) delay; however, summary judgment was warranted because Murphy's (D) affidavit opposing summary judgment contained no factual basis for a claim that Chubb (D) had not been materially prejudiced by the delay. Affirmed.

EDITOR'S ANALYSIS: There exists a split of authority on the issue of whether an insured can attempt to rebut the presumption of prejudice to the insurer. Some states allow the insured to prove lack of prejudice, while other jurisdictions continue to enforce delayed notice provisions literally. This all translates into a question of materiality. Generally, express conditions in a contract must be strictly performed, while constructive, or implied-in-fact conditions can be satisfied by substantial performance. Either type of condition must meet the requirement that it is material to allow a party relief from the other party's noncompliance.

[For more information on adhesion contracts, see Casenote Law Outline on Contracts, Chapter 3, § IV, Defenses Centered on the Deceptive or Coercive Formation Tactics of One of the Parties.]

NOTES:

KINGSTON v. PRESTON

LOFFT 194, 2 Doug. 689, 99 Eng. Rep. 437 (K.B. 1773).

NATURE OF CASE: Action to recover damages for breach of contract.

FACT SUMMARY: Preston (D) agreed to sell his business to Kingston (P), and Kingston (P) agreed to, but did not, give security for the payments.

CONCISE RULE OF LAW: Breach of a covenant by one party to a contract relieves the other party's obligation to perform another covenant which is dependent thereon, the performance of the first covenant being an implied condition precedent to the duty to perform the second covenant.

FACTS: Preston (D) agreed (among other things) to sell his business to Kingston (P). Kingston (P) agreed (among other things) to give sufficient security for his payments. Kingston's (P) personal worth was negligible. Kingston (P) failed to provide sufficient security, and, thereafter, Preston (D) refused to sell.

ISSUE: When one party agrees to sell and a second party agrees to give sufficient security for his payments, are those covenants mutual and independent so that it is no excuse for nonperformance by the first party for him to allege breach of covenant by the second party?

HOLDING AND DECISION: No. When one party covenants to sell and a second party covenants in return to give sufficient security for his payments, those covenants are dependent. Therefore, Kingston (P) must show that he has provided or is ready and willing to provide sufficient security as a condition precedent to Preston's (D) duty to sell. The dependence or independence of covenants is to be determined from the intention of the parties, which in turn will normally be determined by the "order of time in which the intent of the transaction requires their performance." Here, the security was to be given "at and before the sealing and delivery of the deeds" conveying the business. Thus, according to the "temporal sequence" test, Preston's (D) duty to convey his business was dependent on Kingston's (P) giving of sufficient security. Furthermore, "it would be the greatest injustice if the plaintiff [Kingston (P)] should prevail." The giving of sufficient security was the essence of this agreement and, "therefore, must necessarily be a condition precedent."

EDITOR'S ANALYSIS: Although Lord Mansfield in this famous decision focused on the time sequence of the contract provisions (e.g., a provision to be performed after another provision is dependent on that other provision), he was very likely reacting primarily to the personal poverty of Kingston (P) and the "injustice" that would be done by making Preston (D) go through with his performance and then sue poor Kingston (P) for damages. (Kingston (P), presumably, might run the business into the ground very quickly, leaving Preston's (D) court victory a purely theoretical one.) Note that Lord Mansfield, in determining the time sequence (which he felt was so important), apparently looked not only to the contract itself but also to what he thought must have been the reasonable intentions of the parties.

[For more information on constructive conditions, see Casenote Law Outline on Contracts, Chapter 4, § II, Sources of Conditions in a Bargain.]

NOTES:

GOODISON v. NUNN

4 T.R. 762 (1792).

NOTES:

NATURE OF CASE: Action to recover damages for breach of contract to convey land.

FACT SUMMARY: Goodison (P) brought suit to recover the penalty fixed by the contract for nonperformance.

CONCISE RULE OF LAW: A plaintiff must tender his own performance before the defendant's failure to perform his reciprocal duties will be considered a breach.

FACTS: Goodison (P) agreed to convey his estate to Nunn (D) in exchange for £ 210. Nunn (D) refused to complete the contract. Goodison (P) never tendered the property to Nunn (D). Instead, he brought suit for £ 21, the amount specified in the contract as liquidated damages in the event of a breach of contract.

ISSUE: Is a party guilty of breach of contract where the plaintiff has not offered to perform or has not tendered his performance?

HOLDING AND DECISION: (Lord Kenyon, C.J.) No. Nunn's (D) duty to pay was a reciprocal duty. It did not arise until Goodison (P) had tendered his own performance. Since Goodison (P) has not yet conveyed or offered to convey the property to Nunn (D), Nunn's (D) counterperformance is not yet due. Since his duties have never ripened into an obligation to perform, Nunn (D) is not guilty of breach of contract. Judgment for Nunn (D).

EDITOR'S ANALYSIS: A party must complete all conditions precedent to a contract before the other party's reciprocal duties are required to be completed. Where the duties are to be performed simultaneously, they are deemed concurrent conditions. Any complaint for breach of a concurrent duty must contain an allegation that plaintiff has tendered or offered to tender his own performance. This is necessary because the defendant's counterperformance is not due until that time.

[For more information on conditions concurrent, see Casenote Law Outline on Contracts, 4, § I, Classification of Conditions According to Their Impact upon the Modified Promise.]

PALMER v. FOX

274 Mich. 252 (1936).

NATURE OF CASE: Action to recover the balance due on a land sale contract.

FACT SUMMARY: Fox (D) refused to continue making payments on the land sale contract until Palmer (P) cinderized his street as he had covenanted in the contract.

CONCISE RULE OF LAW: Where conditions are concurrent and dependent, the failure of one party to perform exercises the other party's counterperformance.

FACTS: Palmer (P) sold Fox (D) an unimproved lot as an investment. Palmer (P) promised to make certain improvements in the subdivision. The land sale contract was to run for five years, after which Fox (D) would have paid for the land. Palmer (P) made all of the promised improvements except for cinderizing or graveling the street in front of Fox's (D) lot. Fox (D) stopped paying on the lot. Palmer (P) brought suit for the balance due under the contract. Fox (D) claimed that Palmer (P) had breached the contract by not paving the street. This was a dependent concurrent condition, and its breach excused Fox's (D) performance. Palmer (P) argued that the covenant was independent of Fox's (D) duty to pay and that it was an immaterial breach. The court found for Palmer (P).

ISSUE: Does the failure to perform a dependent concurrent condition excuse the other party's counterperformance under the contract?

HOLDING AND DECISION: (Toy, J.) Yes. First, the performance was concurrent. Both Fox's (D) payments and Palmer's (P) performance were to be tendered within five years. Next, Fox (D) was to surrender the contract at the end of five years for the deed. The parties must have contemplated that all covenants would have been completed by that time. Second, the conditions were dependent. There was no showing that the contract specified that they were independent or that the parties had otherwise contemplated that they be deemed independent. Since the acts are concurrent and the parties have not expressly or impliedly made them independent, they will be considered dependent. Third, this is a material breach. The promised improvements were a major consideration in inducing Fox (D) to purchase the property. Fox (D) was purchasing the property for investment purposes, and it seems unlikely that he would have purchased the lot if it were to remain unimproved. Where a party fails to perform a material dependent concurrent condition, the other party's counterperformance is excused. Therefore, Fox (D) was not in breach of the contract. Judgment reversed.

EDITOR'S ANALYSIS: An immaterial breach does not excuse performance. The only action available is for damages. Therefore, the fact that the bathrooms in a 40-story office building were painted the wrong color would not excuse the buyer's duty to pay for the building. Careful drafting of contracts eliminates most of these problems. Normally, the contract makes the duty of the buyer to pay independent of any breaches of covenant by the seller. Therefore, the buyer's only remedy for a breach is an action for damages.

[For more information on conditions concurrent, see Casenote Law Outline on Contracts, Chapter 4, § I, Classification of Conditions According to Their Impact upon the Modified Promise.]

NOTES:

O.W. GRUN ROOFING AND CONSTR. CO.v. COPE

C.C.A. of Texas, 529 S.W.2d 258 (1975).

NATURE OF CASE: Suit to recover damages and to set aside a mechanic's lien.

FACT SUMMARY: Grun (D) contracted to install a new roof on Cope's (P) house but used shingles that were not of uniform color. As a result, Cope (P) refused to pay Grun (D) for the new roof.

CONCISE RULE OF LAW: In order to establish that he has substantially performed a contract, a party must demonstrate that he intended in good faith to comply with his obligations and that any omissions or deviations which did occur were unintentional and comparatively insignificant.

FACTS: O.W. Grun Roofing and Construction Co. (D) agreed to install a new roof on Cope's (P) house at a cost of $648. The roof was to be brown in color, but some of the shingles used by Grun (D) were yellow. When Cope (P) complained, Grun (D) removed at least some of the yellow shingles, but the roof still was not uniformly brown. Cope (P), therefore, refused to pay Grun (D) and ultimately sued for damages and to set aside a mechanic's lien which Grun (D) had filed. Grun (D) cross-claimed for foreclosure of the mechanic's lien and for recovery of the contract price. The trial court set aside the lien and awarded Cope (P) damages in an amount equal to the difference between the price of having a proper roof installed and the contract price. On appeal, Grun (D) claimed that it had substantially performed the agreement.

ISSUE: May a party to a contract claim substantial performance even though he has breached the agreement in a material respect?

HOLDING AND DECISION: (Cadena, J.) No. In order to establish that he has substantially performed a contract, a party must demonstrate that he intended in good faith to comply with his obligations and that any omissions or deviations which did occur were unintentional and comparatively insignificant. While it is impossible to articulate a universal test for determining whether or not substantial performance has occurred, it is obvious that a party has not substantially performed as long as the other party's general plan and purpose in entering into the contract remains unfulfilled. In this case, Cope's (P) general purpose included having a roof of uniform color, and since she can have such a roof only by having Grun's (D) work completely redone, it cannot be said that Grun (D) has substantially performed the contract. Nor may Grun (D) recover on a quantum meruit theory because Cope (P) has received no real benefit from Grun's (D) work. Therefore, the judgment of the trial court must be affirmed.

EDITOR'S ANALYSIS: The doctrine of substantial performance is most frequently invoked in building construction cases. In this context, the contract in question usually involves materials which ultimately are affixed to real estate. Since it is usually impractical, if not impossible, under such a circumstance, to return the parties to their previous status quo by ordering the return of all money and materials expended, courts are anxious to reach a compromise in such cases.

[For more information on substantial performance, see Casenote Law Outline on Contracts, 4, § III, Maturing of Contract Duties: Satisfaction or Excuse of Conditions.]

NOTES:

LOWY v. UNITED PACIFIC INSURANCE CO.

Cal. Sup. Ct., 429 P.2d 577 (1967).

NATURE OF CASE: Appeal from award of damages in a breach of contract action.

FACT SUMMARY: United Pacific (P) refused to pay Lowy (D) the contract price for grading work he performed on a development because the work was not completed by Lowy (D).

CONCISE RULE OF LAW: A contractor may recover for work actually performed under a construction contract if he has substantially performed his contractual duty in good faith.

FACTS: United Pacific (P) entered into a contract whereby Lowy (D), a contractor, would perform certain excavation and grading work on lots and streets. The contract also required Lowy (D) to perform street improvement work, including paving and installing curbs and gutters. Payment for the grading work and for street improvements was to be made separately and was calculated on different scales. A separate surety bond was to be posted by Lowy (D) for each phase of the work. Lowy (D) completed 98% of the grading work before refusing to continue due to a dispute with United Pacific (P). United Pacific (P) hired another contractor to finish the grading and sued Lowy (D) for breach of contract. Lowy (D) cross-complained for breach, contending he could recover for his substantial performance of the grading portion of the contract. The trial court granted recovery to Lowy (D), holding the contract was severable and that United Pacific's (P) failure to pay Lowy (D) for his substantial performance of the grading work excused Lowy's (D) further perfomance of the contract. United Pacific (P) appealed.

ISSUE: May a contractor recover for work actually performed on a contract if he has substantially performed his contractual duty in good faith?

HOLDING AND DECISION: (McComb, J.) Yes. A contractor may recover for work actually performed under a construction contract if he has substantially performed his contractual duties in good faith. In this case, Lowy (D) ceased work due to a good-faith dispute over his responsibility for work not covered by the contract. At the time he stopped work, only 2% of the grading remained incomplete. Clearly, he had substantially performed the grading portion of the contract. Because the consideration under the contract was apportioned, the contract was severable. Therefore, even though no work was performed on the street improvement portion, this does not defeat recovery for the grading work. As a result, Lowy (D) was entitled to recover under the contract. Affirmed.

EDITOR'S ANALYSIS: The Restatement Second on Contracts, in § 240, states that the determination whether a contract is severable or not rests on whether the "performances to be exchanged under an exchange of promises can be apportioned into corresponding pairs of part performances so that the parts of each pair are properly regarded as agreed equivalents." Another approach to severability, used in the present case, looks to the apportionability of the consideration. The parties' intent to create a severable contract is implied where consideration is easily apportionable.

[For more information on substantial performance, see Casenote Law Outline on Contracts, Chapter 4, § III, Maturing of Contract Duties: Satisfaction or Excuse of Conditions.]

NOTES:

BRITTON v. TURNER

N.H. Sup. Ct., 6 N.H. 481 (1834).

NATURE OF CASE: Action to recover in quantum meruit for work done.

FACT SUMMARY: Britton (P) contracted to work for Turner (D) for an entire year but left without cause before the year was up.

CONCISE RULE OF LAW: A defaulting party, although unable to recover on a contract, may recover under a quasi-contractual theory the reasonable value of his services less any damages to the other party arising out of the default.

FACTS: Britton (P) was under contract to labor for Turner (D) for one year and to be paid $120 for the work. Britton (P), without cause, left Turner's (D) employ after nine and one-half months and sought to recover the reasonable value of his labor. A jury awarded Britton (P) a verdict for $95.

ISSUE: Can one who performs work under an entire contract but leaves without cause before the expiration of the term of the contract recover in quantum meruit the reasonable value of the work he has performed?

HOLDING AND DECISION: (Parker, J.) Yes. Although it is clear that one who has labored for only a portion of the contract term may not recover on the contract, he may recover in quantum meruit the reasonable value of his services to the extent that the other party has received a benefit in excess of damages arising from the breach. A contrary result would be unjust and unequal in its operation. By that result, "the party who attempts performance may be placed in a much worse situation than he who wholly disregards his contract, and the other party may receive much more, by the breach of the contract, than the injury, which he sustained by such breach, and more than he could be entitled to were he seeking to recover damages by an action." In the present case, Turner (D) has been receiving benefit from day to day which he cannot now reject, and the circumstance is not distinguishable from those circumstances surrounding contracts to build houses where quantum meruit recoveries have been allowed despite deviations from the building contracts. Since Turner (D) has alleged no damages arising from Britton's (P) breach, the jury's verdict should be affirmed.

EDITOR'S ANALYSIS: The Court here acknowledges the contrary rule which will not allow a breaching party any recovery after only part performance (subject to the doctrine of substantial performance). Even today the present case still represents the minority view, although the trend is in its direction. The Court emphasizes the injustice of the prevailing role that one who attempts performance is in a worse position than one who totally ignores the contract. Although there is a temptation to respond, "So what?" courts following Britton's lead have pointed to the arbitrary forfeitures which breachers would suffer and the pure windfalls to the breachees. Further, the current trend in contract law is not to treat a "breach" as an inherently evil thing; the effect of allowing an unabashed forfeiture would be to sanction a kind of punitive damage.

[For more information on substantial performance, see Casenote Law Outline on Contracts, Chapter 4, § III, Maturing of Contract Duties: Satisfaction or Excuse of Conditions.]

NOTES:

MAXTON BUILDERS, INC. v. LO GALBO

N.Y. Ct. App., 68 N.Y.2d 373, 509 N.Y.S.2d 507, 502 N.E.2d 184 (1986).

NATURE OF CASE: Appeal from summary judgment awarding damages for breach of real estate purchase contract.

FACT SUMMARY: Maxton Builders (P) retained a 10% down payment on a contract with Lo Galbo (D) to purchase a newly constructed house after Lo Galbo (D) improperly canceled the contract.

CONCISE RULE OF LAW: If the buyer defaults under or improperly cancels an agreement to purchase real property, the seller has the right to retain the buyer's down payment as liquidated damages.

FACTS: Maxton Builders (P) contracted to sell a newly constructed home to Lo Galbo (D). Lo Galbo (D) made a down payment of 10% of the purchase price. The contract required Lo Galbo (D) to notify Maxton Builders (P) within three days of an intent to cancel, but Lo Galbo (D) canceled after the three-day period and stopped payment on its down payment check. The purchase and sale contract between Maxton Builders (P) and Lo Galbo (D) provided that Maxton (P) would be allowed to retain Lo Galbo's (D) down payment in the event of default. Maxton (P) then sued to recover the down payment and won summary judgment. Lo Galbo (D) appealed.

ISSUE: If the buyer defaults under or improperly cancels an agreement to purchase real property, does the seller have the right to retain the buyer's down payment as liquidated damages?

HOLDING AND DECISION: (Wachtler, C.J.) Yes. If the buyer defaults under or improperly cancels an agreement to purchase real property, the seller has the right to retain the buyer's down payment as liquidated damages if the agreement expressly provides that the seller could retain it upon default. Further, a 10% down payment has been traditionally accepted as a reasonable amount, unless the buyer proves that this amount exceeds the actual damages suffered by the seller. Although the "modern" rule applicable to contracts generally that a party in default may recover for part performance in excess of actual damages suffered by the other party has much to commend it, it is not workable when applied to real estate contracts. If buyers in default could seek restitution for part performance, it would greatly increase litigation costs without saving many parties true financial loss because in most instances 10% is not much greater than the damage suffered by the buyer's breach. Here, Maxton Builders (P) and Lo Galbo (D) agreed to retention of a 10% down payment in the event of Lo Galbo's (D) default, and Lo Galbo (D) made no effort to show that Maxton's (P) actual damages were less than the down payment. Therefore, Lo Galbo's (D) belated cancellation of the purchase contract constituted a breach, entitling Maxton (P) to retention of the down payment. Affirmed.

EDITOR'S ANALYSIS: The "modern" rule rejected in this case allows restitution to the breaching party only of the net benefit retained after full compensation for the breach. Under Restatement (First) of Contracts § 357(1), however, the breaching party's right to this "net benefit" was unavailable if its breach was "willful and deliberate." A breach was not considered "willful and deliberate" if it was "due to hardship, insolvency, or circumstances that tend appreciably toward moral justification." Comment e. However, § 374(1) of Restatement (Second) of Contracts, which restates the "net benefit" rule, does away completely with this "morality" requirement.

[For more information on liquidated damage, see Casenote Law Outline on Contracts, Chapter 7, § III, Remedies for Breach of Contract.]

NOTES:

HENNINGSEN v. BLOOMFIELD MOTORS

N.J. Sup. Ct., 32 N.J. 358, 161 A.2d 69 (1960).

NATURE OF CASE: Appeal in personal injury suit for damages.

FACT SUMMARY: An express warranty in a vehicle sales contract disclaimed all other warranties and severely limited the express warranty coverage.

CONCISE RULE OF LAW: An express warranty that seeks to severely limit the manufacturer's liability and that disclaims all other warranties can be voided as against public policy.

FACTS: Helen Henningsen (P), the wife of the purchaser of a car, was injured in a Chrysler (D) automobile purchased at Bloomfield Motors (D). Included in the purchase agreement for the car was a clause limiting warranty protection to the purchaser and to the replacement of defective parts. Henningsen (P) filed suit against Bloomfield Motors (D), the dealer, and Chrysler (D), the manufacturer. The trial court invalidated the warranty disclaimers and granted her recovery. Chrysler (D) and Bloomfield Motors (D) appealed the case to the New Jersey Supreme Court.

ISSUE: Can an express warranty that seeks to severely limit the manufacturer's liability and that disclaims all other warranties be voided as against public policy?

HOLDING AND DECISION: (Court) Yes. An express warranty that seeks to severely limit the manufacturer's liability and that disclaims all other warranties can be voided as against public policy. Generally, a person is bound by his signed agreement. However, where certain equities in bargaining position exist, courts retain the power to void enforcement of unconscionable terms. In this case, the warranty in the contract offered little and took away much of a purchaser's potential recourse. Warranties originated in the law to protect the buyer. Here, the warranty served solely to negate liability for the manufacturer. The gross inequality of bargaining power and the unreasonableness of the warranty disclaimer justifies voiding the warranty provision.

EDITOR'S ANALYSIS: The U.C.C. prohibits contracts from disclaiming liability for consequential damages resulting from a breach of warranty. In the relevant provisions, the U.C.C. defines contracts attempting to disclaim such liability as prima facie unconscionable. However, the tension that exists between tort law and contracts in disputes over property has yet to be entirely resolved.

[For more information on disclaimer of warranties, see Casenote Law Outline on Contracts, Chapter 3, § III, Defenses Rooted in Social Objection to the Content of the Bargain.]

MURRAY v. HOLIDAY RAMBLER, INC.

Wis. Sup. Ct., 83 Wis.2d 406, 265 N.W.2d 513 (1978).

NATURE OF CASE: Appeal of jury verdict in suit for damages.

FACT SUMMARY: Murray (P) signed a motor home sales contract that included a limitation of all express or implied warranties other than a warranty against defect, which limited the remedy to repair of defects.

CONCISE RULE OF LAW: Where the remedies in a limited warranty fail to correct a seller's breach, the limitations will be disregarded in favor of ordinary U.C.C. remedies.

FACTS: Murray (P) purchased a motor home from Holiday Rambler (D). The sales contract purported to exclude all warranties express or implied. The remedies for defects were limited to repair or replacement. The motor home purchased had numerous problems, including electrical defects, improperly vented gasoline tanks, and a defective air suspension system. Requests for repairs were never refused, but the motor home spent most of its time undergoing corrective measures. Murray (P) finally revoked acceptance and sued for loss of use of the vehicle. The jury awarded $2,500 for loss of use of the vehicle. Holiday Rambler (D) appealed.

ISSUE: Where the remedies in a limited warranty fail to correct a seller's breach, will the limitations be disregarded in favor of ordinary U.C.C. remedies?

HOLDING AND DECISION: (Hansen, J.) Yes. Where the rememdies in a limited warranty fail to correct a seller's breach, the limitations will be disregarded in favor of ordinary U.C.C. remedies. If a seller has been given a reasonable time to correct defects and fails to do so, then the limited warranty that restricts remedies to repair of defects has failed in its purpose. In such a case, ordinary remedies under the U.C.C. can be sought to correct defects. In this case, the motor home sold to the Murrays (P) was barely functional. After repeated requests to repair the vehicle, the Murrays (P) finally surrendered and revoked acceptance. As they had been denied use of the vehicle, consequential damages were appropriately awarded. The limited warranty failed to correct the defects, leaving other remedies under the U.C.C. as their only available recourse. Affirmed.

EDITOR'S ANALYSIS: Many states have passed laws that allow new vehicles that cannot be repaired to be returned by the buyer. These laws supercede any limited warranties. Such "lemon laws" recognize that an unreasonable number of defects makes relying on a repair remedy impossible and impractical for the buyer.

[For more information on disclaimer of warranties, see Casenote Law Outline on Contracts, Chapter 3, § III, Defenses Rooted in Social Objection to the Content of the Bargain.]

MINERAL PARK LAND CO. v. HOWARD

Cal. Sup. Ct., 134 Cal. 289, 156 P. 458 (1916).

NATURE OF CASE: Appeal from award of damages for breach of contract.

NOTES:

FACT SUMMARY: Mineral Park (D) contended it was not bound to remove gravel from Howard's (P) land that would be commercially impracticable to haul away.

CONCISE RULE OF LAW: A party is excused from performing under a contract where such performance is so much more expensive than contemplated that it would be impracticable to complete.

FACTS: Mineral Park (D) agreed to obtain its gravel requirements for building a bridge from Howard's (P) land and to pay for it at 5 cents per yard. It hauled away all the gravel above the water level but refused to go below that because to do so would cost 10 to 12 times the usual cost of hauling gravel. Howard (P) sued to require Mineral Park (D) to perform fully. The trial court held that because it was merely commercially disadvantageous to remove the gravel, and not physically impossible, Mineral Park (D) was bound to perform and had breached the contract. Mineral Park (D) appealed, contending it was excused from performing due to impracticability.

ISSUE: May a party be excused from performing under a contract on the basis of impracticability?

HOLDING AND DECISION: (Sloss, J.) Yes. A party may be excused from performing under a contract where such performance has become impracticable because its cost would greatly exceed that contemplated. In this case, although it would have been physically possible to remove gravel below the water level, for practical purposes no further gravel was available due to the severe increased cost. Therefore, Mineral Park (D) must be excused from further performance due to the nonexistence of the contractual subject matter for practical purposes. Reversed.

EDITOR'S ANALYSIS: With this case, California led the way toward relaxation of the strict common law rule which required virtual physical impossibility to excuse performance. Today, modern courts equate extreme impracticability with impossibility, and this was the approach adopted in the First Restatement in § 454. U.C.C. § 2-615 defines "impracticable" as including impossibility, and the Restatement Second adopts a similar approach.

[For more information on commercial impracticability, see Casenote Law Outline on Contracts, Chapter 6, § I, Excusable Non-Performance under the Common Law.]

UNITED STATES v. WEGEMATIC CORP.

360 F.2d 674 (2d Cir. 1966).

NATURE OF CASE: Action for damages for breach of a contract for the sale of goods.

FACT SUMMARY: In response to an invitation from the Federal Reserve Board [United States (P)], Wegematic (D) submitted a bid to supply an ALWAC 800 computer. Delivery, which was offered nine months from the date of the contract, was received, but it appeared that the ALWAC 800 was beyond the technology of the day and would not be able to be built. United States (P) obtained another computer and sued for the extra cost.

CONCISE RULE OF LAW: Usually with the production of new products or use of new processes where the manufacturer has contended that compliance under existing technology is impossible, the contractor has assumed the risk that production was possible.

FACTS: In June 1956, the Federal Reserve Board of the United States (P) invited five companies to submit bids on a digital computing system, stressing the importance of early delivery. Wegematic (D), a relative newcomer in the field, proposed the sale or lease of an ALWAC 800, billed as a revolutionary concept and a great step beyond its ALWAC III-E, with which it had enjoyed great success. Delivery was promised within nine months of receipt of contract or purchase order. United States (P) ordered an ALWAC 800 for $231,800 in September 1956 for delivery in June 1957, with liquidated damages of $100 per day for delay. If Wegematic (D) failed in any provision, the Government (P) could contract elsewhere and charge the extra cost to Wegematic (D). In March 1957, Wegematic (D) requested a delay in delivery for redesign and in April suggested delivery in October with waiver of damages. After other requests for delay, Wegematic (D) stated that development of the computer was beyond technological capacities. United States (P), on October 6, 1958, obtained an IBM 650 serving relatively the same purpose as the ALWAC 800 at a rental of $102,000 with an option to purchase for $410,450.

ISSUE: Did the practical impossibility of time and expense of correcting technological problems release Wegematic (D) from performance?

HOLDING AND DECISION: (Friendly, C.J.) No. While under U.C.C. § 2-615 a delay in delivery or nondelivery is not a breach under a sales contract if performance has been made impracticable by the occurrence of a contingency, the nonoccurrence of which was a basic assumption on which the contract was made, the risk of the technological breakthrough did not fall on the purchaser. This was because it was reasonable to suppose that it already had occurred or, at least, that Wegematic (D) had assured the Government (P) that it would be found in order to permit delivery. The purchaser otherwise would be forced to accept whatever the contractor develops while he had selected the contractor on a different basis. If the contractor's technological gamble failed, the purchaser would still have to accept it. This does not appear to be the understanding particularly where Wegematic (D) agreed to liquidated damages for delay and to allowing the Government (P) to find another source in case delivery could not be made.

EDITOR'S ANALYSIS: Cases involving manufacture of new products or the use of new manufacturing processes mostly involve government contract cases, and, generally, where compliance has proved impossible under technology of the day, the contractor has been held to have assumed the risk that production was possible. If the Government has provided detailed specifications for manufacturing (as opposed to the specifications which the end product must meet), the Government has warranted that the specifications will meet the desired result. If the Government has merely suggested the manufacturing process, it has been held not to have warranted the process. Of course, when as to a material fact there is mutual mistake, the risk of which was not assumed, reallocation is justified if it appears that the Government would have assented to it at the outset if it had known the truth.

[For more information on the failure of presupposed conditions, see Casenote Law Outline on Contracts, Chapter 6, § II, Excusable Non-Performance under the U.C.C.]

NOTES:

TAYLOR v. CALDWELL

King's Bench, 3 B.&S. 826, 122 Eng. Rep. 309 (1863).

NATURE OF CASE: Action for damages for breach of a contract for letting of premises.

FACT SUMMARY: Taylor (P) contracted to let Caldwell's (D) hall and gardens for four fetes and concerts, for four days, for £ 100 per day. Taylor (P) expended money in preparation and for advertising, but Caldwell (D) could not perform when the hall burned down without his fault.

CONCISE RULE OF LAW: In contracts in which the performance depends on the continued existence of a given person or thing, a condition is implied that the impossibility of performance arising from the perishing of the person or thing shall excuse the performance.

FACTS: By written agreement, Caldwell (D) agreed to let the Surrey Gardens and Musical Hall at Newington, Surrey for four days for giving four "Grand Concerts" and "Day and Night Fetes." Taylor (P) was to pay £ 100 at the end of each day. Before any concerts were held, the hall was completely destroyed by fire without any fault of either of the parties. Taylor (P) alleged that the fire and destruction of the hall was a breach and that it resulted in his losing large sums in preparation and advertising for the concerts and fetes.

ISSUE: In contracts in which the performance depends on the continued existence of a given person or thing, is a condition implied that the impossibility of performance arising from the perishing of the person or thing shall excuse the performance?

HOLDING AND DECISION: (Blackburn, J.) Yes. In contracts in which the performance depends on the continued existence of a given person or thing, a condition is implied that the impossibility of performance arising from the perishing of the person or thing shall excuse the performance. Caldwell (D) was excused from performance. First, the agreement was not a lease but a contract to "let." The entertainments that were planned could not be made without the existence of the hall. Ordinarily, when there is a positive contract to do something that is not unlawful, the contractor must perform or pay damages for not doing it even if an unforeseen accident makes performance unduly burdensome or even impossible. This is so when the contract is absolute and positive and not subject to either express or implied conditions and that it appears that the parties must have known from the beginning that the contract could not be fulfilled unless a particular, specified thing continued to exist; and when there is no express or implied warranty that the thing shall exist, the contract is not positive and absolute. It is subject to the implied condition that the parties shall be excused in case, before breach, performance becomes impossible from the perishing of the thing without fault of the contractor. This appears to be within the intention of the parties when they enter into a contract. The excuse from the contract's performance is implied in law because from the nature of the contract it is apparent it was made on the basis of the continued existence of the particular, specified thing.

EDITOR'S ANALYSIS: It was important for J. Blackburn not to find the agreement to be a lease; otherwise, the decision would come within direct conflict of Paradine v. Jane, K.B., 82 Eng. Rep. 897 (1647), which held that a lease must be performed to the letter despite unforeseen hardship or good fortune. Next, performance is excused only if the destruction of the specified thing is without fault. Had Caldwell (D) been shown to be guilty of arson in the destruction of the hall, he would not have been excused. If there is impossibility of performance due to no one's fault, the one seeking to enforce performance takes the risk. It might be said that the court was actually apportioning the loss if the contract was, in effect, a joint venture with Taylor (P) paying Caldwell (D) £ 100 out of each day's admission fees to the concerts (Caldwell (D) was supplying the band). The view of this case is found in U.C.C. § 2-613, where for total destruction of the specified thing, the contract is avoided, or, if the specified thing is goods which have so deteriorated as to no longer conform, the contract can be avoided or the goods can be accepted with an allowance for their lesser value. Note that there is not a satisfactory distinction between a contract to let and a lease.

[For more information on impossibility of performance, see Casenote Law Outline on Contracts, Chapter 6, § I, Excusable Non-Performance under the Common Law.]

NOTES:

CANADIAN INDUSTRIES ALCOHOL CO. v. DUNBAR MOLASSES CO.

N.Y. Ct. of App., 179 N.E. 383 (1932).

NATURE OF CASE: Action for damages for breach of a contract for the sale of goods.

FACT SUMMARY: Alcohol Co. (P) contracted to buy Dunbar's (D) usual run of refined blackstrap molasses, about 1,500,000 wine gallons. That year, Dunbar (D) produced less than half its usual capacity, under 500,000 gallons, and could not fulfill its contracted quantity.

CONCISE RULE OF LAW: If the promisor is in some respects responsible for the event which makes performance of his promise impossible, justice does not dictate that he be excused.

FACTS: At the end of 1927, Alcohol Co. (P) contracted to buy from Dunbar (D) about 1,500,000 wine gallons of refined blackstrap molasses, about 60% sugar, of the usual run from the National Sugar Refinery, Yonkers, New York. Delivery was to begin April 1, 1928 "to be spread out during the warm weather." The refinery that year produced far less than its capacity, less than a half-million gallons. Dunbar (D) shipped its entire allotment, 344,083 gallons, to Alcohol Co. (P). Alcohol Co. (P) sued for damages, but Dunbar (D) contended that its duty was conditioned by an implied term, the refinery's producing enough molasses to fill Alcohol's (P) order. Dunbar (D) had no contract with the refinery.

ISSUE: Was performance implicitly conditioned by the refinery's producing enough molasses to fill Alcohol Co.'s order?

HOLDING AND DECISION: (Cardozo, C.J.) No. The contract as read in the light of circumstances did not keep Dunbar's (D) duty within such narrow boundaries. Dunbar (D) never even attempted to get a contract with the refinery between the time of acceptance and the start of shipments. Accordingly, contributory fault is implied to Dunbar (D), which put its faith in the mere chance that the refinery's output would remain as in past years. Dunbar's (D) customer did not take that chance; only Dunbar (D) did.

EDITOR'S ANALYSIS: There is no one rule for allowing the unforeseen risk, but the basis of all existing rules is the attempt to place the risk where the parties would have if they had foreseen it. If it is reasonably foreseeable, the promisor will have been deemed to have accepted it. Excuse of performance on grounds of impossibility involves, in the interests of justice, the creation of a condition. If the promisor is in some respects responsible for the event making performance impossible, that is, if he is guilty of contributory fault, performance will not be excused. Had the refinery in this case been destroyed without the fault of Dunbar (D), Dunbar (D) would have been excused from performance. The destruction of the refinery would not have been a risk assumed by the promisor, Dunbar (D). Even had Dunbar (D) made a contract with the refinery, it would still appear that Alcohol (P) would have a cause of action and that Dunbar (D) would still not be excused, as Dunbar (D) would have a cause of action against the refinery. The refinery would then have been liable for Dunbar's (D) loss.

[For more information on impossibility of performance, see Casenote Law Outline on Contracts, Chapter 6, § I, Excusable Non-Performance under the Common Law.]

NOTES:

DILLS v. TOWN OF ENFIELD

210 Conn. 705, 557 A.2d 517 (1989).

NATURE OF THE CASE: Appeal from denial of damages for breach of contract action.

FACT SUMMARY: Enfield (D) sold land to Dills (P) to be developed into an industrial park, but when Dills (P) later terminated the contract after he could not obtain financing, Enfield (D) refused to return his deposit, and Dills (P) filed suit for breach of contract.

CONCISE RULE OF LAW: The occurrence of a foreseeable event that was contemplated at the time of the contract does not render the obligor's performance impractical and excused.

FACTS: Enfield (D) agreed to convey to Dills (P) property to be developed into an industrial park. The agreement required Dills (P) to submit acceptable construction plans and proof of financial capacity. The contract allowed Dills (P) to withdraw and reclaim his $100,000 deposit if, after approval of the plans, he failed to get financing. The contract also allowed Enfield (D) to terminate the contract and withhold the deposit if Dills (P) failed to submit an acceptable construction plan. Dills (P) failed to submit an acceptable construction plan when he could not obtain the financing. Enfield (D) voted to terminate the contract, but three days later Dills (P) withdrew from the contract himself. Enfield (D) refused to return the deposit, and Dills (P) filed suit. The case was decided by a referee who held for Dills (P). The trial court rejected the decision and held for Enfield (D). Dills (P) appealed.

ISSUE: Does the occurrence of a foreseeable event, contemplated by the parties at the time of the contract, render the promised performance impractical and thereby excused?

HOLDING AND DECISION: (Peters, J.) No. The occurrence of a foreseeable event that was contemplated at the time of the contract does not render the defendant's performance impracticable and excused. A party who wants his performance to be excused has to show that the nonoccurrence of the event was the basic presumption of the contract. Here, the parties expressly contemplated the financial difficulties that Dills (P) might encounter. Thus, Dills' (P) failure to obtain financing was foreseeable and contemplated at the time of the contract and cannot excuse his performance. Affirmed.

EDITOR'S ANALYSIS: It is necessary to learn which party assumed the risk of the occurrence of an event in order to determine whether its nonoccurrence was a basic presumption of the contract. The case above was one dealing with the sale of land and thus outside the U.C.C. The doctrine of impracticability, embodied in U.C.C. § 2-615, concerning the sale of goods, should be referred to for the approach to be taken to the events which may or may not excuse performance of commercial sales contracts for items other than real property.

[For more information on the failure of presuppposed conditions, see Casenote Law Outline on Contracts, Chapter 6, § II, Excusable Non-Performance under the U.C.C.]

KAISER-FRANCIS OIL CO. v. PRODUCER'S GAS CO.

870 F.2d 563 (10th Cir. 1989).

NATURE OF THE CASE: Appeal from partial summary judgment denying liability for breach of contract.

FACT SUMMARY: Gas Co. (D) agreed to take or pay for certain quantities of gas that were partially owned by Kaiser (P), but breached the contract when he refused to take or pay for the gas due to a decrease in market demand.

CONCISE RULE OF LAW: Fluctuations in the market price or demand of the goods do not excuse the obligor's promised performance.

FACTS: Gas Co. (D) entered into two contracts with Kaiser (P), a partial owner of the gas wells, to take or pay for certain quantity of gas to be pumped from the wells. Provisions in both contracts stated that neither party would be liable for breach if their performance was affected by an unexpected event. Gas Co. (D), relying on these provisions, did not take or pay for the agreed quantity when the gas market price decreased. Kaiser (P) filed suit and moved for summary judgment, arguing that market demand is not an unexpected event excusing Gas Co.'s (D) performance. Summary judgment was granted on liability, and Gas Co. (D) appealed.

ISSUE: Are fluctuations in the market demand or price of goods unexpected events excusing the obligor's promised performance?

HOLDING AND DECISION: (Baldock, J.) No. Fluctuations in the market demand or price of goods are not unexpected events excusing obligor's promised performance. The Oklahoma Supreme Court in interpreting contractual force majeure provisions, similar to the ones in the instant case, has held that a decline in the market price of goods or inability to make a profit after the sale of goods are not unexpected events. Since the seller is the one who bears the risk of production, it is the buyer who should bear the risk of market demand. Affirmed.

EDITOR'S ANALYSIS: Force majeure provisions were not meant to create a buffer against the normal risks involved in a contractual relationship. Seller gains at the expense of the buyer when the market price has decreased, while the buyer gains at the expense of the seller when the market price has increased. Thus, fluctuations in market price are normal risks taken by all parties to a contract.

[For more information on the role of foreseeability, see Casenote Law Outline on Contracts, Chapter 6, § II, Excusable Non-Performance under the U.C.C.]

PARADINE v. JANE

King's Bench, Aleyn 26, 82 Eng. Rep. 837 (1647).

NATURE OF CASE: Action on a lease for rent past due.

FACT SUMMARY: Jane (D) argued that he should not have to pay rent owing on land he leased from Paradine (P) because he had been deprived of the land's use when it was occupied by the invading army of German Prince Rupert.

CONCISE RULE OF LAW: When a party by his own contract creates a charge or duty upon himself, he is bound to make it good notwithstanding any frustration because he might have provided against it in the contract.

FACTS: Paradine (P) brought suit upon a lease for years declaring that Jane (D) had failed to pay rent for three years on the lands held under the lease. Jane (D) answered that the lands had been occupied by the invading army of Prince Rupert of Germany and that, as a result, Jane (D) had been unable to take the profits from the land. Jane (D) argued that he was frustrated in the performance of his duties under the lease.

ISSUE: When a party by his own contract creates a charge or duty upon himself, is he bound to make good notwithstanding any frustration?

HOLDING AND DECISION: Yes. When a party by his own contract creates a charge or duty upon himself, he is bound to make it good notwithstanding any frustration because he might have provided against it in the contract. "Now the rent is a duty created by the parties ... and had there been a covenant to pay it, there had been no question but the lessee must have made it good, notwithstanding the interruption by enemies, for the law would not protect him beyond his own agreement." Judgment for Paradine (P).

EDITOR'S ANALYSIS: Another report of this same case said that the decision was placed principally on the ground that "[i]f the tenant for years covenants to pay rent, though the lands let him be surrounded with water, yet he is chargeable with the rent, much more here." Style 47, 82 Eng. Rep. 519 (1647). This case is cited as the leading case in support of the strict seventh century English Rule that impossibility will not be recognized as an excuse for the promisor's nonperformance of his duty. Corbin writes that Jane (D) had no covenant of quiet enjoyment. "The agreed equivalent for the defendant's promise to pay rent was the conveyance of the leasehold property interest and delivery of possession. There was merely a frustration of the tenant's purpose of enjoying the profits of use and occupation." 6 Corbin § 1322.

[For more information on frustration of purpose, see Casenote Law Outline on Contracts, Chapter 6, § I, Excusable Non-Performance under the Common Law.]

NOTES:

KRELL v. HENRY

Ct. of App., 2 K.B. 740 (England 1903).

NATURE OF CASE: Action for damages for breach of a contract for a license for use.

FACT SUMMARY: Henry (D) paid a deposit of £25 to Krell (P) for the use of his apartment in Pall Mall, London, for the purpose of a viewing sight for King Edward VII's coronation procession. The King became ill, causing a delay of the coronation, upon which Henry (D) refused to pay a £50 balance, for which Krell (P) sued.

CONCISE RULE OF LAW: Where the object of one of the parties is the basis upon which both parties contract, the duties of performance are constructively conditioned upon the attainment of that object.

FACTS: In two letters of June 20, 1902, Henry (D) contracted through Krell's (P) agent, Bisgood, to use Krell's (P) flat in Pall Mall, London, to view the coronation procession of King Edward VII, which had been advertised to pass along Pall Mall. The contract made no mention of this purpose. The period of use of the flat was the daytime only of June 26, 27, 1902, for £75, £25 paid in deposit, with the £50 remainder due on June 24, 1902. Henry (D) became aware of the availability of Krell's (P) flat, as an announcement to that effect had been made, which was reiterated by Krell's (P) housekeeper, who showed Henry (D) the rooms. When the king became very ill, the coronation was delayed, and Henry (D) refused to pay the £50 balance, for which Krell (P) brought suit.

ISSUE: Was the defeat of the basis upon which Henry contracted a defeat of the contract?

HOLDING AND DECISION: (Darling, J.) Yes. It can be inferred from the surrounding circumstances that the rooms were taken for the purpose of viewing the processions and that that was the foundation of the contract. It was not a lease of the rooms — they could not be used at night — but a license for use for a particular purpose. With the defeat of the purpose to the contract, the performance is excused.

CONCURRENCE: (Romer, J.) The parties to this contract should have foreseen the possibility that the coronation might not occur, but since the court, as a matter of fact, finds to the contrary, the appeal was properly dismissed.

EDITOR'S ANALYSIS: This case is an extension of Taylor v. Caldwell, and as in that case, it was necessary to remove the roadblock of a lease in order to avoid a conflict with Paradine v. Jane. The rule explained here is "frustration of purpose" or "commercial frustration." It has not been made clear whether this doctrine rests upon the failure of consideration or the allocation of the risks. While there is a frustration, performance is not impossible. No constructive condition of performance has failed, as Krell (P) made no promise that the condition would occur. Rather, a constructive condition based upon the attainment of the purpose or object has arisen. Note that the frustration should be total or nearly total, though that is a matter of degree.

[For more information on frustration of purpose, see Casenote Law Outline on Contracts, Chapter 6, § I, Excusable Non-Performance under the Common Law.]

NOTES:

WASHINGTON STATE HOP PRODUCERS, INC. v. GOSCHIE FARMS INC.

112 Wash.2d 694, 773 P.2d 70 (1989).

NATURE OF THE CASE: Appeal from summary judgment excusing contractual performance.

FACT SUMMARY: Goschie (D) contracted with Washington (P) to purchase a hop base but later refused to perform the contract after the USDA's termination of marketing orders for hop bases.

CONCISE RULE OF LAW: A drastic decrease in market demand or price is to be considered evidence supporting the frustration of a contractual purpose which excuses the obligor's performance.

FACTS: Washington (P), trustee, accepted bids for the sale of two hop base pools. Pool A was to be sold in 1985, while pool B was to be sold in 1986. Goschie (D) was one of the bidders. Five days after notice of acceptance by Washington (P), the USDA terminated the marketing orders for all hop bases. This termination caused a drastic drop in the price of the existing hop base. As a result, Goschie (D) refused to pay for the hop base claiming that the termination frustrated the purpose of the contract and, thus, excused his obligation. Washington (P) unsuccessfully sued to recover the agreed price. Both the trial and appellate court agreed that the purpose of the contract was frustrated and rescinded the contract.

ISSUE: Does a drastic price reduction, resulting from a supervening governmental act, frustrate the purpose of a contract thereby excusing the performance of the obligor?

HOLDING AND DECISION: No. A drastic decrease in market demand or price is to be considered evidence supporting the frustration of a contractual purpose which excuses the obligor's performance. The Restatement (Second) of Contracts requires the frustrated purpose to be the principal purpose of the contract. In this case, the main purpose of the contract was the control and franchising of the hop base. A 92% price decrease, resulting from the USDA's termination, was not the frustrated purpose itself, but only evidence of the frustration of the contractual purpose. Furthermore, foreseeability of the frustrating event is also a factor in deciding whether the nonoccurrence of that event was a basic assumption of the parties entering into a contract. Washington (P) claimed that the USDA's termination was foreseeable, but failed to show any supportive facts. On the contrary, the inference drawn by the court was that the event was not foreseeable. This notion was supported by the lack of incorporating language in the contract allocating the risk of termination. Affirmed.

EDITOR'S ANALYSIS: Frustration differs from impossibility in that supervening events may occur that destroy one's purpose in entering into a contract, even when the actual performance of the contract is not rendered impossible. The frustration doctrine is also incorporated in U.C.C. § 2-615.

[For more information on frustration of purpose, see Casenote Law Outline on Contracts, Chapter 6, § I, Excusable Non-Performance under the Common Law.]

NOTES:

CENTRONICS CORPORATION v. GENICOM CORPORATION

N.H. Sup. Ct., 132 N.H. 133, 562 A.2d 187 (1989).

NATURE OF CASE: Appeal from summary judgment denying damages for breach of implied obligation of good faith and fair dealing.

FACT SUMMARY: Centronics (P) agreed to sell its business assets to Genicom (D) for an amount to be determined in arbitration once a portion of the estimated price had been placed in escrow; Centronics (P), however, demanded that Genicom (D) release part of the escrow funds before arbitration had been concluded, a demand Genicom (D) rejected.

CONCISE RULE OF LAW: A party to a contract is not bound by the implied obligation of good faith and fair dealing to do something not expressly required by the contract.

FACTS: Centronics (P) agreed to sell its business assets to Genicom (D) for an amount to be determined in arbitration according to the consolidated closing net book value of the assets (CCNBV). The agreement between Centronics (P) and Genicom (D) required Genicom (D) to deposit in escrow a portion of the price claimed by Centronics (P) pending this final valuation. Genicom (D) made such a deposit. However, as it became apparent that arbitration would drag on given the parties' disputes over CCNBV, Centronics (P) demanded that a portion of the amount deposited in escrow which it claimed was "free from dispute" should be paid to it immediately. This demand was made despite the fact that the agreement required that the funds be retained in escrow until the conclusion of arbitration. Genicom (D) refused to release any funds, and Centronics (P) sued Genicom (D) for breach of the implied covenant of good faith and fair dealing in refusing to release any moneys. Genicom's (D) motion for summary judgment was granted, and Centronics (P) appealed.

ISSUE: Is a party to a contract bound by the implied covenant of good faith and fair dealing to do something not expressly required by the contract?

HOLDING AND DECISION: (Souter, J.) No. A party to a contract is not bound by the implied covenant of good faith and fair dealing to do something not expressly required by the contract. Where an agreement invests one party with discretion which if wrongfully exercised could effectively deprive the other of the practical benefits of the agreement, the party invested with the discretion has an implied obligation to observe reasonable limits in exercising it consistent with the parties' purposes in contracting. Here, however, Genicom (D) had no discretion under its contract with Centronics (P) to release funds from escrow prior to the conclusion of arbitration, even if they were, as alleged by Centronics (P), "free from dispute." Centronics (P) cannot now rewrite a contract which did not provide for a partial disbursal of funds from escrow; if it had been concerned about receiving a portion of the purchase price by a certain date, it should have demanded a mechanism for partial payments if the arbitration process lagged. However, the court will not renegotiate the contract for the parties to obtain such a result. Because Genicom (D) was not invested with discretion to release payments early, it is not necessary to decide whether a hypothetical release would have exceeded the limits of reasonableness. Accordingly, Genicom (D) did not breach the implied covenant of good faith and fair dealing in refusing to do something the contract did not require it to do. Affirmed.

EDITOR'S ANALYSIS: The covenant of good faith and fair dealing is also implied in two other principal categories of cases: ones concerned with contract formation and those concerned with termination of at-will employment contracts. The standard of conduct required in contract formation cases amounts to the traditional duty of cure to refrain from misrepresentation and to correct known misperceptions of the other party to the contract which concern material matters relating to the contract. In at-will employment cases, the implied covenant limits the power of an employer to terminate a wage contract by discharging the employee out of malice or bad faith in retaliation for action taken or refused by the employee in consonance with public policy. Seminal cases of these types are collected and addressed in Summers, The General Duty of Good Faith — Its Recognition and Conceptualization, 67 Cornell L. Rev. 810 (1982).

[For more information on breach of covenant of good faith, see Casenote Law Outline on Contracts, Chapter 7, § I, Breach — Disappointment of Reasonable Expectations.]

NOTES:

NEUMILLER FARMS, INC. v. CORNETT
Ala. Sup. Ct., 368 So.2d 272 (1979).

NATURE OF CASE: Appeal from award of damages for breach of contract.

FACT SUMMARY: Cornett (P) contended Neumiller (D) rejected nine loads of potatoes in bad faith and thereby breached its contract.

CONCISE RULE OF LAW: U.C.C. § 2-104 requires a merchant's claim of dissatisfaction with tendered goods be made in good faith, that he judge objectively based on honesty in fact, and observance of reasonable commercial standards of fair dealing in the trade.

FACTS: Neumiller (D), a corporation which acted as a broker of potatoes, contracted to purchase 12 loads of potatoes from Cornett (P) at $4.25 per hundredweight. The contract provided that Neumiller's (D) acceptance of the potatoes was conditioned upon the potatoes' suitability for use in making of potato chips. Such suitability was subject to Neumiller's (D) satisfaction with the potatoes. Subsequently, the market price of potatoes fell to $2.00 per hundredweight, and Neumiller (D) rejected all subsequent deliveries on the basis the potatoes would not chip satisfactorily. Cornett (P) tendered a load it purchased from another grower, from whom Neumiller (D) had recently purchased for $2.00 per hundredweight, yet Neumiller (D) rejected it at a price of $4.25, saying they were unfit. Cornett (P) sued for breach of contract due to Neumiller's (D) rejection of the remaining nine loads, and Neumiller (D) contended it simply was dissatisfied with the goods. The jury returned a verdict for Cornett (P), and Neumiller (D) appealed.

ISSUE: Does U.C.C. § 2-104 require a merchant's claim of dissatisfaction with tendered goods be made in objective good faith?

HOLDING AND DECISION: (Shores, J.) Yes. U.C.C. § 2-104 requires a merchant's claim of dissatisfaction with tendered goods, where his satisfaction is a condition precedent to acceptance, be made in good faith. The standard for judging such good faith is an objective standard measured by honesty in fact and observance of reasonable commercial standards of fair dealing in the trade. In this case, Neumiller (D), a potato broker, clearly qualified as a merchant. The fact that it accepted potatoes from a field at $2.00 per hundredweight and rejected potatoes from the same field at the higher contract price shows Neumiller (D) did not reject the potatoes for their chipping potential but to avoid the contract. As a result, Neumiller (D) failed to use good faith, and its rejection constituted a breach of contract. Affirmed.

EDITOR'S ANALYSIS: This case illustrates the application of the objective test of a party's good faith rejection of tendered goods as unsatisfactory to it. The objective test is imposed by the U.C.C. upon merchants, those normally dealing in goods of the kind involved. The test is normally applied to contracts involving satisfaction as to mechanical utility or fitness, areas which are objectively measurable. In contracts involving nonmerchants and calling for subjective satisfaction, a duty of good faith is imposed to prevent arbitrary rejection.

[For more information on good faith dealing obligations, see Casenote Law Outline on Contracts, Chapter 2, § I, Valuable Consideration: The Bargained-for Incursion of Legal Detriment.]

NOTES:

REID v. KEY BANK OF SOUTHERN MAINE, INC.

831 F.2d 9 (1st Cir. 1987).

NATURE OF CASE: Appeal of damages for breach of implied covenant of good faith.

FACT SUMMARY: Reid (P) asserted that Depositors acted in bad faith after cutting off Reid's (P) credit line.

CONCISE RULE OF LAW: The implied covenant of good faith is measured by an objective standard.

FACTS: From 1976 to 1979, Depositors Trust Co (Depositors), Key Bank of Southern Maine's (D) predecessor in interest, made a series of loans to Reid (P) for the operation of his painting business. In March 1979, Reid (P) and Depositors entered into a $25,000 commercial credit agreement. In May, Reid (P) was informed that he would not receive any more advances on his credit line. Reid (P) testified at trial and Depositors denied among other things that deposits to Reid's (P) account were improperly handled in an attempt to recover collateral on the loan made in March. Reid (P) further contended that Depositors' actions in terminating the credit arrangement were in bad faith and without cause. Depositors relied on an "on demand" clause in the agreement to accelerate the loan payments, but did not point to any triggering occurrences enumerated in the contract that caused the arrangement to be terminated. Reid (P) sued key Bank (D), as the successor of Depositors, and received an award of damages. This appeal followed.

ISSUE: Is the implied covenant of good faith measured by an objective standard?

HOLDING AND DECISION: (Bownes, C.J.) Yes. The implied covenant of good faith is measured by an objective standard. Although the note seemed to grant Depositors the right to immediate repayment of $25,000 "on demand." Reid (P) had not received and never was to receive this amount. According to testimony as to normal banking practices, Depositors neither relied on any default on Reid's (P) part nor followed any customary practice in registering complaints to him or asking him to alter his conduct in some manner. In short, Depositors could not explain why it abruptly terminated its arrangement with Reid (P). Affirmed.

EDITOR'S ANALYSIS: Inquiry into whether lender institutions have exercised bad faith focuses on the contract terms. Since it would be virtually impossible to provide for every contingency in a contract, the interpretation of a good faith requirement becomes important to the party who feels he was treated unfairly. A fairly intermediate and widely used definition of good faith would be a prohibition of opportunistic behavior. In the lender-borrower context, however, would it be reasonable to imagine that a lender would ever admit that its actions were based on anything but the borrower's ability to repay the loan?

[For more information on conditions implied-in-fact, see Casenote Law Outline on Contracts, Chapter 4, § II, Sources of Conditions in a Bargain.]

NOTES:

FELD v. HENRY S. LEVY & SONS, INC.
37 N.Y.2d 466, 373 N.Y.S.2d 102, 335 N.E.2d 320 (1975).

NATURE OF CASE: Suit alleging breach of an output contract.

FACT SUMMARY: Feld (P) contracted to purchase all bread crumbs produced by Levy (D) during a certain period. Levy (D) then dismantled its crumb-making machinery because the operation proved to be "uneconomical."

CONCISE RULE OF LAW: Implicit in every output contract is the understanding that the supplier will act in good faith in determining the quantity of goods which he will produce.

FACTS: Feld (P) entered into a written contract to purchase all bread crumbs produced by Henry S. Levy & Sons, Inc. (D) between June 19, 1968 and June 18, 1969. The contract included an automatic renewal provision but also gave each party the right to terminate the agreement upon six months' written notice. At the outset of the contract, Feld (P) delivered a performance bond and later presented a bond continuation certificate. Levy (D) sold bread crumbs to Feld (P) for nearly a year but then stopped producing the crumbs, explaining that the operation was "very uneconomical." Levy (D) finally dismantled its crumb-producing machinery, although offering to resume production if Feld (P) would agree to a price increase. Feld (P) instead filed suit, claiming that the output contract between the parties obligated Levy (D) to continue producing bread crumbs. Levy (D) argued that the contract required Levy (D) to sell its entire output, if any, of bread crumbs to Feld (P) but imposed no duty upon Levy (D) to produce any bread crumbs at all. The trial court denied motions for summary judgment by both parties, and the appellate court affirmed. Both Feld (P) and Levy (D) then appealed.

ISSUE: Does an output contract impose any duty upon the seller to continue producing the item which is the subject matter of the contract?

HOLDING AND DECISION: (Cooke, J.) Yes. Implicit in every output contract is the understanding that the supplier will act in good faith in determining the quantity of goods which he will produce. The Uniform Commercial Code clearly states that output contracts are not invalid for want of mutuality or because of indefiniteness. But, the Code does impose a requirement that both parties to such a contract act in good faith. In the context of this case, the good-faith rule obligates Levy (D) to continue producing bread crumbs unless that conduct would threaten the viability of Levy's (D) entire operation, including the related food-producing activities in which the company (D) is engaged. A showing that Levy's (D) profits from the contract were less than had been anticipated is not sufficient to relieve Levy (D) of the obligation to perform the contract. Since the extent to which Levy (D) has acted in good faith must be determined by the trial court, the motions for summary judgment were properly denied.

EDITOR'S ANALYSIS: The validity of output and requirement contracts was once very much in doubt. Today, the Uniform Commercial Code has foreclosed virtually all arguments against the validity of such contracts. The good-faith requirement imposed by the Code has also reduced the hazards which such contracts once entailed. No longer can the buyer demand, pursuant to a requirement contract, more goods than the seller can reasonably produce. Nor, as the Feld case illustrates, can the seller under an output contract produce an unreasonably small (or large) amount of merchandise.

[For more information on output contracts, see Casenote Law Outline on Contracts, Chapter 2, § I, Valuable Consideration: The Bargained-for Incursion of Legal Detriment.]

NOTES:

ROTH STEEL PRODUCTS v. SHARON STEEL CORP.

705 F.2d 134 (6th Cir. 1983).

NATURE OF CASE: Appeal from a breach of contract award.

FACT SUMMARY: Sharon (D) contended it was excused from performing under a contract with Roth (P) because of a modification that Roth (P) agreed to under Sharon's (D) threat to discontinue supplying steel completely.

CONCISE RULE OF LAW: A court must, in determining whether a particular modification was obtained in good faith, determine whether: (1) a party's conduct was consistent with reasonable commercial standards of fair dealing in the trade and (2) the parties were in fact motivated to seek modification by an honest desire to compensate for commercial exigencies.

FACTS: In 1972, during a slump in the steel industry, Roth (P) contracted to purchase 200 tons of hot rolled steel per month from Sharon (D) for $148 per ton. Subsequently, the industry experienced an increased demand, and all producers were soon operating at full capacity. Sharon (D) notified Roth (P) that it would discontinue all price concessions given in 1972. The parties renegotiated the contract, and Roth (P) agreed to a price modification primarily because they could not obtain steel elsewhere. Sharon (D) had experienced several cost increases on raw materials and was unable to get a sufficient supply of steel slab at an affordable price to allow it to operate profitably without the modification. Subsequently, Sharon (D) was unable to meet Roth's (P) steel needs, and Roth (P) sued for breach when it discovered Sharon (D) had been allocating steel to a subsidiary for sale at premium prices. Sharon (D) defended on the ground that the modification was valid and allowed it to raise prices, and Roth's (P) refusal to pay excused Sharon's (D) performance. The trial court found the modification unenforceable as not sought in good faith, and Sharon (D) appealed.

ISSUE: Must a court, in determining the validity of a modification, determine (1) a party's conduct was consistent with reasonable commercial standards of fair dealing; and (2) the parties were in fact motivated to seek the modification by an honest desire to compensate for commercial exigencies?

HOLDING AND DECISION: (Celebreeze, J.) Yes. A court must, in determining whether a modification was obtained in good faith, determine whether: (1) a party's conduct was consistent with reasonable commercial standards of fair dealing in the trade and (2) the parties were in fact motivated to seek modification by an honest desire to compensate for commercial exigencies. In this case, continued performance under the original contract would cause Sharon (D) to incur a loss. Therefore, it acted consistently with reasonable commercial standards in seeking a modification. However, under the second requirement, Sharon (D) had to demonstrate its honesty in fact. Sharon (D) failed to assert its alleged right to raise prices until the trial on this matter. Its failure to give this as a justification for its failure to supply Roth (P) indicates a lack of honesty in fact in seeking the modification. As a result, the modification was not made in good faith and was invalid. Therefore, Sharon's (D) failure to ship under the original contract was a breach. Affirmed.

EDITOR'S ANALYSIS: Some jurisdictions ignore questions of good or bad faith is assessing the validity of a contract modification. In Austin Instrument, Inc. v. Loral Corp., 272 N.E.2d 533 (1971), a New York court held that the question turns entirely upon concepts of economic duress. Such economic duress is shown where the threatened party is forced into a modification because he cannot obtain the goods elsewhere.

[For more information on modification of an existing contract, see Casenote Law Outline on Contracts, Chapter 2, § I, Valuable Consideration: The Bargained-for Incursion of Legal Detriment.]

NOTES:

AFC INTERIORS v. DICELLO

46 Ohio St. 3d 1, 544 N.E.2d 869 (1989).

NATURE OF THE CASE: Appeal from the court's denial that a balance of a debt was due.

FACT SUMMARY: DiCello, (D), debtor, sent a check for partial payment to AFC (P) and marked it "payment in full" in satisfaction of his debt, but AFC (P) crossed out the marking before depositing the check and sued for the balance.

CONCISE RULE OF LAW: In conditional check situations, § 1-207 of the Uniform Commercial Code supersedes the common law rule of accord and satisfaction.

FACTS: DiCello (D) sent a check to AFC (P) for a portion of his debt. However, the check was marked "payment in full." AFC (P) deposited the check after crossing out the marking and replacing it with the words "payment on account." AFC (P) filed suit to recover the balance of the debt when DiCello (D) refused to pay, arguing that the debt was satisfied by the deposit of the check. The court considered AFC's (P) deposit of the check as acceptance of the satisfaction, and AFC (P) appealed, arguing the U.C.C. § 1-207 should have been applied.

ISSUE: Does U.C.C. § 1-207 supersede the common law doctrine of accord and satisfaction in conditional check situations?

HOLDING AND DECISION: (Sweeny, J.) Yes. U.C.C. § 1-207 supersedes the common law doctrine of accord and satisfaction in conditional check situations. Common law treats the deposit of a conditional check as acceptance, unless the condition is waived or the check is fully rejected by the creditor. Consequently, a creditor is at loss if he either deposits a conditional check marked "payment in full" or if he rejects the check. The drafters of § 1-207 intended to prevent such injustice suffered by a creditor. This section allows for a creditor to reserve his right to collect the balance due when he deposits the check under protest. AFC (P) wrote the words "payment on account" on the check received, thus putting DiCello (D) on notice of intent to reserve his right to collect the balance owed. Reverse and remanded.

DISSENT: (Brown, J.) The common law doctrine should be preserved within the language of U.C.C. § 1-207 and not replaced. Section 1-207 should not be applied to these facts for several reasons. First, the code refers to one who "performs or promises performance or assents to performance in a manner demanded on offered by the other party." Here, AFC (P), creditor, crossed out the "payment in full" notation but did not perform or promise to perform. Furthermore, he was not consenting to performance in the manner requested by DiCello (D). Second, the majority interprets this section narrowly. Third, U.C.C. Article 3 does not allow a creditor to alter a check by changing its material term without consent of the drawer. Lastly, common law rule makes good policy.

EDITOR'S ANALYSIS: Replacing the common law doctrine of accord and satisfaction by the U.C.C. § 1-207 is the modern trend. States such as New York, Delaware, Florida, Massachusetts, and New Hampshire have joined this trend and have replaced the common law doctrine in conditional check situations. With this case, Ohio has followed, but only narrowly; the decision was reached by a 4-3 vote.

[For more information on accord and satisfaction, see Casenote Law Outline on Contracts, Chapter 2, § I, Valuable Consideration: The Bargained-for Incursion of Legal Detriment.]

NOTES:

SEUBERT v. McKESSON CORPORATION

223 Cal. App. 3d 1514 (1990).

NATURE OF THE CASE: Appeal from breach of implied covenant of good faith and dealing.

FACT SUMMARY: Seubert (P), who was hired by McKesson (D) to sell computer systems, was fired because his sales quota dropped when clients returned the incomplete system.

CONCISE RULE OF LAW: Covenants of good faith and fair dealing can be inferred from an at-will employment contract in order to limit the employer's power to discharge an employee.

FACTS: McKesson (D) hired Seubert (P) to sell its computer system to retail pharmacies. Prior to his acceptance of employment, Seubert (P) signed an application stating that his employment could be terminated at any time without notice. One year later, Seubert (P) accepted a promotion to become the sales manager for the western region after relying on McKesson's (D) assurance that the system was operational in that area. However, the system was not operational, and as a result Seubert (P) lost sales. A similar situation happened a year later when Seubert (P) was sent to Hawaii. In 1984, McKesson (D) adopted a nonretroactive policy requiring its sales personnel to meet a certain sales quota to maintain their employment. Three months later, Seubert (P) was fired for not meeting his quota. Seubert (P) won a $240,000 judgment against McKesson (D), which appealed.

ISSUE: Can covenants of good faith and dealing be inferred from an at-will employment contract to limit an employer's power to discharge an employee?

HOLDING AND DECISION: (Perley, J.) Yes. Covenants of good faith and dealing can be inferred from an at-will employment contract to limit an employer's right to discharge an employee. The application signed by Seubert (P) was a standardized two-page form that did not state his position or salary. The application further lacked an integration clause. Thus, it was not intended to be the entire employment agreement between the parties. The evidence of the informal practice of sales quotas before the actual adoption of the express sales quota policy supports the inference that Seubert (P) could not be fired without cause. Affirmed.

EDITOR'S ANALYSIS: In this case, McKesson (D) argued that the awarded damages were erroneous in light of the Foley case. This argument was rejected by the court since Foley only denied recovery of tort damages in a contract action. However, express or implied bad-faith discharge of an employee is a breach of contract. Thus, a discharged employee can seek compensatory damages where applicable.

[For more information on good faith, see Casenote Law Outline on Contracts, Chapter 4, § II, Sources of Conditions in a Bargain.]

NOTES:

CHAPTER 6
BREACH OF CONTACT AND PERMISSIBLE REMEDIAL RESPONSES

QUICK REFERENCE RULES OF LAW

1. **Right to Suspend Performance or Cancel upon Prospective Inability or Breach.** A party to a contract who renounces his intention to perform may not complain if the other party, instead of waiting until performance is due, elects to sue immediately for breach of contract. (Hochster v. De La Tour)

   [For more information on anticipatory repudiation, see Casenote Law Outline on Contracts, Chapter 4, § III, Maturing of Contract Duties: Satisfaction or Excuse of Conditions.]

2. **Right to Suspend Performance or Cancel upon Prospective Inability or Breach.** Anticipatory breach occurs only when one of the parties to a contract has expressly or impliedly repudiated the agreement. (Taylor v. Johnston)

   [For more information on anticipatory breach, see Casenote Law Outline on Contracts, Chapter 4, § III, Maturing of Contract Duties: Satisfaction or Excuse of Conditions.]

3. **Right to Suspend Performance or Cancel upon Prospective Inability or Breach.** Where reasonable grounds for insecurity exist, a party to a contract may demand adequate assurance of performance, and if such assurance is not forthcoming, that party may cancel the contract with impunity. (AMF, Inc. v. McDonald's Corp.)

   [For more information on assurance of performance, see Casenote Law Outline on Contracts, Chapter 4, § III, Maturing of Contract Duties: Satisfaction or Excuse of Conditions.]

4. **Right to Suspend Performance or Cancel upon Prospective Inability or Breach.** The failure of a buyer to make a payment on a (severable) installment contract will constitute a material breach of contract, excusing the seller from any further duty to perform, only where it is shown that such failure has either: (1) made such performance unreasonably economically burdensome for the seller or (2) made such performance an unreasonable economic risk for the seller to take. (Plotnick v. Pennsylvania Smelting & Refining Co.)

   [For more information on installment contracts, see Casenote Law Outline on Contracts, Chapter 7, § I, Breach — Disappointment of Reasonable Expectations.]

5. **Basic Policies of Compensatory Damages.** Damages for mental distress may be recovered for breach of a contract which so affects the vital concerns of the individual that severe mental distress is a foreseeable result of a breach. (Allen v. Jones)

   [For more information on the expectation interest, see Casenote Law Outline on Contracts, Chapter 7, § III, Remedies for Breach of Contract.]

6. **Basic Policies of Compensatory Damages.** Punitive damages are recoverable in breach of contract actions accompanied by defendant's tortious conduct. (F.D. Borkholder Co. v. Sandock)

   [For more information on punitive damages, see Casenote Law Outline on Contracts, Chapter 7, § III, Remedies for Breach of Contract.]

7. **Basic Policies of Compensatory Damages.** Although an award of punitive damages must be reasonably proportionate to the amount of actual damages suffered by the plaintiff, a judge or jury is entitled to exercise considerable discretion in determining the amount of punitive damages to be assessed. (Boise Dodge, Inc. v. Clark)

[For more information on punitive damages, see Casenote Law Outline on Contracts, Chapter 7, § III, Remedies for Breach of Contract.]

8. **Breach or Repudiation by Payor.** The doctrine of anticipatory breach is inapplicable to a suit to enforce contracts for future payment of money only, in installments or otherwise. (John Hancock Mutual Life Insurance Co. v. Cohen)

[For more information on anticipatory breach, see Casenote Law Outline on Contracts, Chapter 4, § III, Maturing of Contract Duties: Satisfaction or Excuse of Conditions.]

9. **Breach or Repudiation by Payor.** For breach of a real estate purchase contract, an injured party is entitled to recover his actual losses when the traditional recovery formula is inadequate. (American Mechanical Corp. v. Union Machine Co. of Lynn, Inc.)

[For more information on the recovery of foreseeable damages, see Casenote Law Outline on Contracts, Chapter 7, § III, Remedies for Breach of Contract.]

10. **Breach or Repudiation by Payor.** The inclusion of a provision in a construction contract for partial payments to be made as the work progresses does not, generally, render the contract divisible unless it is clear from the contract terms that each progress payment is intended to be so apportioned to the corresponding portion of the work as to be the full consideration for that portion of work. (New Era Homes Corp. v. Forster)

[For more information on installment contracts, see Casenote Law Outline on Contracts, Chapter 7, § I, Breach — Disappointment of Reasonable Expectations.]

11. **Breach or Repudiation by Payor.** An injured party is not entitled to a restitutionary remedy where the breaching party has not been enriched and cannot be put back in the position he would have been before the contract. (Bernstein v. Nemeyer)

[For more information on the restitution interest, see Casenote Law Outline on Contracts, Chapter 7, § III, Remedies for Breach of Contract.]

12. **Breach or Repudiation by Payor.** Where a lessee defaults on an agreement to lease an article, the supply of which is not limited, the lessor is not required to reduce his damages by the amount he actually did, or reasonably could, realize on a reletting of the article. (Locks v. Wade)

[For more information on recovery in restitution, see Casenote Law Outline on Contracts, Chapter 7, § III, Remedies for Breach of Contract.]

13. **Direct Damages.** Whether a seller breaches a contract by giving the buyer notice of renunciation or simply fails to perform, the damages awarded the buyer shall be measured as the difference between the contract price and the market price on the date delivery was due. (Reliance Cooperage Corp. v. Treat)

[For more information on the measure of damages, see Casenote Law Outline on Contracts, Chapter 7, § II, Affirmative Obligations of the Aggrieved Party.]

14. **Direct Damages.** In the case of faulty construction, the proper measure of damages is the market value of the cost to repair the faulty construction. (Rivers v. Deane)

[For more information on remedies for breach of contract, see Casenote Law Outline on Contracts, Chapter 7, § III, Remedies for Breach of Contract.]

15. **Direct Damages.** Only where the cost of completing the contract would entail unreasonable economic waste will the measure of damages for breach of a construction contract be diminution in value of the property in relation to what its value would have been if performance had been properly completed. (American Standard, Inc. v. Schectman)

[For more information on the measure of damages, see Casenote Law Outline on Contracts, Chapter 7, § III, Remedies for Breach of Contract.]

16. **Consequential Damages.** The injured party may recover those damages as may reasonably be considered arising naturally from the breach itself and, second, may recover those damages as may reasonably be supposed to have been in contemplation of the parties, at the time they made the contract, as the probable result of a breach of it. (Hadley v. Baxendale)

[For more information on foreseeability of damages, see Casenote Law Outline on Contracts, Chapter 7, § III, Remedies for Breach of Contract.]

17. **Consequential Damages.** A party who breaches a contract may be held liable for all damages which could reasonably have been anticipated at the time the agreement was entered into. (Spang Industries, Inc., Fort Pitt Bridge Division v. Aetna Casualty & Surety Co.)

[For more information on foreseeable damages, see Casenote Law Outline on Contracts, Chapter 7, § III, Remedies for Breach of Contract.]

18. **Consequential Damages.** Consequential damages must be reasonably foreseeable, ascertainable, and unavoidable. (Hydraform Products Corp. v. American Steel & Aluminum Corp.)

[For more information on limitations on consequential damages, see Casenote Law Outline on Contracts, Chapter 7, § III, Remedies for Breach of Contract.]

19. **Consequential Damages.** A promisee may recover costs incurred in reliance on the promisor's promise to perform, subject to the privilege of the promisor to reduce such recovery by as much as he can show that the promisee would have lost if the contract had been performed. (L. Albert & Son v. Armstrong Rubber Co.)

[For more information on reliance recoveries, see Casenote Law Outline on Contracts, Chapter 7, § III, Remedies for Breach of Contract.]

20. **Prevention, Hindrance, and the Duty of Cooperation.** To be released from performance based on the plaintiff's actions hindering such, the defendant must show he did as much as he could to perform in spite of the plaintiff's hindrance. (Blandford v. Andrews)

[For more information on good faith dealing obligations, see Casenote Law Outline on Contracts, Chapter 2, § I, Valuable Consideration: The Bargained-for Incursion of Legal Detriment.]

21. **Prevention, Hindrance, and the Duty of Cooperation.** In every contract there is an implied promise on the part of each party that he will not intentionally and purposely do anything to prevent the other party from carrying out the agreement on his part. (Patterson v. Meyerhoff)

[For more information on impossibility of performance, see Casenote Law Outline on Contracts, Chapter 6, § I, Excusable Non-Performance under the Common Law.]

22. **Prevention, Hindrance, and the Duty of Cooperation.** Mere difficulty of performance will not excuse a breach of contract even though that difficulty was created by the other contracting party. (Iron Trade Products Co. v. Wilkoff Co.)

[For more information on excusable non-performance, see Casenote Law Outline on Contracts, Chapter 6, § II, Excusable Non-Performance under the U.C.C.]

23. **Prevention, Hindrance, and the Duty of Cooperation.** A clause in a real estate sales contract which makes the buyer's obtaining financing a condition precedent to his duty to perform imposes on the buyer an implied duty to make reasonable good-faith efforts to satisfy the condition. (Billman v. Hensel)

[For more information on conditions precedent, see Casenote Law Outline on Contracts, Chapter 4, § I, Classification of Conditions According to Their Impact upon the Modified Promise.]

24. **Equitable Remedies for Breach of Contract.** Specific performance of a contract for personalty will be granted where the goods cannot be obtained elsewhere and they are necessary to the plaintiff's business. (Curtice Brothers Co. v. Catts)

[For more information on equitable intervention, see Casenote Law Outline on Contracts, Chapter 7, § III, Remedies for Breach of Contract.]

25. **Equitable Remedies for Breach of Contract.** Specific performance will be imposed where the terms of the contract clearly express the duties of the parties and the conditions under which performance is due. (Laclede Gas Co. v. Amoco Oil Co.)

[For more information on decrees of specific performance, see Casenote Law Outline on Contracts, Chapter 7, § III, Remedies for Breach of Contract.]

26. **Equitable Remedies for Breach of Contract.** Specific performance is not available if damages are an adequate remedy, and it is unlikely the order would ever be implemented. (Northern Indiana Public Service Co. v. Carbon County Coal Co.)

[For more information on specific performance, see Casenote Law Outline on Contracts, Chapter 7, § III, Remedies for Breach of Contract.]

27. **Equitable Remedies for Breach of Contract.** Where the costs of injunctive relief are less than the costs of a damages remedy, injunctive relief is an appropriate remedy, even when the damage remedy is not shown to be inadequate. (Walgreen Co. v. Sara Creek Property Co.)

[For more information on equitable relief, see Casenote Law Outline on Contracts, Chapter 7, § III, Remedies for Breach of Contract.]

28. **Equitable Remedies for Breach of Contract.** Negative enforcement of an employment contract may only be granted, once the contract has terminated, to prevent injury from unfair competition or to enforce an express and valid anticompetitive covenant. (American Broadcasting Companies v. Wolf)

[For more information on decrees of specific performance, see Casenote Law Outline on Contracts, Chapter 7, § III, Remedies for Breach of Contract.]

29. **Liquidated Damages.** The situation existing at the time of the contract's execution is controlling in determining the reasonableness of liquidated damages. (Southwest Engineering Co. v. United States)

[For more information on liquidated damage provisions, see Casenote Law Outline on Contracts, Chapter 7, § III, Remedies for Breach of Contract.]

30. **Liquidated Damages.** Liquidated damage clauses will be upheld if they bear a reasonable proportion to the probable loss and the amount of actual loss is incapable of precise estimation. (United Air Lines, Inc. v. Austin Travel Corp.)

    [For more information on liquidated damages clause, see Casenote Law Outline on Contracts, Chapter 7, § III, Remedies for Breach of Contract.]

31. **Liquidated Damages.** Equity will not enforce a liquidated damages clause if to allow the seller to retain the specified sum would shock the court's conscience. (Leeber v. Deltona Corp.)

    [For more information on liquidated damages clause, see Casenote Law Outline on Contracts, Chapter 7, § III, Remedies for Breach of Contract.]

32. **Agreed Remedies.** Contractual limitations on the recovery of consequential damages for breach are valid unless it is established that the limitations were unconscionable. (Lewis Refrigeration Co. v. Sawyer Fruit, Vegetable and Cold Storage Co.)

    [For more information on consequential damages, see Casenote Law Outline on Contracts, Chapter 7, § III, Remedies for Breach of Contract.]

33. **Role of Architect or Engineer.** Parties to a contract may agree that their disputes will be determinatively settled by a third party. (Bolton Corp. v. T.A. Loving Co.)

34. **Arbitration.** A claim of fraud in the inducement goes to the making of a contract and thus falls within an arbitration clause covering controversies arising out of relating to the making of a contract. (Michael-Curry Co. v. Knutson Shareholders)

35. **Arbitration.** An arbitrator's decisions about contract interpretation or the merits of the claims presented to him shall not be reviewed during a hearing to judicially confirm the arbitration award. (Container Technology Corp. v. J. Gadsden Pty., Ltd.)

HOCHSTER v. DE LA TOUR

Q.B., 2 E. & B. 678, 118 Eng. Rep. 922 (1853).

NATURE OF CASE: Action to recover damages for breach of contract.

FACT SUMMARY: Before Hochster (P) was due to perform his contract of employment for De La Tour (D), De La Tour (D) announced his intention to repudiate the contract, whereupon Hochster (P) immediately commenced an action for breach of contract.

CONCISE RULE OF LAW: A party to a contract who renounces his intention to perform may not complain if the other party, instead of waiting until performance is due, elects to sue immediately for breach of contract.

FACTS: In April, Hochster (P) contracted to serve as De La Tour's (D) employee beginning on June 1. On May 11, De La Tour (D) wrote to Hochster (P) that he had changed his mind and declined Hochster's (P) services. On May 22, Hochster (P) brought this action for breach of contract.

ISSUE: When the time for performance has not arrived, but one party nevertheless indicates his intention not to perform, must the other party wait until the performance should have occurred before bringing action for breach of contract?

HOLDING AND DECISION: (Lord Campbell) No. "The man who wrongfully renounces a contract into which he has deliberately entered cannot justly complain if he is immediately sued for compensation in damages by the man whom he has injured; and it seems reasonable to allow an option to the injured party, either to sue immediately, or to wait till the time when the act was to be done." If Hochster (P) had to wait until June 1 to sue, he would not be able to enter any employment which would interfere with his promise to begin work at that time. But it is surely more rational that after renunciation by De La Tour (D), Hochster (P) should be at liberty to consider himself absolved from any future performance. Thus, he would be free to seek other employment in mitigation of damages. De La Tour's (D) renunciation may be treated as a breach of contract.

EDITOR'S ANALYSIS: This is the leading case on the so-called doctrine of anticipatory breach. The court's reasoning is erroneous insofar as it felt that Hochster (P) would otherwise be caught in a dilemma: to remain idle and hope for a favorable future judgment or to obtain other employment and thereby forfeit his rights against De La Tour (D). The court overlooked the rule that where a party manifests prospective unwillingness to perform, the other party may suspend his performance and change his position without surrendering his right to sue after the breach occurs. In other words, the court could have considered the repudiation as (1) a defense to an action brought by De La Tour (D) and (2) an excuse of the constructive condition that Hochster (P) be ready, willing, and able to perform on June 1.

[For more information on anticipatory repudiation, see Casenote Law Outline on Contracts, Chapter 4, § III, Maturing of Contract Duties: Satisfaction or Excuse of Conditions.]

NOTES:

TAYLOR v. JOHNSTON

Cal. Sup. Ct., 15 Cal. 3d 130 (1975).

NATURE OF CASE: Suit seeking damages for breach of contract.

FACT SUMMARY: Taylor (P) contracted to breed his mares with the Johnstons' (D) stallion. The Johnstons (D) later sold their stallion, and the horse was never bred with Taylor's (P) mares.

CONCISE RULE OF LAW: Anticipatory breach occurs only when one of the parties to a contract has expressly or impliedly repudiated the agreement.

FACTS: Taylor (P) entered into a contract to breed two of his mares, Sunday Slippers and Sandy Fork, with a stallion owned by the Johnstons (D). The agreement provided that breeding with the stallion, Fleet Nasrullah, would take place in the following year, 1966, and contained a clause allowing a free breeding the next year for a mare which failed to produce a live foal as a result of the 1966 breeding. Late in 1965, the Johnstons (D) sold Fleet Nasrullah, and the horse was shipped to Kentucky, where various shareholders acquired the right to breed their mares with him. The Johnstons (D) notified Taylor (P) of the sale, advising Taylor (P) that they considered themselves released from their agreement with him by reason of the sale. When Taylor (P) threatened litigation, the Johnstons (D) agreed to allow Sunday Slippers and Sandy Fork to breed with Fleet Nasrullah in Kentucky. During early 1966, both mares were in foal, and Sunday Slippers gave birth on April 17 and Sandy Fork did likewise on June 5. Taylor's (P) agent tried three times to arrange for Fleet Nasrullah to breed with Sunday Slippers while the mare was in heat and tried once to arrange for the breeding of Fleet Nasrullah and Sandy Fork. No appointments could be made for Taylor's (P) horses because shareholders of Fleet Nasrullah had booked his services for the days that the Taylor (P) mares were to be in heat. Taylor (P) eventually gave up trying to book Fleet Nasrullah and, in June of 1966, bred each mare with Chateaugay, a former Kentucky Derby winner. Both mares became pregnant by Chateaugay but were subsequently aborted when it was discovered that they were carrying twins. Taylor (P) eventually sued the Johnstons (D) for breach of contract, and the Johnstons (D) counterclaimed for stud fees. The trial court, concluding that the sale of Fleet Nasrullah coupled with the subsequent inability of the Johnstons' (D) agents to arrange for the stallion to breed with the two mares constituted a repudiation and a breach of the contract, rendered judgment for Taylor (P) in the amount of more than $103,000. On appeal, the Johnstons (D) claimed that they had not repudiated or breached the contract and that it had been Taylor's (P) conduct in breeding his horses with Chateaugay which had made performance of the agreement impossible.

ISSUE: Should a party be deemed to have anticipatorily breached a contract if he has caused the other party to believe that he will not perform the agreement?

HOLDING AND DECISION: (Sullivan, J.) No. Anticipatory breach occurs only when one of the parties to a contract has expressly or impliedly repudiated the agreement. An express repudiation requires a clear, positive, unequivocal refusal to perform. And an express repudiation results when one party puts it out of his power to perform the contract. In this case, the Johnstons (D) did initially repudiate the contract by telling Taylor (P) that the sale of Fleet Nasrullah made performance impossible. But, Taylor (P) elected to treat the agreement as still in force, and the Johnstons (D) retracted their prior repudiation when they made Fleet Nasrullah available for breeding with Taylor's (P) mares in Kentucky. Once the contract had been thus reinstated, the Johnstons (D) had until the end of 1966 or, at a minimum, until the end of the 1966 breeding season to mate Fleet Nasrullah with Sunday Slippers and Sandy Fork. The Johnstons (D), for all that the evidence discloses, stood willing to perform their contractual obligation. Performance became impossible only when Taylor (P) elected to breed his mares with Chateaugay instead of with Fleet Nasrullah. It follows that the Johnstons (D) did not repudiate or commit an anticipatory breach and therefore are not liable to Taylor (P) for damages.

EDITOR'S ANALYSIS: Even when it is clear that an anticipatory breach has occurred, the nonbreaching party has a choice of remedies to pursue. He may treat the contract as at an end and sue for damages immediately. However, he may also wait until the time fixed for performance has arrived and may sue for damages at that time if the prescribed performance is not tendered. The latter course may be advantageous in that it allows the breaching party an additional opportunity to perform, but if that party cures the breach, the aggrieved party may not, of course, recover damages for the anticipatory breach which occurred but was condoned.

[For more information on anticipatory breach, see Casenote Law Outline on Contracts, Chapter 4, § III, Maturing of Contract Duties: Satisfaction or Excuse of Conditions.]

NOTES:

AMF, INC. v. McDONALD'S CORP.

536 F.2d 1167 (7th Cir. 1976).

NATURE OF CASE: Suit to recover damages; suit to recover the price of allegedly defective merchandise.

FACT SUMMARY: AMF (P) contracted to sell computerized cash registers to McDonald's (D) and some of its licensees but was unable to manufacture enough workable cash registers to fill the order.

CONCISE RULE OF LAW: Where reasonable grounds for insecurity exist, a party to a contract may demand adequate assurance of performance, and if such assurance is not forthcoming, that party may cancel the contract with impunity.

FACTS: McDonald's Corporation (D) was interested in installing AMF, Inc. (P) Model 72C computerized cash registers in its restaurants. It was agreed that a 72C unit would be installed in a subsidiary of McDonald's (D) located in Elk Grove, Illinois. Later, McDonald's (D) ordered 16 72C units for its restaurants, and orders were subsequently received from seven McDonald's (D) licensees. Furthermore, McDonald's (D) paid approximately $20,000 for the unit which had previously been installed in the Elk Grove restaurant. Soon after accepting the orders, AMF (P) revised existing schedules to provide for later deliveries of the cash registers. Then, McDonald's (D) had AMF (P) remove the unit from the Elk Grove restaurant because of a continuing lack of effective performance. Representatives of the two companies met, and AMF (P) agreed to formulate performance standards, which the parties were never able to agree upon, and to hold up production of the machines which McDonald's (D) had ordered. AMF (P) then learned that satisfactory 72C units could not be produced at its Vandalia, Ohio plant, where production of McDonald's (D) machines was to have taken place. After that, it was apparently mutually understood that the McDonald's (D) order would not be filled. AMF (P) then sued for damages, alleging wrongful cancellation and repudiation of the contracts to sell 72C units to McDonald's (D) and its licensees. The Elk Grove restaurant then sued to recover the price of the register installed by AMF (P) as well as the amount of losses occasioned by the failure of the machine to function properly. The two cases were tried together, and in each case the relief sought was denied. AMF (P) appealed from the orders denying it relief against McDonald's (D) and its licensees.

ISSUE: May a party cancel a contract if there is no satisfactory response to his proper and reasonable demand that the other party provide adequate assurance of performance?

HOLDING AND DECISION: (Cummings, C.J.) Yes. Where reasonable grounds for insecurity exist, a party to a contract may demand adequate assurance of performance, and if such assurance is not forthcoming, that party may cancel the contract with impunity. In this case, McDonald's (D) clearly had the "reasonable grounds for insecurity" contemplated by § 2-609 of the Uniform Commercial Code. Therefore, McDonald's (D) was entitled to demand adequate assurance of performance and was not required to do so in writing since AMF (P) knew that McDonald's (D) had suspended its own performance pending receipt of adequate assurance. When AMF (P) provided "assurance" of a clearly inadequate nature, it effectively repudiated the contract according to § 2-609(4) of the Code. At that point, § 2-610(h) permitted McDonald's (D) to cancel its outstanding orders. McDonald's (D) ultimately did so and thereby was absolved of further liability to perform.

EDITOR'S ANALYSIS: At common law, his counterpart's apparent anticipatory breach or prospective inability to perform left a party to a contract in something of a quandary. He was forced to elect between terminating his own performance, thereby inviting an action for breach of contract, and continuing his own performance despite the prospect of receiving no quid pro quo. It was in an effort to establish some kind of middle ground that the Uniform Commercial Code developed the procedure of demanding assurance of performance, justifiable cancellation being the remedy of the party who receives no adequate assurance. The Code approach is both reasonable and commercially realistic.

[For more information on assurance of performance, see Casenote Law Outline on Contracts, Chapter 4, § III, Maturing of Contract Duties: Satisfaction or Excuse of Conditions.]

NOTES:

PLOTNICK v. PA. SMELTING & REFINING CO.

194 F.2d 859 (1952).

NATURE OF CASE: Action for breach of contract.

FACT SUMMARY: Plotnick (P) refused to make further shipments of lead after Pennsylvania (D) failed to make an installment payment pursuant to a contract for that lead.

CONCISE RULE OF LAW: The failure of a buyer to make a payment on a (severable) installment contract will constitute a material breach of contract, excusing the seller from any further duty to perform, only where it is shown that such failure has either: (1) made such performance unreasonably economically burdensome for the seller or (2) made such performance an unreasonable economic risk for the seller to take.

FACTS: Plotnick (P) was a Canadian supplier of battery lead. In 1947, he entered into a series of installment contracts with Pennsylvania Smelting (D) for the sale of such lead. The shipments of lead and installment payments for the lead were frequently late. On the last contract, Pennsylvania (D) refused to pay for a shipment until Plotnick (P) promised to ship the entire balance of the contract lead within 30 days. Plotnick (P) refused to ship further lead until earlier shipment installment was paid. Finally, after a series of communications, Plotnick (P) gave notice that he considered the contract to have been canceled by Pennsylvania (D) and instituted this action to recover the third installment. Pennsylvania (D) counterclaimed for damages for breach of contract by Plotnick (P) for failing to complete the contract shipments. From judgment granting both the claim and the counterclaim, Plotnick (P) appealed.

ISSUE: Is the seller of goods in an installment contract automatically excused from the duty to complete performance by the buyer's failure to make an installment payment?

HOLDING AND DECISION: (Hastie, C.J.) No. The failure of a buyer to make a payment on a (severable) installment contract will constitute a material breach of contract, excusing the seller from any further duty to perform, only where it has shown that such failure has either: (1) made such performance unreasonably economically burdensome for the seller or (2) made such performance an unreasonable economic risk for the seller to take. Not all breaches of contract excuse counterperformance. Here, Plotnick (P) failed to establish a material breach which would excuse his performance. No evidence was produced that Pennsylvania's (D) failure to pay placed any real economic burden on Plotnick (P). Furthermore, the fact that Pennsylvania's (D) credit rating remained sound, that it needed the lead badly due to a fluctuation in the market price at the time, and that it offered payment at the end of each delivery (by sight draft) all suggest that there was no real risk involved for Plotnick (P) in further shipments. As such, his failure to perform was a material breach itself. The counterclaim was proper. Judgment affirmed.

EDITOR'S ANALYSIS: This case points up the essential distinction between material (i.e., discharging the duty of counterperformance) and minor breaches of contract. In either type, a right to damages and the duty to cooperate to cure (within a reasonable time) and to mitigate damages arise for the aggrieved party. Only where a breach is material, however, will the duty of counterperformance be excused. Though no set criteria for making the distinction between material and minor breaches is readily definable, it is generally stated that a material breach occurs when damages alone (i.e., without excusing counterperformance) are not likely to protect the aggrieved party or where he will not or is not substantially likely to be able to enjoy the benefit of the bargain which he has made.

[For more information on installment contracts, see Casenote Law Outline on Contracts, Chapter 7, § I, Breach – Disappointment of Reasonable Expectations.]

NOTES:

ALLEN v. JONES

Cal. Ct. of App., 104 Cal. App. 3d 207 (1980).

NATURE OF CASE: Appeal from denial of damages for mental anguish caused by a breach of contract.

FACT SUMMARY: The trial court held that Allen (P) failed to state a cause of action in his suit against Jones (D) for mental anguish suffered as a result of Jones' (D) negligence in performing a contract to cremate Allen's (D) brother's remains.

CONCISE RULE OF LAW: Damages for mental distress may be recovered for breach of a contract which so affects the vital concerns of the individual that severe mental distress is a foreseeable result of a breach.

FACTS: Allen (P) entered into an oral contract whereby Jones' (D) mortuary would cremate the remains of Allen's (P) brother and ship them from California to Illinois for $516. Allen (P) sued, contending that as a result of Jones' (D) negligence, the remains were lost, causing Allen (P) to suffer mental anguish and emotional distress. The trial court sustained Jones' (D) demurrer, and Allen (P) appealed.

ISSUE: May damages for mental distress be recovered in a breach of contract action?

HOLDING AND DECISION: (Tamura, J.) Yes. Damages for mental distress may be recovered for the breach of a contract which so affects the vital concerns of the individual that mental distress is a foreseeable result of the breach. It is clear that a mortician contracting with the bereaved relatives of the deceased to prepare the remains for interment could reasonably foresee that breach of the contract would cause great mental distress. As a result, such a contract so affects the bereaved's vital concerns that breach will give rise to recovery for emotional distress even where such is not evidenced by physical injuries. Therefore, Jones' (D) demurrer should have been overruled. Reversed.

EDITOR'S ANALYSIS: Section 868 of the Restatement Second of Torts establishes a cause of action for the intentional, reckless, or negligent conduct preventing proper interment of a dead body. The cause of action rests on the interference with the exclusive right of control over the body. This right has been recognized as a property right. This case falls within a borderland between tort and contract. The injury incurred is clearly a tort injury, yet it is caused by a breach of contract. Allen (P) not only lost the benefit of his bargain but also suffered physical injury.

[For more information on the expectation interest, see Casenote Law Outline on Contracts, Chapter 7, § III, Remedies for Breach of Contract.]

NOTES:

F. D. BORKHOLDER COMPANY, INC. v. SANDOCK

274 Ind. 612, 413 N.E.2d 567 (1980).

NATURE OF THE CASE: Appeal from award of damages for breach of a contract.

FACT SUMMARY: Borkholder (D) agreed to build an addition to Sandock's (P) showroom in accordance with certain specifications, but Borkholder (D) breached the contract when the addition did not conform to the specifications agreed upon.

CONCISE RULE OF LAW: Punitive damages are recoverable in breach of contract actions accompanied by defendant's tortious conduct.

FACTS: Borkholder (D) agreed to add a showroom/warehouse to Sandock's (P) furniture store. The contract provided that the addition be in accordance with certain specifications that were required to eliminate recurring moisture problems. However, the addition was constructed contrary to the specifications. Upon notification by Sandock (P) of the moisture problem, Borkholder's (D) president reassured that the situation would be remedied. In reliance, Sandock (P) withheld $1,000 from the contract price and tendered the remaining balance. Borkholder (D) breached the contract when the problem was not corrected. As a result, Sandock (P) was awarded compensatory and punitive damages.

ISSUE: Can punitive damages be recovered in an action for breach of contract accompanied with defendant's tortious conduct?

HOLDING AND DECISION: (Hunter, J.) Yes. Punitive damages are an appropriate remedy in a breach of contract actions accompanied by a separate tort or a tortious act of defendant. Awarding punitive damages furthers the public interest by punishing and deterring the wrongdoer from engaging in similar conduct. Such awards are particularly appropriate in consumer fraud cases where one relies on the expertise of the seller. Here, after discussing the moisture problem, Sandock (P) relied on the expertise of Borkholder (D) and its construction plans for the showroom addition. Borkholder (D) knowingly deviated from the plan and was deceitful and grossly negligent in its dealings with Sandock (P). Thus, the punitive and compensatory award of damages were appropriate. Affirmed.

DISSENT: (DeBruler, J.) The deviations in the construction constituted a simple breach of contract. There was no misrepresentation of facts to create a tortious conduct by Borkholder (D). Thus, punitive damages were inappropriate.

EDITOR'S ANALYSIS: Punitive damages or exemplary damages are almost never awarded in breach of contract cases. The idea behind awards of damages in breach of contract cases is to restore the wronged party to his original position by compensating him for his losses that resulted from the breach. On the other hand, the purpose of punitive damages is to punish the wrongdoer and not to compensate the injured party. However, punitive damages may be recovered when the breach of contract also constitutes a tort.

[For more information on punitive damages, see Casenote Law Outline on Contracts, Chapter 7, § III, Remedies for Breach of Contract.]

NOTES:

BOISE DODGE, INC. v. CLARK

Idaho Sup. Ct., 92 Idaho 902, 453 P.2d 551 (1969).

NATURE OF CASE: Suit to recover pursuant to a contract; counterclaim to recover damages.

FACT SUMMARY: Boise Dodge (P) sold Clark (D) what was supposedly a new car. Clark (D) later discovered that the car was used and that Boise Dodge (P) had turned back the odometer.

CONCISE RULE OF LAW: Although an award of punitive damages must be reasonably proportionate to the amount of actual damages suffered by the plaintiff, a judge or jury is entitled to exercise considerable discretion in determining the amount of punitive damages to be assessed.

FACTS: Clark (D) purchased a car from Boise Dodge, Inc. (P). The car's odometer registered 165 miles, and the salesman described the vehicle as "new." Clark (D) later learned that the car had been used as a demonstrator and that the odometer had registered nearly 7,000 miles before Boise Dodge (P) had turned it back. Clark (D) then stopped payment on two checks which, together with a trade-in car worth $1,100, had been given as consideration for the "new" car. Boise Dodge (P) sued on the checks, but Clark (D) counterclaimed for actual and punitive damages, alleging breach of contract and deceit. A jury awarded Clark (D) $350 in actual damages, representing the difference between the purported value of the car and its true worth, and also awarded $12,500 in punitive damages. On appeal, Boise Dodge (P) challenged the award of punitive damages.

ISSUE: May punitive damages be awarded which are substantially in excess of the actual damages suffered by a plaintiff?

HOLDING AND DECISION: (McQuade, J.) Yes. Although an award of punitive damages must be reasonably proportionate to the amount of actual damages suffered by the plaintiff, a judge or jury is entitled to exercise considerable discretion in determining the amount of punitive damages to be assessed. In this case, it was proper to assess punitive damages against Boise Dodge (P) despite its corporate status. A corporation may not insulate itself from punitive damages merely by disavowing the acts of its employees, especially when, as in the present case, management personnel were apparently aware of and responsible for deceitful conduct. And it cannot be said that the amount of punitive damages assessed against Boise Dodge (P) was unreasonable. All jury instructions relating to punitive damages were properly issued, and the jury was entitled to consider various factors in determining the appropriate amount of those damages. Boise Dodge (P) perpetrated a particularly reprehensible fraud, not only against Clark (D) but against the consuming public generally. In fixing punitive damages at $12,500, the jury was apparently motivated not by passion or prejudice but by a desire to deter similar conduct in the future. Therefore, the award of the court below must be affirmed.

EDITOR'S ANALYSIS: Ordinarily, punitive damages are not recoverable for breach of contract. However, such damages may be awarded for wanton and malicious breach or when a claim sounds in both tort and contract. Most courts are reluctant to articulate or employ any mechanical formula for fixing the appropriate amount of punitive damages. Since a major purpose of punitive damages is to deter a wrongdoer from repeating his unlawful conduct, the amount of punitive damages which should be awarded in a particular case may depend on the financial status of the defendant. In other words, a comparatively large punitive damage assessment may be necessary in order to deter a multimillion dollar-corporation from engaging in deceitful practices, whereas a smaller award may serve as an effective deterrent if a tiny company or an individual is involved.

[For more information on punitive damages, see Casenote Law Outline on Contracts, Chapter 7, § III, Remedies for Breach of Contract.]

NOTES:

JOHN HANCOCK MUTUAL LIFE INS. CO. v. COHEN

254 F.2d 417 (9th Cir. 1958).

NATURE OF CASE: Action against an insurer by a beneficiary.

FACT SUMMARY: Cohen (P) was the beneficiary of a John Hancock (D) life insurance policy under which she was to receive monthly payments for 20 years. After 15 years, John Hancock (D) refused to continue making payments on the ground that the policy was issued for 20 years by mistake.

CONCISE RULE OF LAW: The doctrine of anticipatory breach is inapplicable to a suit to enforce contracts for future payment of money only, in installments or otherwise.

FACTS: Cohen (P) was the beneficiary of a John Hancock (D) life insurance policy under which she was to receive monthly payments for 20 years and a final lump sum. John Hancock (D) made payments for 15 years and then tendered the lump-sum payment. It alleged that the policy was issued for 20 years by mistake and that both parties intended 15-year protection. The trial court found for Cohen (P) on the mistake issue and held that John Hancock (D) had breached the contract by anticipatory repudiation. It awarded Cohen (P) the installments due and to become due and the final payment.

ISSUE: Is the doctrine of anticipatory breach applicable to a case of an unconditional unilateral contract for the payment of money in installments?

HOLDING AND DECISION: (Barnes, C.J.) No. The general rule is that the doctrine of anticipatory breach has no application to suits to enforce contracts for future payments of money only, in installments or otherwise. That doctrine is not applicable to enforce unconditional unilateral contracts such as the one involved here, under which an insurer has promised to pay definite sums of money at a specified future date. To allow a present recovery for all future benefits would change the terms of such contracts and would force the insurer to pay now what it contracted to pay later. Here, Cohen (P) should recover all payments due, but future payments should not be paid until they fall due. It is decreed that they shall so be paid.

EDITOR'S ANALYSIS: Corbin argued that it is wrong to limit the doctrine of anticipatory repudiation to cases where the plaintiff still has part of the exchange to perform. With regard to Cohen, Corbin stated that justice would also have been achieved if Cohen (P) had been given judgment for the full amount of the future installments property discounted to "present value." He argued, "These were definite in number and amount and could be adequately discounted. This would be a judgment for `damages' and not accelerated specific performance."

[For more information on anticipatory breach, see Casenote Law Outline on Contracts, Chapter 4, § III, Maturing of Contract Duties: Satisfaction or Excuse of Conditions.]

NOTES:

AMERICAN MECHANICAL CORP. v. UNION MACHINE CO. OF LYNN INC.

21 Mass. App. Ct. 97, 485 N.E.2d 680 (1985).

NATURE OF THE CASE: Appeal from award of nominal damages for breach of contract action.

FACT SUMMARY: When Union's (D) repudiation of its contract with American Mechanical Corp. (P) to purchase its real estate and machinery led to the foreclosure of its property, American (P) filed suit for breach of contract.

CONCISE RULE OF LAW: For breach of a real estate purchase contract, an injured party is entitled to recover his actual losses when the traditional recovery formula is inadequate.

FACTS: American (P) agreed to sell its real property to Union (D) for $135,000. Union (D) entered into the contract knowing that American (P) was in financial difficulty and was pressed by the bank to sell the real property. One month later, Union (D) repudiated the contract. After American (P) was unable to find another purchaser, the bank foreclosed and sold the property for $55,000. The machinery was sold for $35,000. In an action brought by American (P), the court concluded that there was a breach of contract but awarded only nominal damages.

ISSUE: Should actual losses suffered in a breach of a contract for real estate purchase be awarded to the injured party when the traditional recovery formula is inadequate?

HOLDING AND DECISION: (Fine, J.) Yes. For breach of a real estate purchase contract, the injured party can recover for the actual losses he suffered. The general rule is to place the injured party in the position he would have been had the contract been performed. Thus, in case of a breach, the injured party can recover foreseeable damages that were contemplated by the parties at the time of the contract. In an action for breach of a real estate purchase contract, the damages are measured by calculating the difference between the contract price and the market price at the time of the breach. When this formula creates an inadequate remedy, as in this case, the injured party should be compensated for the actual losses he has incurred. Here, the property was sold at a foreclosure sale for below the full market value. Thus, to give an adequate remedy, the correct measure of damages should be the difference between the contract price and the foreclosure sale price. American (P) proved that it suffered a $45,000 loss after receiving only $90,000 after the foreclosure of the property and sale of his machinery. [The judgment was vacated, and American (P) was awarded $46,000.]

EDITOR'S ANALYSIS: The amount of damages awarded could have been reduced to the extent that American (P) could have mitigated its damages. The breaching party has the burden of proving that certain losses could have been avoided. The court found as a matter of fact that American (P) was unable to secure another purchaser on time. It should also be noted that the formula assessing damages by the difference between the contract price and the market price has generally been applied to contracts for sale of improved property or for lease of realty.

[For more information on the recovery of foreseeable damages, see Casenote Law Outline on Contracts, Chapter 7, § III, Remedies for Breach of Contract.]

NOTES:

NEW ERA HOMES CORP. v. FORSTER
N.Y. Ct. of App., 299 N.Y. 303, 86 N.E.2d 757 (1949).

NATURE OF CASE: Action to recover payment due under a contract.

FACT SUMMARY: Under its contract to remodel Forster's (D) home, New Era (P) was to be paid certain amounts at certain stages. When Forster (D) refused to make the third payment, New Era (P) brought this action to recover the amount of the payment.

CONCISE RULE OF LAW: The inclusion of a provision in a construction contract for partial payments to be made as the work progresses does not, generally, render the contract divisible unless it is clear from the contract terms that each progress payment is intended to be so apportioned to the corresponding portion of the work as to be the full consideration for that portion of work.

FACTS: New Era's (P) construction contract with Forster (D) fixed a total price for the work, but payments were to be paid upon the signing of the contract, upon New Era's (P) starting work, upon its completion of the rough carpentry, and upon completion of the whole job. When the rough carpentry was done, Forster (D) refused to make the third payment, and New Era (P) brought suit to recover the amount of the payment. New Era (P) offered no other proof of damages, and Forster (D) contended that New Era (P) could only recover the actual loss if sustained due to Forster's (D) breach.

ISSUE: Does the inclusion of a provision in a construction contract for partial payments to be made as the work progresses generally render the contract divisible?

HOLDING AND DECISION: (Desmond, J.) No. The inclusion of a provision in a construction contract for partial payments to be made as the work progresses does not generally render the contract divisible unless it is clear from the contract terms that each progress payment is intended to be so apportioned to the corresponding portion of the work as to be the full consideration for that portion of work. The parties to a construction contract may make it divisible and stipulate the value of each divisible part, but there is no sign here that New Era (P) and Forster (D) so intended. Hence, New Era (P) can recover either in quantum meruit for what had been finished or in contract for the value of what New Era (P) had lost — the contract price, less payments made and less the cost of completion — but it cannot simply recover the amount of the payment.

DISSENT: I conclude the contract was divisible. Hence, New Era (P) should be able to recover the amount of the third payment.

EDITOR'S ANALYSIS: The tendency of many cases is to view provisions for progress payments in construction contracts as being designed for the convenience of the contractor, by providing him with funds as the work progresses or for the mutual convenience of both parties rather than as being intended to apportion the consideration into parts equivalent to corresponding parts of the work. Hence, such contracts have been held to be entire rather than divisible. There are, however, several cases which agree with the dissent in New Era.

[For more information on installment contracts, see Casenote Law Outline on Contracts, Chapter 7, § I, Breach – Disappointment of Reasonable Expectations.]

NOTES:

BERNSTEIN v. NEMEYER

213 Conn. 665, 570 A.2d 164 (1990).

NATURE OF THE CASE: Appeal from denial of rescission and restitution.

NOTES:

FACT SUMMARY: Bernstein (P) sought to rescind his partnership agreement with Nemeyer (D) after Nemeyer (D) breached his negative cash flow guarantee, leading to the loss of their entire investment.

CONCISE RULE OF LAW: An injured party is not entitled to a restitutionary remedy where the breaching party has not been enriched and cannot be put back in the position he would have been before the contract.

FACTS: Nemeyer (D) induced Bernstein (P) to invest $1,050,000 for the purchase and renovation of two apartment complexes by guaranteeing a negative cash flow. Although Bernstein (P) was aware of the risks of foreclosure due to the negative cash flow, he entered into this partnership for the purpose of creating a tax shelter. Nemeyer (D) defaulted on their obligations, which resulted in foreclosure of the apartment complexes. Thus, both parties lost their investment. Bernstein (P) filed suit to rescind the contract and requesting restitution of his initial investment. The trial court denied relief, holding that Nemeyer's (D) breach of guarantee was not material. Bernstein (P) appealed.

ISSUE: Does an injured party have a right to restitution when the breaching party has not been enriched and cannot be put back in the position he would have been but for the contract?

HOLDING AND DECISION: (Peters, J.) No. The objective of a restitutionary remedy is to prevent unjust enrichment of the breaching party and to put him back in the position he would have been but for the contract. The courts have the discretion to award a restitutionary remedy. A material breach of a contract does not automatically entitle the injured party to restitution; it only discharges the injured party's duty to perform and allows recovery of damages. Thus, the plaintiff has to prove his right to a restitutionary remedy. The court of appeal reversed the lower court, holding that the breach of the guarantee was material. However, Bernstein (P) was not entitled to recover restitutionary damages because the record was unclear as to whether he made any efforts to tender back his partnership interests to Nemeyer (D), as required for rescission and restitution. Furthermore, the facts indicated that Nemeyer (D) was not unjustly enriched but that he suffered a great loss himself. Affirmed.

EDITOR'S ANALYSIS: The Restatement (Second) of Contracts provides a formula to measure the restitutionary remedy available to an injured party. It allows the injured party to recover the reasonable value of his performance less any benefits he may have received.

[For more information on the restitution interest, see Casenote Law Outline on Contracts, Chapter 7, § III, Remedies for Breach of Contract.]

LOCKS v. WADE

N.J. Sup. Ct., 36 N.J. Sup. 128, 114 A.2d 875 (1955).

NATURE OF CASE: Action to recover for breach of contract.

FACT SUMMARY: Wade (D) breached its contract to rent a jukebox from Locks (P). Locks (P) was able to rent the jukebox to someone else. There was evidence that jukeboxes were readily available on the market but that locations were hard to get.

CONCISE RULE OF LAW: Where a lessee defaults on an agreement to lease an article, the supply of which is not limited, the lessor is not required to reduce his damages by the amount he actually did, or reasonably could, realize on a reletting of the article.

FACTS: Under a contract between them, Locks (P) leased to Wade (D) a jukebox for two years. Before the machine was installed, Wade (D) repudiated the contract. Locks (P) was awarded the total rent less his costs and depreciation. After the breach, Locks (P) rented the same machine to another person. He introduced evidence that jukeboxes were readily available on the market but that locations were difficult to get.

ISSUE: Where a lessee defaults on an agreement to lease an article, the supply of which is not limited, is the lessor required to reduce his damages by the amount he actually did, or reasonably could, realize on a reletting of the article?

HOLDING AND DECISION: (Clapp, J.) No. Where a lessee defaults on an agreement to lease an article, the supply of which is not limited, the lessor is not required to reduce his damages by the amount he actually did, or reasonably could, realize on a reletting of the article. For if there had been no breach and another customer had appeared, the lessor could as well have secured another such article and entered into a second lease. In the case of realty which is specific and cannot be duplicated on the market, the lessor should not recover two profits merely because of the first lessee's default since that default enabled him to make the second lease. Gains made by a lessor on a lease entered into after the lessee's breach should not be deducted from his damages unless the breach enabled him to make the gains.

EDITOR'S ANALYSIS: In Locks v. Wade, the court computed lost profit by subtracting the cost to the plaintiff of purchasing the machine from the contract price. This figure was adjusted to reflect savings to Locks (P) from being relieved of performance and depreciation on the machine. This approach, rather than a simple comparison of contract and market price, is often employed in contracts for the manufacture and sale of goods where the seller is in the middle of performance at the time of the buyer's repudiation and elects to stop work and sue for damages. This method has a built-in mitigation feature — to compute actual loss caused by the breach, the plaintiff must first deduct from the contract price any savings realized by the breach.

[For more information on recovery in restitution, see Casenote Law Outline on Contracts, Chapter 7, § III, Remedies for Breach of Contract.]

NOTES:

RELIANCE COOPERAGE CORP. v. TREAT

175 F.2d 977 (8th Cir. 1968).

NATURE OF CASE: Action for damages for breach of a contract for the sale of goods.

FACT SUMMARY: Reliance (P), a cooperage, contracted to buy barrel staves for Treat (D) at $450 per thousand for bourbon quality and $40 per thousand for oil grade quality. When the price rose during the four months between the contracting date and delivery date, Treat (D) did not perform.

CONCISE RULE OF LAW: Whether a seller breaches a contract by giving the buyer notice of renunciation or simply fails to perform, the damages awarded the buyer shall be measured as the difference between the contract price and the market price on the date delivery was due.

FACTS: Reliance (P), a cooperage, contracted to buy barrel staves from Treat (D) at $450 per thousand for bourbon quality and $40 per thousand for oil grade quality. The contract was signed July 12, 1950, with delivery set for no later than December 31, 1950. On August 12, 1950, Treat (D) wrote Reliance (P), stating its inability to deliver staves at the contract price, as the market price had risen from $475 to $500 per thousand for bourbon quality. On October 6, 1950, after receiving notice by telephone in either August or September from Treat (D) that staves would not be delivered, Reliance (P) wrote Treat (D), stating its expectation that Treat (D) would fulfill its obligation. The market price of staves on December 31, 1950, was about $750 per thousand. Treat (D) never delivered.

ISSUE: Whether a seller breaches a contract by giving the buyer notice of renunciation or simply fails to perform, shall the damages awarded the buyer be measured as the difference between the contract price and the market price on the date delivery was due?

HOLDING AND DECISION: (Sanborn, C.J.) Yes. Whether a seller breaches a contract by giving the buyer notice of renunciation or simply fails to perform, the damages awarded the buyer shall be measured as the difference between the contract price and the market price on the date delivery was due. Treat's (D) notice of repudiation in no way affected his liability. The measure of damages remained the same as for simple nonperformance. Reliance (P) should receive the difference between the contract price and the market price on the date of delivery. This measure would have remained the same had Reliance (P) accepted the anticipatory repudiation as an actionable breach of the contract. Under Restatement (First) § 338, repudiation does not accelerate the time fixed for performance, nor does it change the measure of damages. A party has no duty to mitigate damages until there are damages to mitigate. Damages did not arise until December 31, 1950. To hold Reliance (P) had to mitigate before December 31, 1950, while still holding itself open to accept Treat's (D) performance during the same period has no justification. To so hold would encourage repudiations as the market rose and fell.

EDITOR'S ANALYSIS: The rule of this case has been changed by U.C.C. § 2-713 (1). While the measure is still the difference between the market price and the contract price, it is applied to the day notice of breach was made rather than to the day of delivery because of an additional code provision. Under the new provision, the buyer may cover, that is, make a good-faith purchase or contract to purchase substitute goods without unreasonable delay. Buyer may then recover the difference between the contract price and the cover price. This helps to remove the difficulty of proving market price at trial. By measuring damages under the U.C.C. on the day notice of breach was made (or the day the buyer learned of the breach), that day is the time when buyer should cover the market for substitute goods. Note, however, that if buyer breaches, the day of measure remains the day set for delivery.

[For more information on the measure of damages, see Casenote Law Outline on Contracts, Chapter 7, § II, Affirmative Obligations of the Aggrieved Party.]

NOTES:

RIVERS v. DEANE

N.Y. Sup. Ct., App. Div., 209 A.D.2d 936, 619 N.Y.S.2d 419 (1994).

NATURE OF CASE: Appeal of damage award calculation in an action for breach of contract.

FACT SUMMARY: An addition to a home was constructed in such a faulty manner as to render it unusable, and damages were awarded at trial based upon diminution of value.

CONCISE RULE OF LAW: In the case of faulty construction, the proper measure of damages is the market value of the cost to repair the faulty construction.

FACTS: Deane (P) contracted with Rivers (D) to build an addition to Deane's (P) home. The addition was so faulty that the third floor of the addition was unusable. Deane (P) filed suit. At trial, the court awarded Deane (P) damages for the diminution in value of the home, the difference between market value with proper construction and market value as completed. Rivers (D) appealed the calculation method of damages.

ISSUE: In the case of faulty construction, is the proper measure of damages the market value of the cost to repair the faulty construction?

HOLDING AND DECISION: (Court) Yes. In the case of faulty construction, the proper measure of damages is the market value of the cost to repair the faulty construction. In cases where a builder's failure to perform is very trivial, the cost of repair can be greater than the diminution of value to the house on the market. Where that is the situation, diminution of value is the proper manner to calculate damages. In this case, however, the failure to perform was severe. A portion of the house was unusable. Here, the proper manner to calculate damages is the cost to correct the work, not the diminution of market value. Reversed and remanded for calculation of damages.

EDITOR'S ANALYSIS: When construction is defective, contract law generally favors awarding the injured party sufficient compensation to correct the defect. However, contract law attempts to avoid needless waste by declining to award correction damages when the cost to repair a minor defect is much greater than the diminution of value. Economic efficiency is balanced against the expectations of the aggrieved party.

[For more information on remedies for breach of contract, see Casenote Law Outline on Contracts, Chapter 7, § III, Remedies for Breach of Contract.]

AMERICAN STANDARD, INC. v. SCHECTMAN

N.Y. Sup. Ct. 80 A.D. 318, 427 N.E.2d 512 (1981).

NATURE OF CASE: Appeal from award of damages for breach of contract.

FACT SUMMARY: Schectman (D) contended that the correct measure of damages for his failure to complete grading American's (P) land was the diminution in value of the land, rather than the cost of completion.

CONCISE RULE OF LAW: Only where the cost of completing the contract would entail unreasonable economic waste will the measure of damages for breach of a construction contract be diminution in value of the property in relation to what its value would have been if performance had been properly completed.

FACTS: Schectman (D) contracted to grade and to take down certain foundations to one foot below grade on American's (P) land. Schectman's (D) performance substantially deviated from the grading specifications in the contract. American (P) sued for breach and was awarded damages equal to the cost of completing the grading properly. Schectman (D) appealed, contending the trial court erred by refusing to admit evidence that American (P) sold the property for only $3,000 less than its full market value and therefore suffered no appreciable loss due to the breach. As a result, Schectman (D) argued, the correct measure of damages was this $3,000 diminution in value of the property due to the breach, rather than the cost of completion.

ISSUE: Will the measure of damages for breach of a construction contract be diminution in property value only where the cost of completion would entail unreasonable economic waste?

HOLDING AND DECISION: (Hancock, J.) Yes. The generally accepted measure of damages for breach of a construction contract is the cost of completing performance properly. Only where such cost of completion would entail unreasonable economic waste will the measure of damages be the diminution in the value of the property caused by the breach. Completing the job properly in this case would not require destruction of past work, only that performance be completed. The fact that the sale price of the property was not markedly affected by the breach is irrelevant to the measure of damages determination. No unreasonable economic waste would result from awarding cost of completion damages; therefore, that measure was properly used. Affirmed.

EDITOR'S ANALYSIS: Some commentators criticize the result in this case as bestowing upon American (P) a windfall recovery. Not only was it able to sell the property for virtually its fair market value, $183,000, it also received a judgment against Schectman (D) for $90,000. Other commentators justify cost of completion awards as protecting the plaintiff's subjective value ascribed to the property.

[For more information on the measure of damages, see Casenote Law Outline on Contracts, Chapter 7, § III, Remedies for Breach of Contract.]

HADLEY v. BAXENDALE

Ct. of Exchequer, 7 Ex. 341, 156 Eng. Rep. 145 (1854).

NATURE OF CASE: Action for damages for breach of a carrier contract.

FACT SUMMARY: Hadley (P), a mill operator in Gloucester, arranged to have Baxendale's (D) company, a carrier, ship his broken mill shaft to the engineer in Greenwich for a copy to be made. Hadley (P) suffered a £300 loss when Baxendale (D) unreasonably delayed shipping the mill shaft, causing the mill to be shut down longer than anticipated.

CONCISE RULE OF LAW: The injured party may recover those damages as may reasonably be considered arising naturally from the breach itself and, second, may recover those damages as may reasonably be supposed to have been in contemplation of the parties, at the time they made the contract, as the probable result of a breach of it.

FACTS: Hadley (P), a mill operator in Gloucester, arranged to have Baxendale's (D) shipping company return his broken mill shaft to the engineer in Greenwich, who was to make a duplicate. Hadley (P) delivered the broken shaft to Baxendale (D), who, in consideration for his fee, promised to deliver the shaft to Greenwich in a reasonable time. Baxendale (D) did not know that the mill was shut down while awaiting the new shaft. Baxendale (D) was negligent in delivering the shaft within a reasonable time. Reopening of the mill was delayed five days, costing Hadley (P) lost profits and paid-out wages of £300. Hadley (P) had paid Baxendale (D) £24 to ship the mill shaft. Baxendale (D) paid into court £25 in satisfaction of Hadley's (P) claim. The jury awarded an additional £25 for a total £50 award.

ISSUE: May the injured party recover those damages as may reasonably be considered arising naturally from the breach itself, and, may damages as may reasonably be supposed to have been in contemplation of the parties, at the time they made the contract, as the probable result of a breach of it, be recovered?

HOLDING AND DECISION: (Alderson, B.) Yes. The jury requires a rule for its guidance in awarding damages justly. When a party breaches his contract, the damages he pays ought to be those arising naturally from the breach itself and, in addition, those as may reasonably be supposed to have been in contemplation of the parties, at the time they made the contract, as the probable result of the breach of it. Therefore, if the special circumstances under which the contract was made were known to both parties, the resulting damages upon breach would be those reasonably contemplated as arising under those communicated and known circumstances. But if the special circumstances were unknown, then damages can only be those expected to arise generally from the breach. Hadley's (P) telling Baxendale (D) that he ran a mill and that his mill shaft which he wanted shipped was broken did not notify Baxendale (D) that the mill was shut down. Baxendale (D) could have believed reasonably that Hadley (P) had a spare shaft or that the shaft to be shipped was not the only defective machinery at the mill. Here, it does not follow that a loss of profits could fairly or reasonably have been contemplated by both parties in case of breach. Such a loss would not have flowed naturally from the breach without the special circumstances having been communicated to Baxendale (D).

EDITOR'S ANALYSIS: This case lays down two rules guiding damages. First, only those damages as may fairly and reasonably be considered arising from the breach itself may be awarded. Second, those damages which may reasonably be supposed to have been in contemplation of the parties at the time they made the contract as the probable result of a breach of it may be awarded. The second is distinguished from the first because with the latter, both parties are aware of the special circumstances under which the contract is made. Usually, those special circumstances are communicated by the plaintiff to the defendant before the making of the contract. But that is not an absolute condition. If the consequences of the breach are foreseeable, the party which breaches will be liable for the lost profits or expectation damages. Foreseeability and assumption of the risk are ways of describing the bargain. If there is an assumption of the risk, the seller or carrier must necessarily be aware of the consequences. A later English case held that there would be a lesser foreseeability for a common carrier than a seller, as a seller would tend to know the purpose and use of the item sold while the common carrier probably would not know the use of all items it carried. If all loss went on to the seller, this would obviously be an incentive not to enter into contracts. Courts balance what has become a "seller beware" attitude by placing limitations on full recovery. The loss must be foreseeable when the contract is entered into. It cannot be overly speculative. The seller's breach must be judged by willingness, negligence, bad faith, and availability of replacement items. Restatement (First) § 331(2) would allow recovery in the situation in this case under an alternative theory. If the breach were one preventing the use and operation of property from which profits would have been made, damages can be measured by the rental value of the property or by interest on the value of the property. U.C.C. § 2-715(2) allows the buyer consequential damages for any loss which results from general or particular needs of which the seller had reason to know.

[For more information on foreseeability of damages, see Casenote Law Outline on Contracts, Chapter 7, § III, Remedies for Breach of Contract.]

NOTES:

SPANG INDUSTRIES v. AETNA CASUALTY & SURETY

512 F.2d 365 (2d Cir. 1975).

NATURE OF CASE: Suit to recover money due on a contract.

FACT SUMMARY: Fort Pitt (P) agreed to supply steel to Torrington (D) for use on a construction project, but delays in delivery resulted in inconvenience and extra work for Torrington's (D) employees.

CONCISE RULE OF LAW: A party who breaches a contract may be held liable for all damages which could reasonably have been anticipated at the time the agreement was entered into.

FACTS: Spang Industries, Inc., Fort Pitt Bridge Division (P), promised to supply Torrington Construction Co., Inc. (D) with steel Torrington (D) needed to erect a bridge. Their agreement was confirmed by a letter from Fort Pitt (P) which stated, "Delivery to be mutually agreed upon." Torrington (D), in November of 1969, advised Fort Pitt (P) that the steel would be needed late in June 1970, and Torrington (D) verified that date in the middle of January. On January 29, Fort Pitt (P) informed Torrington (D) that the June delivery date could probably not be met, but, pursuant to Torrington's (D) threat to cancel the contract, Fort Pitt (P) agreed to ship the steel early in August. Delivery finally commenced in late August, although not until September 16 was there enough steel on hand to begin work on the bridge. This delayed the pouring of concrete until late October, by which time threats of freezing weather made it necessary for Torrington (D) to make use of extra equipment and pay its employees overtime. This resulted in additional expenses for Torrington (D), which had already incurred unexpected expenses when it had to unload some of the steel itself because Fort Pitt (P) had failed to notify the subcontractor responsible for the unloading. Fort Pitt (P) sued the Aetna Casualty & Surety Co. (D), which had posted a general contractor's bond, to recover money due under the contract. Torrington (D) then sued in a different court to recover for damages sustained as a result of Fort Pitt's (P) delay in delivering the steel. Fort Pitt (P) counterclaimed for the amount Torrington (D) owed on the contract. The two actions were consolidated for trial, and the judge ruled that Fort Pitt's (P) tardy delivery of the steel constituted breach of the contract and entitled Torrington (D) to recover more than $7,600 in damages. The judge also ruled that Fort Pitt (P) was entitled to recover the amount Torrington (D) owed on the contract, less the $7,600. Judgment was then entered against Torrington (D) and Aetna (D) in the amount of nearly $16,000. Fort Pitt (P), however, appealed, contending that Torrington (D) should not have been allowed to recover any damages because the expenses it suffered had not been reasonably within the contemplation of the parties at the time that they had entered into the contract.

ISSUE: Is a party who breaches a contract responsible for all damages suffered by the nonbreaching party?

HOLDING AND DECISION: (Mulligan, C.J.) No. But a party who breaches a contract may be held liable for all damages which could reasonably have been anticipated at the time the agreement was entered into. This is the rule which was established by the well-known case of Hadley v. Baxendale. Fort Pitt (P) argued that it did not know, at the time the contract was entered into, that delivery of the steel would be expected in June 1970. However, the parties both agreed that a mutually acceptable delivery date would be arranged, and Fort Pitt (P) acquiesced on the June date. In so doing, Fort Pitt (P) must have realized that any extensive delays in shipment would, by reason of unsatisfactory weather conditions which might arise, occasion added efforts and costs on the part of Torrington (D). Since the costs incurred by Torrington (D) were entirely foreseeable, the trial court quite properly awarded damages to Torrington (D).

EDITOR'S ANALYSIS: It seems fair to require a breaching party to bear the cost of damages which are caused by his conduct. But, in order to prevent liability from being imposed in an amount totally disproportionate to the nature and extent of the breaching party's conduct, the courts have developed the rule that a party may be held liable only for anticipated damages. Some courts have modified the Hadley v. Baxendale rule by imposing no liability for damages which, though foreseeable, would occur only under extremely unusual circumstances. The Hadley v. Baxendale rule is virtually identical with the rule which holds a tortfeasor liable for the natural and probable (foreseeable) consequences of his acts and is embodied, in slightly different language, in § 2-715(2) of the Uniform Commercial Code.

[For more information on foreseeable damages, see Casenote Law Outline on Contracts, Chapter 7, § III, Remedies for Breach of Contract.]

NOTES:

HYDRAFORM PRODUCTS CORP. v. AMERICAN STEEL & ALUMINUM CORP.

New Hamp. Sup. Ct., 127 N.H. 187, 498 A.2d 339 (1985).

NATURE OF CASE: Appeal in action for negligent misrepresentation and breach of contract.

FACT SUMMARY: American Steel (D), supplying steel to Hydraform Products (P), attempted to enforce a limitation of damages clause in its contract which barred consequential damages.

CONCISE RULE OF LAW: Consequential damages must be reasonably foreseeable, ascertainable, and unavoidable.

FACTS: Hydraform (P) entered into a contract with American (D) to supply steel used in the fabrication of wood stoves. The delivery receipt, signed by agents of Hydraform (P), disclaimed liability for consequential damages. Some of the steel deliveries were late. When Hydraform (P) complained, American (D) promised that if steel for 400 stoves was ordered, American (D) would stockpile steel in advance. Deliveries continued to be slow or defective. Hydraform (P) finally attempted to obtain steel elsewhere, but it was unsuccessful. Hydraform (P) sold its wood stove division for $150,000 after selling only 250 stoves. Hydraform (P) then filed suit for breach of contract, claiming $100,000 for lost profits and $220,000 for the loss on the sale. The jury at trial awarded consequential damages of $80,245.12. American (D) appealed the award of consequential damages.

ISSUE: Must consequential damages be reasonably foreseeable, ascertainable, and unavoidable?

HOLDING AND DECISION: (Souter, J.) Yes. Consequential damages must be reasonably foreseeable, ascertainable, and unavoidable. First, a seller must know of general or particular requirements and needs of the buyer to be bound by foreseeability. Second, damages sought must be reasonable consequences of the breach. Third, consequential damages may only be recovered if they could not be prevented by cover or otherwise. In this case, the contract with American (D) contemplated the sale of 400 stoves. Thus, lost profits up to 400 stoves were foreseeable and ascertainable. Hydraform (P) attempted to cover, so the lost profits were not avoidable. However, damages beyond the 400 stoves were not clearly foreseeable. And damages for subsequent years were not readily ascertainable. Furthermore, the diminution of value on the sale of the business was based upon future profits, which were not readily ascertainable. The jury should only have been entitled to consider a claim for lost profits on stoves, the difference between the 400 referenced in the contract and the 250 actually sold. Reversed.

EDITOR'S ANALYSIS: Proving loss of future profits is a difficult proposition. However, the history of business is one source for such proof if the business has a long track record upon which to infer lost profits. Of course, even a new business can recover lost future profits if they can be ascertained with reasonable certainty.

[For more information on limitations on consequential damages, see Casenote Law Outline on Contracts, Chapter 7, § III, Remedies for Breach of Contract.]

NOTES:

L. ALBERT & SON v. ARMSTRONG RUBBER CO.

178 F.2d 182 (2d Cir. 1949).

NATURE OF CASE: Appeal from dismissal of counterclaim for costs incurred in reliance on a contract.

FACT SUMMARY: Armstrong (D) counterclaimed for Albert's (P) breach, seeking recovery for costs it incurred in reliance on Albert's (P) promise to deliver the refining machines on time.

CONCISE RULE OF LAW: A promisee may recover costs incurred in reliance on the promisor's promise to perform, subject to the privilege of the promisor to reduce such recovery by as much as he can show that the promisee would have lost if the contract had been performed.

FACTS: Armstrong (D) contracted to purchase four refiners, machines designed to recondition old rubber, from L. Albert & Son (Albert) (P). In reliance on the contract, Armstrong (D) expended $3,000 in laying a foundation for the machines. Albert (P) failed to deliver the machines on time yet delivered them within a few days, when Armstrong (D) refused acceptance. Albert (P) sued to recover the purchase price, and Armstrong (D) counterclaimed for breach, seeking recovery of the $3,000 expended in reliance on the contract. The trial court dismissed both the complaint and the counterclaim, yet it entered judgment for Albert (P) for the cost of a portion of the equipment. Armstrong (D) appealed.

ISSUE: May a promisee recover costs incurred in reliance on the promisor's performance?

HOLDING AND DECISION: (Hand, J.) Yes. A promisee may recover costs incurred in reliance on the promisor's promise to perform. However, such recovery is subject to the promisor's privilege to reduce it by as much as he can show that the promisee would have lost if the contract had been performed. It was not shown by Armstrong (D) that the purchase of the machines would result in a net profit to it. As a result, it cannot be established that if Albert (P) had in fact performed, Armstrong (D) would have realized $3,000 to cover the cost of the foundations. To award Armstrong (D) that amount without affording Albert (P) a chance to prove the amount of loss Armstrong (D) would have incurred if the contract were performed would make Albert (P) an insurer of the success of Armstrong's (D) transaction. Therefore, the trial court's judgment for Albert (P) for the price of the portion of the equipment must be modified to allow Armstrong (D) a setoff of $3,000 less any amount Albert (P) can prove would have been lost had the contract been performed. Remanded.

EDITOR'S ANALYSIS: This case illustrates the rule set forth in U.S. v. Beham, 110 U.S. 338 (1884), wherein the plaintiff was allowed to recover expenditures made in reliance on the defendant's contractual promises. In that case, Beham was granted recovery even though he could not prove the venture would have been profitable because he sought an amount less than the contract price.

[For more information on reliance recoveries, see Casenote Law Outline on Contracts, Chapter 7, § III, Remedies for Breach of Contract.]

BLANDFORD v. ANDREWS

Queen's Bench, 78 Eng. Rep. 930 (1599).

NATURE OF CASE: Action to recover on a debt.

FACT SUMMARY: Andrews (D) contended he was released from his debt to Blandford (P), repayment of which was made waivable if Andrews (D) procured Palmer to marry Blandford (P) because Blandford (P) acted to prevent the marriage.

CONCISE RULE OF LAW: To be released from performance based on the plaintiff's actions hindering such, the defendant must show he did as much as he could to perform in spite of the plaintiff's hindrance.

FACTS: Andrews (D) incurred a debt to Blandford (P). The parties agreed that repayment would be excused if Andrews (D) could arrange a marriage between Blandford (P) and Bridget Palmer before the next Feast of St. Bartholomew. Andrews (D) was unable to arrange the marriage, and Blandford (P) sued to recover on the debt. Andrews (D) contended that he was prevented from arranging the marriage by Blandford's (P) insulting behavior toward Palmer, and, therefore, he should be excused from his obligation. Blandford (P) contended that this was not enough to release the debt, that Andrews (D) had to show he used his best efforts to procure the marriage.

ISSUE: Must a defendant show he did as much as he could to perform on the contract before he may be excused due to the plaintiff's hindrance?

HOLDING AND DECISION: (Per curiam) Yes. To be released from performance based on the plaintiff's hindrance, a defendant must show he did all he could to complete his performance and that such hindrance actually precluded performance. In this case, the woman and Blandford (P) may have married despite his insults had Andrews (D) used his best efforts to procure the marriage. Andrews' (D) failure to prove he did all he could rendered him bound to perform. Judgment for Blandford (P).

EDITOR'S ANALYSIS: Today, contracting parties are considered to owe each other a duty of good faith in that they will not act so as to prevent the other's performance. This is a rule commonly traced back to the case of Hochster v. De La Tour, 118 Eng. Rep. 922 (1853). A breach of this duty excuses the other party's performance and gives rise to a cause of action in damages.

[For more information on good faith dealing obligations, see Casenote Law Outline on Contracts, Chapter 2, § I, Valuable Consideration: The Bargained-for Incursion of Legal Detriment.]

PATTERSON v. MEYERHOFF

N.Y. Ct. of App., 204 N.Y. 96, 97 N.E. 472 (1912).

NATURE OF CASE: Action for damages and to have a lien declared on property allegedly held in constructive trust.

FACT SUMMARY: After Meyerhoff (D) had agreed to purchase from Patterson (P) four houses he did not then own but would acquire at a foreclosure sale, Meyerhoff (D) outbid Patterson (P) at the sale.

CONCISE RULE OF LAW: In every contract there is an implied promise on the part of each party that he will not intentionally and purposely do anything to prevent the other party from carrying out the agreement on his part.

FACTS: Meyerhoff (D) agreed to buy from Patterson (P) four parcels of land which Patterson (P) did not then own but planned to purchase at a foreclosure sale. Before the foreclosure occurred, Meyerhoff (D) renounced the contract. At the sale, Meyerhoff (D) outbid Patterson (P) and acquired the four parcels in her own name. As a result, Meyerhoff (D) acquired the parcels for $620 less than she had obligated herself to pay under the contract with Patterson (P). Patterson (P) filed an action to recover damages equal to the difference between the contract price and the auction price for the parcels and to establish a lien on the parcels on a trust theory.

ISSUE: May a party who causes or sanctions the breach of an agreement interpose the other party's nonperformance as a defense to an action on the contract?

HOLDING AND DECISION: (Willard, Bartlett, J.) No. In every contract there is an implied promise on the part of each party to refrain from hindering the performance of the other. Here, although no relation of trust can be found, Patterson (P) is not precluded from recovering his anticipated profits on the contract merely because he has also asked for too much equitable relief. Patterson (P) is excused from his nonperformance, and Meyerhoff (D) is liable in damages for breaching her implied promise. The damages may fairly be measured as Patterson's (P) lost anticipated profits.

DISSENT: Patterson's (P) prayer for damages is only incidental to his complaint, which is essentially one in equity. No trust being established, Patterson (P) should not now be allowed to expand his remedy. Furthermore, Patterson (P), who had not specifically excluded Meyerhoff (D) from acquiring the parcels he himself did not own, could have simply outbid her at the foreclosure sale.

EDITOR'S ANALYSIS: Where one party has breached all implied promise of cooperation, the other party will be excused from any nonperformance on the theory that performance on his part, although a condition precedent to the other's obligation, has been actively prevented. The aggrieved party, nonetheless, must still be ready to show that but for the hindrance he would have been ready, willing, and able to honor his side of the contract.

[For more information on impossibility of performance, see Casenote Law Outline on Contracts, Chapter 6, § I, Excusable Non-Performance under the Common Law.]

NOTES:

IRON TRADE PROD. CO. v. WILKOFF CO.
Pa. Sup. Ct., 272 Pa. 172, 116 A. 150 (1922).

NATURE OF CASE: Action to recover damages for breach of contract.

FACT SUMMARY: Wilkoff (D) contracted to deliver rails to Iron Trade (P) but refused to do so after Iron Trade (P) reduced the available supply and made Wilkoff's (D) performance more difficult.

CONCISE RULE OF LAW: Mere difficulty of performance will not excuse a breach of contract even though that difficulty was created by the other contracting party.

FACTS: Iron Trade (P) contracted to purchase 2,600 tons of rails from Wilkoff (D) at the rate of $41 per ton. Iron Trade (P) thereafter purchased additional rails from one of the very few rail suppliers, thereby reducing the overall rail supply and driving up the market price. Because of the reduced supply and increased price of rails, it became difficult and unprofitable for Wilkoff (D) to procure rails for Iron Trade (P). Wilkoff (D) failed to deliver. Iron Trade (P) subsequently covered at a higher price and sued for damages.

ISSUE: Does one party's conduct, which renders performance by the second party more difficult, excuse that second party's refusal to perform?

HOLDING AND DECISION: (Walling, J.) No. "If a party seeking to secure all the merchandise which he could entered into a contract for a quantity of the required goods and subsequently made performance of the contract by the seller more difficult by making other purchases which increased the scarcity of the available supply, his conduct would furnish no excuse for refusal to perform the prior contract" (Williston). Here, Iron Trade's (P) conduct did not render performance by Wilkoff (D) impossible but only more difficult. Mere difficulty of performance will not excuse a breach of contract. (The case of U.S. v. Peck, 102 U.S. 64, in which one party cut off the other party's only available source of supply, thus rendering performance impossible, is not parallel.) Finally, there was no restriction in the contract on subsequent purchases by Iron Trade (P).

EDITOR'S ANALYSIS: Although there is no straightforward rule which explains the result in all the cases similar to the present one, perhaps the connecting thread is an assumption-of-risk notion. The court here undoubtedly felt that a deflated supply (and the resulting inflated market price) was a foreseeable commercial risk which Wilkoff (D) undertook when he entered the contract. However, if Iron Trade (P) had interfered with what it knew to be Wilkoff's (D) only source of supply, Wilkoff's (D) duty might have been discharged since Wilkoff (D) would not be held to have assumed the risk of Iron Trade's (P) knowing interference. [See Patterson v. Meyerhoff, 204 N.Y. 96 (1912).] A court will use its instinct for "justice" in each case.

[For more information on excusable non-performance, see Casenote Law Outline on Contracts, Chapter 6, § II, Excusable Non-Performance under the U.C.C.]

NOTES:

BILLMAN v. HENSEL

Ind. Ct. of App., 181 Ind. App. 272, 391 N.E.2d 671 (1979).

NATURE OF CASE: Appeal from recovery of earnest money deposit.

FACT SUMMARY: The Hensels (P) sought to recover a $1,000 earnest money deposit pursuant to a contract to sell their home which was not fulfilled by the Billmans (D) after they were unable to secure financing.

CONCISE RULE OF LAW: A clause in a real estate sales contract which makes the buyer's obtaining financing a condition precedent to his duty to perform imposes on the buyer an implied duty to make reasonable good-faith efforts to satisfy the condition.

FACTS: The Billmans (D) contracted to purchase the Hensel's (P) house and gave the Hensels (P) a check for a $1,000 earnest money/ liquidated damage deposit, as required by the contract. The contract provided that it was conditioned by the Billmans' (D) ability to secure a $35,000 mortgage within 30 days. Following execution of the contract, Billman (D) met with an agent of a bank and was told he had to have the balance of the purchase price to secure the mortgage. Billman (D) was $6,500 short, and he told Hensel (P) he could not obtain the mortgage without a $5,000 loan, which he had been denied. Hensel (P) offered to reduce the sale price by $5,000, but Billman (D) then said he needed another $1,500 and stopped payment on the earnest money check. The Hensels (P) sued to recover the earnest money, and judgment was entered in their favor. The Billmans (D) appealed on the basis that they were not liable because the condition precedent to their duty to perform was never fulfilled.

ISSUE: Does a condition subjecting the enforcement of a contract to the ability of a party to obtain financing impose on that party an implied obligation to make a reasonable good-faith effort to satisfy the condition?

HOLDING AND DECISION: (Garrard, J.) Yes. A clause in a real estate sales contract which makes the buyer's ability to obtain financing a condition precedent to his duty to perform imposes an implied duty to make a reasonable good-faith effort to satisfy the condition. In this case, the Billmans (D) contacted only one financial institution and applied for a mortgage of $35,000 although they in fact required more. They then turned down the Hensels' (P) offer to reduce the sales price. These facts show the Billmans (D) breached their implied duty to make a good-faith effort to obtain financing, and therefore, the Hensels (P) were entitled to the earnest money deposit. Affirmed.

EDITOR'S ANALYSIS: This case illustrates the general rule applied to so-called "subject to financing" clauses in contracts. The rationale for the rule seems to be that it promotes the reasonable expectations of the parties. Some commentators argue it is an extension of the basic rule of contract law that a promisor cannot rely upon the existence of a condition precedent to excuse his performance of the condition.

[For more information on conditions precedent, see Casenote Law Outline on Contracts, Chapter 4, § I, Classification of Conditions According to Their Impact upon the Modified Promise.]

NOTES:

CURTICE BROS. CO. v. CATTS

72 N.J. Eq. 831 (1907).

NATURE OF CASE: Action to specifically perform a contract for the sale of services and personalty.

FACT SUMMARY: After Catts (D) defaulted on his contract to supply Curtice Bros. (P) with tomatoes for its canning company, Curtice Bros. (P) was unable to purchase any replacement tomatoes elsewhere.

CONCISE RULE OF LAW: Specific performance of a contract for personalty will be granted where the goods cannot be obtained elsewhere and they are necessary to the plaintiff's business.

FACTS: Curtice Canning (P) contracted with Catts (D) to buy his tomato crop. Catts (D) then repudiated the contract and said he would not sell to Curtice (P). Curtice (P) attempted to buy replacement tomatoes elsewhere; however, none could be purchased. Curtice (P) brought an action in equity to specifically enforce the contract. Curtice (P) alleged that its canning operation required an adequate supply of tomatoes and that it would be severely injured by Catts' (D) refusal to perform the contract since no replacements were available. Catts (D) defended on the basis that specific performance was normally denied for contracts to convey personalty and that the contract also involved Catts' (D) personal services, which were also an inappropriate subject for specific performance. Curtice (P) alleged that damages would be an inadequate remedy.

ISSUE: Where damages are inadequate, replacements cannot be found, and they are necessary for plaintiff's business, is specific performance available for a contract to convey personalty?

HOLDING AND DECISION: (Leaming, V.C.) Yes. Under these circumstances, specific performance will be granted. Here, the tomatoes are necessary for Curtice's (P) business. Curtice (P) cannot operate profitably without an adequate supply, and it could not obtain replacements elsewhere. Curtice (P) cannot honor its commitments without an adequate supply. The distinction between specific enforcement of realty and personalty has been on the decline. Where there is no adequate remedy at law, equity will grant specific performance. The fact that services are involved is immaterial to this case. An injunction may be issued forbidding Catts' (D) selling his crop to another. Finally, if appropriate, a receiver may be appointed to harvest the crops. Specific performance is granted.

EDITOR'S ANALYSIS: Specific performance may also be granted in other situations involving personalty. Uniqueness of chattel (e.g., a rare painting or custom goods) and avoidance multiple lawsuits are examples of adequate grounds for decreeing specific performance. Personal service contracts may or may not be specifically enforced, depending on the nature of the services. If the court can adequately compel or supervise performance, it may be specifically enforceable.

[For more information on equitable intervention, see Casenote Law Outline on Contracts, Chapter 7, § III, Remedies for Breach of Contract.]

NOTES:

LACLEDE GAS CO. v. AMOCO OIL CO.

522 F.2d 33 (8th Cir. 1975).

NATURE OF CASE: Suit seeking a mandatory injunction or, alternatively, damages.

FACT SUMMARY: Laclede (P) and Amoco (D) had a written agreement under which Amoco (D) supplied propane gas to Laclede (P). Laclede (P) had a right to cancel the agreement, but Amoco (D) did not. When Amoco (D) terminated the agreement, Laclede (P) sought specific performance of the contract.

CONCISE RULE OF LAW: Specific performance will be imposed where the terms of the contract clearly express the duties of the parties and the conditions under which performance is due.

FACTS: Laclede Gas Company's (P) predecessor and Amoco Oil Co. (D) entered into a written agreement on September 21, 1970. Under the terms of the agreement, Amoco (D) was to be a supplier of propane gas for Laclede (P), and Laclede (P) was to be a distributor for various residential developments in Missouri. As each development applied to Laclede (P) for a propane system, Laclede (P) would request that Amoco (D) supply the propane, and both Laclede (P) and Amoco (D) would sign a form letter which was supplementary to their original written agreement. Both Laclede (P) and Amoco (D) recognized that the propane systems would eventually be converted into natural gas systems, so Laclede (P) was given, under the 1970 agreement, the right to cancel the agreement by giving Amoco (D) 30 days' written notice of the conversion to natural gas. Another paragraph also gave Laclede (P) the right to cancel the agreement, which, if not canceled, continued for additional periods of one year. Amoco (D) had no right of termination under the 1970 agreement. Difficulties between Laclede (P) and Amoco (D) arose in early 1973, and in May of that year, Amoco (D) advised Laclede (P) that it was terminating the 1970 agreement because it lacked "mutuality." Laclede (P) brought suit in federal district court for breach of contract and sought a mandatory injunction prohibiting the continued breach or damages. The district court held a bench trial and ruled that in the absence of mutuality, there was no contract, and, therefore, no injunction could issue. Laclede (P) appealed.

ISSUE: Where the terms of a contract are fair and plain and other equitable requirements are met, should specific performance be ordered?

HOLDING AND DECISION: (Ross, J.) Yes. Specific performance will be imposed where the terms of the contract clearly express the duties of the parties and the conditions under which performance is due. Specific performance will not be imposed when the party claiming breach has an adequate remedy at law, especially where the contract involves personalty rather than real property. However, in Missouri, specific performance of a contract involving personalty has been ordered in the proper circumstances, as when the replacement of the item could be made only at considerable expense, trouble, or loss which cannot be calculated in advance. Amoco (D) argued that specific performance should not be decreed in the absence of mutuality of that remedy or when supervision by the court would be difficult. Neither contention merits much discussion since mutuality of the remedy is not a prerequisite for the decree of specific performance and because supervision by the court would not be a particular hardship on the court. However, Amoco's (D) third argument, that Laclede (P) had an adequate remedy at law, deserves discussion. Although it is agreed that Laclede (P) presently had contracts with other suppliers of propane and that propane is available on the open market, neither of these solutions will give Laclede (P) the long-term, assured supply of propane contemplated by the 1970 agreement. Such a long-term contract would be extremely difficult to obtain at this time, and were it attainable, Laclede (P) would, nevertheless, incur considerable expense and trouble which cannot be estimated in advance. The contract was clear and certain in its terms. Therefore, specific performance is the proper remedy. Accordingly, the judgment of the district court is reversed and the cause remanded for the issuance of injunctive relief in the form of a decree of specific performance.

EDITOR'S ANALYSIS: Historically, decrees of specific performance are rarely issued except in cases involving real estate or unique personal property. In the commercial sphere, the usual remedy for breach of contract was damages rather than a mandatory injunction. The court in the instant case adopted an extremely liberal test for determining the appropriateness of specific performance, examining primarily the issue of whether or not replacement would put the party to trouble and expense which could not be calculated in advance. Such a test is consistent with U.C.C. § 2-716, which provides that specific performance may be decreed when goods are unique or in other proper circumstances. However, this rule, which emphasizes the commercial ease of replacement, does not sufficiently weigh the availability of legal remedies prior to the resort to equity.

[For more information on decrees of specific performance, see Casenote Law Outline on Contracts, Chapter 7, § III, Remedies for Breach of Contract.]

NOTES:

NORTHERN INDIANA PUBLIC SERVICE CO. v. CARBON COUNTY COAL CO.

799 F.2d 265 (7th Cir. 1986).

NATURE OF CASE: Appeal from award of damages on defense counterclaim and from denial of specific performance.

FACT SUMMARY: NIPSCO (P), who had agreed to buy 1.5 million tons of coal every year for 20 years from Carbon County (D), sought to be excused from the contract, when the price of electricity fell dramatically.

CONCISE RULE OF LAW: Specific performance is not available if damages are an adequate remedy, and it is unlikely the order would ever be implemented.

FACTS: NIPSCO (P) and Carbon County (D) signed a 20-year contract which required Carbon County (D), the owner and operator of a coal mine, to sell, and NIPSCO (P) to buy, about 1.5 million tons of coal every year. The price, initially set at $24/ton, could and did go up under the contract terms, to $44/ton. But when oil prices and the cost of electricity plummeted, NIPSCO (P) had alternative sources of fuel available at much lower costs. It filed a declaratory relief action against Carbon County (D), seeking to be excused from the contract. Carbon County (D) counterclaimed for damages due to breach and won a jury verdict for $181 million, but its request for specific performance was denied.

ISSUE: Will the remedy of specific performance be awarded only when damages at law are inadequate to compensate the injured party?

HOLDING AND DECISION: (Posner, J.) Yes. Specific performance is not available if damages are an adequate remedy, and it is unlikely the order would ever be implemented. Here, the damage award of $181 million was not argued to be an unreasonable estimate of the loss suffered by Carbon County (D), calculated as the difference between the contract price times quantity, and the cost of mining coal. Therefore, damages were adequate to compensate Carbon County (D) and specific enforcement was unnecessary. Specific performance would also have been undesirable because the breach by NIPSCO (P) was economically efficient, halting a production process was no longer cost-justified. A decree of specific performance would have been unenforceable in any event because NIPSCO (P) and Carbon County (D) would have independently negotiated a cancellation of the contract given NIPSCO's (P) interest in minimizing its losses under the contract. Finally, the miners of Carbon County (D) were not third party real parties in interest to the contract such that the consequences of denying specific performance should have been considered; they assumed the risk that the coal mine would close down if uneconomical. Affirmed.

EDITOR'S ANALYSIS: Posner is well known for his economist's approach to the resolution of legal issues such as this. However, his denial of specific performance on the grounds that the jury award was not shown to be unreasonable ignored the fact that the contract at issue had many years to run and that the price of coal over its course would most likely be highly volatile. In such a case, damages are speculative at best and hard to calculate, and it seems less likely that the award would accurately forecast the future.

[For more information on specific performance, see Casenote Law Outline on Contracts, Chapter 7, § III, Remedies for Breach of Contract.]

NOTES:

WALGREEN CO. v. SARA CREEK PROPERTY CO.

966 F.2d 273 (7th Cir. 1992).

NATURE OF CASE: Appeal from a grant of permanent injunctive relief in suit for breach of contract.

FACT SUMMARY: Walgreen (P) filed suit to enforce a clause contained in its lease agreement that provided that no space in the mall would be rented to a competing pharmacy.

CONCISE RULE OF LAW: Where the costs of injunctive relief are less than the costs of a damages remedy, injunctive relief is an appropriate remedy, even when the damage remedy is not shown to be inadequate.

FACTS: Walgreen (P) operated a pharmacy in a mall under a lease that provided that the landlord, Sara Creek (D), would not lease space to anyone else who wanted to operate a pharmacy or store containing a pharmacy in the mall. After losing its primary tenant, Sara Creek (D) informed Walgreen (P) that it intended to lease space to Phar-Mor, a "deep discount" chain. The Phar-Mor store would include a pharmacy. Walgreen (P) filed a diversity suit for breach of contract and asked for injunctive relief mandating compliance with the nonrental clause. Evidence was offered by Sara Creek (D) that Walgreen's (P) damages were readily ascertainable. The injunction was granted and Sara Creek (D) appealed.

ISSUE: Where the costs of injunctive relief are less than the costs of a damages remedy, is injunctive relief an appropriate remedy even when the damage remedy is not shown to be inadequate?

HOLDING AND DECISION: (Posner, J.) Yes. Where the costs of injunctive relief are less than the costs of a damages remedy, injunctive relief is an appropriate remedy, even when the damage remedy is not shown to be inadequate. Generally, the plaintiff seeking an injunction has the burden of pursuasion. In the case of a permanent injunction, it must be shown that damages are inadequate. If it is likely that the costs of the damages remedy would exceed the costs of the injunction, then for the sake of efficiency, the injunction is the proper remedy. In this case, despite testimony by Sara Creek (D) to the contrary, the damage remedy would have been difficult to compute. It would have required calculation of lost profits for at least ten years into the future. An injunction, on the other hand, removes the evidentiary issue from the court. And since supervision of the injunction would rest with Walgreen (P), the future cost to the court is likewise minimal. By imposing the injunction on Sara Creek (D), the issue becomes one of private bargaining. The parties are free to negotiate a fee for the removal of the injunction. The trial court properly weighed the costs and benefits of injunctive relief. Affirmed.

EDITOR'S ANALYSIS: Certain categories of contracts will regularly win equitable remedies. Where subject matter is unique, such as with real estate, specific performance will usually be granted. The rationale is that money damages cannot adequately compensate for the loss of a unique item. This is, however, something of a fallacy since most individuals would be willing to bargain away rights to a specific item for some price. The problem, however, rests with the trier of fact, as it is next to impossible to determine the appropriate premium to pay for the loss of a unique item.

[For more information on equitable relief, see Casenote Law Outline on Contracts, Chapter 7, § III, Remedies for Breach of Contract.]

NOTES:

AMERICAN BROADCASTING CO., INC. v. WOLF

52 N.Y.2d 394, 420 N.E.2d 363 (1981).

NATURE OF CASE: Action to specifically enforce employment contract.

FACT SUMMARY: Wolf (D) breached a good-faith negotiation clause with ABC (P) and contracted to work for its competitor.

CONCISE RULE OF LAW: Negative enforcement of an employment contract may only be granted, once the contract has terminated, to prevent injury from unfair competition or to enforce an express and valid anticompetitive covenant.

FACTS: Wolf (D), a popular New York sportscaster, entered into an employment contract with ABC (P), whereby he agreed to enter into good-faith negotiations during a 90-day period preceding the contract's termination regarding an extension period. He further agreed that for the first half of that period he would not negotiate with any other company. Moreover, if the negotiations did not prove fruitful, Wolf (D) was required to submit any offer accepted during the 90-day period subsequent to the contract's termination to ABC (P), allowing them to match that offer. This was known as the right of first refusal. Approximately 150 days prior to the contract's termination, Wolf (D) entered into negotiations with CBS, a competitor of ABC (P). He tentatively agreed to CBS' offer of employment, stipulating that such offer would be kept open until the day following the first refusal period. When ABC (P) became aware of the agreement, it brought suit, seeking specific enforcement of its right of first refusal and an injunction against Wolf's (D) beginning employment with CBS. The trial court denied the requested relief, and the Appellate Division affirmed. ABC (P) appealed.

ISSUE: Will an employment contract be specifically enforced, after its termination, through injunction, absent the need to prevent injury from unfair competition or the existence of an express and valid anticompetitive covenant?

HOLDING AND DECISION: (Cooke, C.J.) No. It must first be noted that Wolf's (D) actions constituted a breach of the agreement to negotiate in good faith but not of the first refusal right. That is because the first refusal right only applied to offers accepted during the designated period. His offer with CBS was negotiated prior to the effective period and accepted after it expired. Regardless, the breach of contract by Wolf (D) will not be enforced by injunction. Due to constitutional and policy considerations, employment contracts will not be affirmatively enforced by the courts. However, "negative" injunctions are sometimes used to prevent the employee from working for a competitor during the contract term. But in the instant case, the contract term between ABC (P) and Wolf (D) had expired at the time ABC (P) sought relief. After an employment contract has expired, negative enforcement will be granted only when necessary to prevent injury to the employer from unfair competition (usually involving the theft of trade secrets or customer lists) or to enforce an express and valid anticompetitive covenant. Since neither of these extraordinary factors are present in the instant case, equitable relief is denied. Affirmed.

DISSENT: (Fuchsberg, J.) The majority acted irresponsibly in failing to grant equitable relief in light of Wolf's (D) admitted misconduct. A proper judgment would grant a negative injunction on Wolf's (D) employment for the three-month first-refusal period.

EDITOR'S ANALYSIS: The concept of enforcement of employment contracts through "negative" covenants arose principally out of the notion that affirmative enforcement of such contracts was impractical due to the difficulty in supervising performance and most likely unconstitutional, as violative of the Thirteenth Amendment's prohibition of slavery. Thus, it was determined in certain situations, an order enjoining a breaching employee from competing with his employer for the contractual period, or reasonable time thereafter, was proper. However, as the principal case suggests, the courts are very cautious in issuing such relief.

[For more information on decrees of specific performance, see Casenote Law Outline on Contracts, Chapter 7, § III, Remedies for Breach of Contract.]

NOTES:

SOUTHWEST ENGINEERING COMPANY v. U.S.

341 F.2d 998 (8th Cir. 1965).

NATURE OF CASE: Action to recover sum of money.

FACT SUMMARY: Government (D) withheld from contract price paid to contractor (P) money stipulated for in the event of delay past the completion date, although it admitted that it thereby suffered no harm.

CONCISE RULE OF LAW: The situation existing at the time of the contract's execution is controlling in determining the reasonableness of liquidated damages.

FACTS: Southwest Engineering (P) entered into four contracts with the U.S. Government (D) for the construction of three radio facilities and a high-intensity approach light lane. A liquidated damage clause in the contract provided that for each day's delay past the fixed completion date, the Government (P) would withhold either $100 or $50, depending on the project. No liquidated damages were to be assessed if, in the Government's (D) judgment, the delay was justified. Southwest Engineering (P), upon completion of the projects, was assessed for an aggregate delay of 146 days. Southwest Engineering (P) brought an action to recover the money withheld as liquidated damages. At trial, the Government (D) admitted that it suffered no actual damage on any project as a result of the delays.

ISSUE: Will a contract provision fixing the amount of damages payable on breach be interpreted as an unenforceable liquidated damage clause if, at the time of the breach, the injured party suffered no actual damage?

HOLDING AND DECISION: (Van Ossterhout, J.) No. A provision included in a contract fixing the amount of damages payable on breach will be interpreted as a liquidated damages clause rather than an unenforceable penalty clause if, at the time the contract is entered, (1) the amount so fixed is a reasonable forecast of just compensation for the harm that is caused by the breach, and (2) the harm that is caused by the breach is one that is incapable or very difficult of accurate estimation. Since parties are free to contract, liquidated damages are not viewed with disfavor. Thus, the fact that the damages suffered are shown to be less than the damages contracted for is not fatal so long as, at the time the contract was executed, the liquidated damages clause was reasonable. Each party, in entering into such a contract, took a calculated risk which he is bound to accept. In the present case, since there is no proof that the liquidated damages for delay provided for are beyond damages reasonably contemplated by the parties at the time of the contract, Southwest (P) is not entitled to the return of the sum withheld.

EDITOR'S ANALYSIS: U.C.C. § 2-718(1) provides that liquidated damages may be agreed upon "but only at an amount which is reasonable in the light of the anticipated or actual harm caused by the breach, the difficulties of proof of loss, and the inconvenience or nonfeasibility of otherwise obtaining an adequate remedy." The U.C.C. has thus made one significant departure from the common law rule: a liquidated damages provision will be found, and upheld, even if the sum provided for in the case of breach was not a reasonable forecast of probable harm so long as, judged in the light of the actual harm, it appears reasonable.

[For more information on liquidated damage provisions, see Casenote Law Outline on Contracts, Chapter 7, § III, Remedies for Breach of Contract.]

NOTES:

UNITED AIRLINES, INC. v. AUSTIN TRAVEL CORP.

867 F.2d 737 (2d Cir. 1989).

NATURE OF CASE: Appeal from summary judgment for plaintiff in liquidated damages and unpaid debt for breach of lease.

FACT SUMMARY: Austin (D), a travel agency that leased computerized reservation and accounting systems from United Airlines (P), terminated the lease before the end of its term and balked at paying liquidated damages.

CONCISE RULE OF LAW: Liquidated damage clauses will be upheld if they bear a reasonable proportion to the probable loss and the amount of actual loss is incapable of precise estimation.

FACTS: Austin (D), a travel agency, assumed leases with United Airlines (P) for its ABS and Apollo computer systems at the time it purchased two other agencies. Apollo provided subscribers a data bank for making reservations, issuing tickets, and reserving rental cars and hotel rooms. United (P) charged a monthly subscription fee and a booking fee for use of the system for booking flights on airlines other than United (P). ABS was a back-office accounting and management system. A United (P) rival, Texas Air, offered to install for Austin (D) its competing computer system. Austin (D) accepted Texas Air's offer, and United (P) sued Austin (D) for liquidated damages under the leases. These damages were 80% of remaining monthly fees and variable charges and 50% of booking fee revenues. Austin (D) objected to them as penalties, but the district court held for United (P). Austin (D) appealed.

ISSUE: If a liquidated damages clause is not plainly or grossly disproportionate to the probable loss anticipated when the contract was executed, will it be upheld?

HOLDING AND DECISION: (Miner, C.J.) Yes. Liquidated damage clauses will be upheld if they bear a reasonable proportion to the probable loss and the amount of actual loss is incapable of precise estimation. Here, most of United's (P) costs when providing Apollo service were either fixed or determined in the early stages of the contractual relationship. United (P) was able to avoid less than 20% of its costs if Apollo leases are terminated early. The 20% discount was supported by evidence, such as that United's (P) competitors call for 100% of rent due on an unexpired contract. Furthermore, these liquidated damages were only available in the event, as here, of a material breach. Affirmed.

EDITOR'S ANALYSIS: Liquidated damage clauses benefit society by helping the parties prepare for the future and by reducing caseloads in the court. However, they have met resistance because they are a personal, rather than a societal, response to breach. Damages are intended to compensate the nonbreaching party rather than punish the breaching party, but the amount of liquidated damages may serve to accomplish the latter purpose if left to the discretion of only the parties to the contract. In addition, a noneconomic or economically wasteful bargain should not be immune from breach due to a disproportionately high damage clause.

[For more information on liquidated damages clause, see Casenote Law Outline on Contracts, Chapter 7, § III, Remedies for Breach of Contract.]

NOTES:

LEEBER v. DELTONA CORP.
Maine Sup. Ct., 546 A.2d 452 (1988).

NATURE OF CASE: Appeal from denial of liquidated damages for breach of contract.

FACT SUMMARY: Leeber (P) deposited a down payment on a Florida condominium sold by Deltona (D), but failed to pay the rest of the purchase price at closing.

CONCISE RULE OF LAW: Equity will not enforce a liquidated damages clause if to allow the seller to retain the specified sum would shock the court's conscience.

FACTS: Leeber (P) entered into a subscription and purchase agreement with Deltona (D) for the purpose of buying one unit of a condominium development in a Deltona (D) project on Marco Island, Florida. Under the agreement, Leeber (P) deposited 15% of the purchase price of $150,000 as a down payment, with the remainder due at closing (at a time within four years to be specified by Deltona (D)). Under the agreement, this 15% was to be retained by Deltona (D) as liquidated damages in the event of Leeber's (P) breach. After several notices of closing by Deltona (D) and several extensions at Leeber's (P) request, a final closing date was set which Leeber (P) also missed. Deltona (D) resold the unit in short order at a higher price and kept the 15%. The trial court refused to enforce the liquidated damage clause and ordered Deltona (D) to repay Leeber (P) the deposit.

ISSUE: Will equity relieve the breaching party from a forfeiture if a liquidated damage clause shocks the conscience of the court?

HOLDING AND DECISION: (Clifford, J.) Yes. If damages are ascertainable at the time of contracting, a liquidated damages clause is a penalty and will not be enforced. However, if as here, damages were not ascertainable, a liquidated damages clause still will not be enforced if to allow the seller to retain money under the clause would shock the conscience of the court. A liquidated damages clause of 15% of the contract price is not on its face unreasonable or so extraordinary as to shock. Leeber (P) filed to allege any other grounds for nonenforcement, such as fraud by the seller, mutual rescission, or extreme buyer misfortune resulting in the breach. Parties who try to avoid future litigation by agreeing to liquidated damages clauses should be encouraged. Reversed.

EDITOR'S ANALYSIS: Liquidated damages clauses may also limit a seller's liability for breach of contract or negligence; in such instances they operate more as exculpatory clauses and are known as "underliquidated" damage clauses. These limiting clauses are usually enforced, even in cases where a burglar alarm is installed which fails to promptly report fires or theft and considerable loss results. See, e.g., Feary v. Aaron Burglar Alarm, Inc., 32 Cal. App. 3d 553 (1973).

[For more information on liquidated damages clause, see Casenote Law Outline on Contracts, Chapter 7, § III, Remedies for Breach of Contract.]

NOTES:

LEWIS REFRIGERATED CO. v. SAWYER FRUIT, VEGETABLE, AND COLD STORAGE CO.

709 F.2d 427 (6th Cir. 1983).

NATURE OF CASE: Appeal from award of consequential damages for breach of contract.

FACT SUMMARY: Lewis (P) contended the trial court erred in awarding Sawyer (D) consequential damages on its counterclaim for breach in light of a clause in the contract excluding consequential damages.

CONCISE RULE OF LAW: Contractual limitations on the recovery of consequential damages for breach are valid unless it is established that the limitations were unconscionable.

FACTS: Lewis (P) sued Sawyer (D) to recover the balance of the purchase price of a freezer. Sawyer (D) counterclaimed, asserting Lewis (P) breached the contract. The jury awarded Sawyer (D) damages for lost profits and excess costs of operating the freezer caused by the breach. Lewis (P) appealed, contending the trial court erred in failing to hear evidence and instruct the jury on the validity of a contract clause which purported to exclude the recovery of consequential damages, which would have necessarily denied recovery for lost profits and increased costs if the clause was found not to be unconscionable.

ISSUE: Are contractual limitations on the recovery of consequential damages for breach of contract valid unless determined to be unconscionable?

HOLDING AND DECISION: (Newblatt, J.) Yes. Contractual limitations on the recovery of consequential damages are valid unless it is established that the limitation was unconscionable. This rule, codified in U.C.C. § 2-719(3), is designed to protect consumers against abuse in contract formation and to allow merchants to allocate business risks. This ability to allocate the potential losses is consistent with the U.C.C.'s general purpose to promote freedom in commercial transactions. As a result, it was error for the trial court to hear evidence on the conscionability of the consequential damages exclusion clause in the contract. Verdict vacated, and case remanded.

EDITOR'S ANALYSIS: Generally, clauses attempting to exclude consequential damages are used in conjunction with other clauses as a package of commercial warranties. The other items usually included are: (1) an express warranty to the purchaser of the goods that they are free of defects in workmanship and materials; (2) a disclaimer of all other express or implied warranties; (3) limits on the remedy for breach of any express warranty to replace or repair defects.

[For more information on consequential damages, see Casenote Law Outline on Contracts, Chapter 7, § III, Remedies for Breach of Contract.]

BOLTON CORP. v. T.A. LOVING CO.

N.C. Ct. of App., 94 N.C.App. 392;
review denied, 325 N.C. 545 (1989).

NATURE OF CASE: Appeal from denial damages for breach of contract.

FACT SUMMARY: Bolton Corp. (P), the heating and ventilation contractor on a project to construct a university library, was prevented from timely performing his duties due to the delay of the general contractor, Loving Co. (D).

CONCISE RULE OF LAW: Parties to a contract may agree that their disputes will be determinatively settled by a third party.

FACTS: Loving Co. (D) was the general contractor and "project expediter" on a large public construction project (to build a library on the UNC/Chapel Hill campus). As required by law, another "prime" contractor, Bolton Corp. (P) was hired as heating and ventilation contractor. Under Bolton's (P) contract with Loving (D), Loving (D) as "project expediter" was responsible for scheduling the work of the primes and for maintaining a progress schedule. Under the contract, responsibility for resolving disputes among the prime contractors due to delay was allocated to the architect. Bolton (P) was unable to complete his work on time due to the delay of other prime contractors. In Bolton's (P) suit for breach of contract, the trial judge refused to admit the testimony of the architect.

ISSUE: May the parties to a contract agree to submit their disputes under it to a third party for determinative resolution?

HOLDING AND DECISION: Yes. Parties to a contract may agree that their disputes will be determinatively settled by a third party. Loving (D) specifically contracted to assume the role of project "expediter." As such, it was required to prevent delay by scheduling work by all prime contractors and maintaining a progress schedule. Here Bolton's (P) work depended on the work of other primes who were so late Bolton (P) could not finish on schedule. Under the contract, if the work of a contractor such as Bolton (P) depended on the work of another contractor, the first is required to report to the architect the delay or defect; the architect has final responsibility for settling all disputes and his judgment as to a prime's ability to timely and adequately perform his job is prima facie correct, subject to a showing of fraud or mistake. Although the contract did not contemplate arbitration, they agreed to be bound by the architect's judgment. The trial court erred in disallowing the architect's testimony as to the cause of delay. Reversed and remanded.

EDITOR'S ANALYSIS: The decision of the prime contractor to delegate authority to the architect to resolve disputes was not a decision to submit to arbitration. In fact, the architect's judgment will still be reviewed in court under common law precepts. It is also common to limit an architect's authority to final decisions as to aesthetics and to require parties to a construction contract to submit to arbitration. See Article 10 of Document A107 of the American Institute of Architects.

MICHAEL-CURRY CO. v. KNUTSON SHAREHOLDERS

Minn. Sup. Ct., 449 N.W.2d 139 (1989).

NATURE OF CASE: Appeal from appellate reversal of trial court interpretation of arbitration clause.

FACT SUMMARY: A purchaser alleging seller's fraud in the inducement sought a trial on his claim despite a clause in the purchase and sale agreement providing for arbitration.

CONCISE RULE OF LAW: A claim of fraud in the inducement goes to the making of a contract and thus falls within an arbitration clause covering controversies arising out of relating to the making of a contract.

FACTS: A purchaser alleged seller's fraud in the inducement. The parties had signed an agreement requiring arbitration of "any controversy or claim arising out of, or relating to, this Agreement, or the making...thereof." The trial court held the clause did not require arbitration, but the appeals court reversed, holding that the clause was sufficiently broad to encompass fraud in the inducement.

ISSUE: Does an arbitration clause requiring arbitration of claims relating to the making of the contract encompass claims for fraud in the inducement?

HOLDING AND DECISION: (Keith, J.) Yes. Parties may validly choose to arbitrate all controversies, including fraud in the inducement. To determine whether the parties so intended, the clause itself must mention fraud or must be sufficiently broad to comprehend that a claim of fraudulent inducement be arbitrated. Fraud is not specifically listed in the clause here, but because fraud in the inducement goes to the "making" of the contract, the language is sufficiently broad. The law favors arbitration. Further, a specific list of all possible claims in an arbitration clause would be impractical, and parties would shy from contracts in which fraud was specifically mentioned. Affirmed.

EDITOR'S ANALYSIS: The federal government enacted a national arbitration law in 1925 which is generally in conformity with the Uniform Arbitration Act adopted by most states. The Federal Arbitration Act (FAA) applies to arbitration clauses in maritime contracts or "transactions involving commerce," and has been interpreted by the Supreme Court as controlling state laws that do not allow claims arbitrable under federal law or which make it more difficult to arbitrate claims arbitrable under either state or federal law.

CONTAINER TECHNOLOGY CORP. v. J. GADSDEN PTY., LTD.

Co. Ct. of App., 781 P.2d 119 (1989).

NATURE OF CASE: Appeal from summary judgment confirming an arbitration award for defendant.

FACT SUMMARY: After Gadsden (D) won an award of $44,937 against Container Technology (P) in arbitration pursuant to contract, Container Technology (P) sought to set it aside.

CONCISE RULE OF LAW: An arbitrator's decisions about contract interpretation or the merits of the claims presented to him shall not be reviewed during a hearing to judicially confirm the arbitration award.

FACTS: Container Technology (P) and Gadsden (D) were parties to a contract which contained an arbitration clause. They submitted a dispute to an arbitrator, who awarded Gadsden (D) $44,937. Container (P) applied to set aside the award, and Gadsden (D) applied to have it judicially confirmed. Gadsden (D) prevailed.

ISSUE: May an arbitration award be reviewed on its merits by a trial court deciding whether to judicially confirm it?

HOLDING AND DECISION: (Metzger, J.) No. An arbitration award is tantamount to a judgment and is given such status by the court asked to judicially confirm it. It is not open to review on the merits, including asserted errors in determining the credibility of witnesses, the weight given the testimony, the determination of factual issues, or the ultimate interpretation of the contract itself. The parties agreed that everything necessary to render an ultimate decision was included in the arbitrator's authority. Affirmed.

EDITOR'S ANALYSIS: Arbitration awards are vacated, not confirmed, in three situations: (1) where the award was procured by corruption, fraud, or undue influence; (2) where there was either evident partiality or corruption in the arbitrators; (3) where the arbitrators exceeded or so imperfectly executed their powers that a mutual, final, and definite award upon the subject was not made. In the above case, no sufficient evidence of any of these factors was introduced.

NOTES:

CHAPTER 7
THIRD PARTY INTERESTS

QUICK REFERENCE RULES OF LAW

1. **Assignment of Rights.** The motives of an assignee suing on a debt due and owing are immaterial and the assignment is valid. (Fitzroy v. Cave)

   [For more information on present assignment, see Casenote Law Outline on Contracts, Chapter 5, § II, The Assignment of Contract Rights.]

2. **Assignment of Rights.** A contractual provision clearly prohibiting assignment will be given effect by the courts (unless it violates public policy or a principle of law). (Allhusen v. Caristo Construction Corp.)

   [For more information on the restriction of the right to assign, see Casenote Law Outline on Contracts, Chapter 5, § II, The Assignment of Contract Rights.]

3. **Asignment of Rights.** If, after notification of an assignment, an obligor continues to pay to the assignor any money which, under the assignment, belongs to the assignee, he is liable to the assignee for the resulting damage. (Continental Purchasing Co. v. Van Raalte Co., Inc.)

   [For more information on the status of assignee, see Casenote Law Outline on Contracts, Chapter 5, § II, The Assignment of Contract Rights.]

4. **Delegation of Duties.** An obligor may delegate his duties under an executory agreement unless the obligee refuses his consent because it has a substantial interest in having the original promisor perform or control the contractual acts. (Sally Beauty Co. v. Nexxus Products Co., Inc.)

   [For more information on restraints on delegation, see Casenote Law Outline on Contracts, Chapter 5, § III, The Delegation of Contract Duties.]

5. **Creation of Rights.** It is not necessary that the beneficiary be named and identified as an individual; a third party may enforce a contract if he can show he is a member of a class for whose benefit it was made. (Johnson v. Holmes Tuttle Lincoln-Mercury, Inc.)

   [For more information on the rights of an intended beneficiary, see Casenote Law Outline on Contracts, Chapter 5, § I, The Status and Right of an Intended Beneficiary.]

6. **Creation of Rights.** A third party intended by a testator to be the beneficiary of a bequest by will or trust may sue, in contract or tort, the lawyer who failed to include the bequest. (Hale v. Groce)

   [For more information on the rights of an intended beneficiary, see Casenote Law Outline on Contracts, Chapter 5, § I, The Status and Right of an Intended Beneficiary.]

7. **Creation of Rights.** When the federal government has contracted with landlords to provide apartment financing in return for rent ceilings, tenants have standing to seek enforcement or damages. (Zigas v. Superior Court, Etc.)

   [For more information on the rights of an intended beneficiary, see Casenote Law Outline on Contracts, Chapter 5, § I, The Status and Right of an Intended Beneficiary.]

8. **Nature of Rights.** A third-party beneficiary to a contract has an immediate right of action upon the contract that does not depend upon his acceptance, nor may the contract be rescinded while he is still ignorant of it and before he assents to it. (Tweeddale v. Tweeddale)

[For more information on the rights of a third party beneficiary, see Casenote Law Outline on Contracts, Chapter 5, § I, The Status and Right of an Intended Beneficiary.]

FITZROY v. CAVE

2 K.B. 364 (1905).

NATURE OF CASE: Appeal from finding that an assignment was void as against public policy.

FACT SUMMARY: Fitzroy (P) took an assignment of debts owed by Cave (D) to five tradesmen in Ireland. Fitzroy (P) hoped that a suit on these debts would force Cave (D) into bankruptcy.

CONCISE RULE OF LAW: The motives of an assignee suing on a debt due and owing are immaterial and the assignment is valid.

FACTS: Cave (D) owed some debts to five tradesmen in Ireland. They assigned these debts for collection to Fitzroy (P), who promised to pay any recovery over costs to them. Fitzroy's (P) motive in accepting the assignment was to force Cave (D) into bankruptcy so that he could be removed from the Board of Fitzroy's (P) company. The trial court found that Fitzroy's (P) motives rendered the assignment against public policy and found for Cave (D). Fitzroy (P) appealed on the basis that as long as the money was due and owing, his motives were immaterial.

ISSUE: Will improper motives render an assignment invalid even though the debt is legitimate and is due and owing?

HOLDING AND DECISION: (Lawrance, J.) No. Fitzroy's (P) motives are immaterial. Fitzroy (P) was acting as a mere trustee for the tradesmen. The debt was legitimate and was long past due. A party having a legal right to do so may bring suit regardless of his motive for doing so. The debtor who has not honored his commitments should not be allowed to complain. He is merely being required to do what he has already legally obligated himself to do. The fact that an adverse judgment may cause his removal from a Board of Directors or may throw him into bankruptcy does not affect the validity of either the debt or the assignment. Cave (D) is liable to the tradesmen and cannot complain of Fitzroy's (P) motives in accepting the assignment. Judgment reversed.

EDITOR'S ANALYSIS: An assignee stands in the shoes of the assignor. The debtor can raise any defenses against the assignee that he could raise against the assignor. Fitzroy is important because it stands for a basic principle of contract law. So long as a party is acting in a legal manner, his underlying motive is immaterial. Consider the chaos that would result in most contractual situations if valid contracts could be set aside merely because of impure motives on one side or the other.

[For more information on present assignment, see Casenote Law Outline on Contracts, Chapter 5, § II, The Assignment of Contract Rights.]

CONTINENTAL PURCHASING CO., INC. v. VAN RAALTE CO., INC.

N.Y. Sup. Ct., 251 App. Div. 151, 295 N.Y.S. 867 (1937).

NATURE OF CASE: Action to recover assigned wages.

FACT SUMMARY: Mrs. Potter assigned all of her wages from the Van Raalte Co. (D) to the Continental Purchasing Co. (P), but the Van Raalte Co. (D), even after notification of the assignment, continued to pay all wages to Mrs. Potter.

CONCISE RULE OF LAW: If, after notification of an assignment, an obligor continues to pay to the assignor any money which, under the assignment, belongs to the assignee, he is liable to the assignee for the resulting damage.

FACTS: In 1934, Mrs. Potter assigned to the Continental Purchasing Co. (P) all of her wages earned or to be earned from the Van Raalte Co. (D). Thereafter, the Continental Purchasing Co. (P) gave written notice of this assignment to the Van Raalte Co. (D), which acknowledged receipt of such notice. Subsequently, however, the Van Raalte Co. (D) continued to pay Mrs. Potter's wages directly to her. In response, the Continental Purchasing Co. (P) brought an action against the Van Raalte Co. (D) to recover those wages paid to Mrs. Potter after the assignment. After a judgment for Van Raalte Co. (D), the Continental Purchasing Co. (P) brought this appeal.

ISSUE: If, after notification of an assignment, an obligor continues to pay to the assignor money assigned to the assignee, is he liable to the assignee?

HOLDING AND DECISION: (Edgecomb, J.) Yes. If, after notification of an assignment, an obligor continues to pay to the assignor money which, under the assignment, belongs to the assignee, he is liable to the assignee for the resulting damage. Of course, before such notification, an obligor has no liability to the assignee (i.e., he can continue to pay the money assigned to the assignor). Here, however, the Van Raalte Co. (D), the obligor, received notice of the assignment from Mrs. Potter, the assignor, to the Continental Purchasing Co. (P), the assignee. As such, the Van Raalte Co. (D) is liable to the Continental Purchasing Co. (P) for any wages paid to Mrs. Potter after notice of the assignment. Reversed.

EDITOR'S ANALYSIS: This case points up the importance of the notice requirement in the assignment and delegation areas. Note that at common law, until notice was received, the obligor was under no duty to perform to the assignee whatsoever. Furthermore, the obligor and assignor could alter their contractual agreement at any time prior to notice of the assignment to the obligor. The U.C.C. has retained these common law rules almost completely but has ruled that the basic contractual agreement may still be modified even after notice of the assignment.

[For more information on the status of assignee, see Casenote Law Outline on Contracts, Chapter 5, § II, The Assignment of Contract Rights.]

ALLHUSEN v. CARISTO CONSTR. CORP.

303 N.Y. 446, 103 N.E.2d 891.

NATURE OF CASE: Action by an assignee to recover damages for breach of contract.

FACT SUMMARY: One Kroo assigned to Allhusen (P) rights under his contract in spite of an antiassignment clause.

CONCISE RULE OF LAW: A contractual provision clearly prohibiting assignment will be given effect by the courts (unless it violates public policy or a principle of law).

FACTS: Caristo (D), a general contractor, subcontracted with Kroo to do painting. The subcontract contained the following provision: "The assignment by the second party (Kroo) of this contract or any interests therein or of any money due or to become due by reason of the terms hereof without the written consent of the first party [Caristo (D)] shall be void." Kroo subsequently and without written consent from Caristo (D) assigned rights (including "moneys due and to become due") to a third company, which in turn assigned them to Allhusen (P). The contracts were not "assigned," and no question of improper delegation was involved. Allhusen (P) sought to recover on the assignment, but Caristo (D) contended that the contract prohibition against assignments must be given effect.

ISSUE: Will a contractual provision clearly prohibiting assignment be held effective?

HOLDING AND DECISION: (Froessel, J.) Yes. A term of a contract with language clearly prohibiting assignment will be upheld, although in the absence of such clear language a prohibitory clause will normally be interpreted as merely a covenant not to assign (for which the obligor may have an action for breach). In the present case, it is clearly and unequivocally provided that an "assignment ... shall be void." In such a situation, courts, while striving to uphold freedom of assignability, have recognized the greater interest in freedom of contract. "No sound reason appears why an assignee should remain unaffected by a provision in the very contract which gave life to the claim he asserts." Such a holding is not violative of public policy, and the question of free alienation of property does not deem to be involved.

EDITOR'S ANALYSIS: Although some cases have held an antiassignment clause to be an unlawful restraint on alienation (the present court to the contrary notwithstanding), most courts have refused to interfere with "freedom of contract" so explicitly. Instead, a court, while allowing an antiassignment clause in theory, will tend to find that the particular provision before it is not drafted with sufficient clarity to accomplish its purpose of prohibiting assignment. As such, the provision is held merely a promise not to assign for breach of which the obligor has a theoretical action. ("Theoretical" because damages for such a breach will ordinarily be nominal.) In the present case, the court could not shut its eyes to the clear language and even admitted that "violence" would be done to that language by construing it as a mere promise. [See also U.C.C. § 2-210(2) and Restatement (Second) §§ 149(2)c and 154(2); and cf. U.C.C. § 9-318(4), comments to which expressly reject the present decision.]

[For more information on the restriction of the right to assign, see Casenote Law Outline on Contracts, Chapter 5, § II, The Assignment of Contract Rights.]

NOTES:

SALLY BEAUTY CO. v. NEXXUS PRODUCTS CO., INC.

801 F.2d 1001 (7th Cir. 1986).

NATURE OF CASE: Appeal from summary denial of damages for breach of contract.

FACT SUMMARY: Nexxus (D) hired Best Beauty as its exclusive distributor in Texas of its hair care products, but cancelled the agreement when Best was acquired by Sally Beauty (P), a subsidiary of its competitor, Alberto-Culver.

CONCISE RULE OF LAW: An obligor may delegate his duties under an executory agreement unless the obligee refuses his consent because it has a substantial interest in having the original promisor perform or control the contractual acts.

FACTS: Nexxus (D) hired Best Beauty as its exclusive distributor of its hair care products to barbers and stylists in Texas. When Best merged into Sally Beauty (P), Nexxus cancelled the agreement. Sally Beauty (P) was a subsidiary of Alberto-Culver, a major manufacturer of hair products and a Nexxus (D) competitor. Sally Beauty (P) sued for breach of contract. The district court held that Nexxus' (D) contract was for personal services and was therefore not assignable.

ISSUE: May an obligor delegate his duties under an executory contract without the consent of the obligee?

HOLDING AND DECISION: (Cudahy, D.J.) No. U.C.C. § 2-210(l) allows the delegation of performance under an executory sales contract, but only if it would be satisfactory to the obligee. The obligee may withhold its consent to the delegation if it has a substantial interest in having the original promisor control the acts required by contract. Here, Nexxus (D) contracted for Best's "best efforts" in promoting the sale of its products in Texas. Nexxus (D) should not be required to accept the "best efforts" of Sally Beauty (P) when those efforts are subject to the control of its competitor, Alberto-Culver. Sally Beauty's (P) position as a competitor's subsidiary per se, not the contract's classification as one for personal services, warrants upholding the district court's judgment. Affirmed.

DISSENT: (Posner, C.J.) If Nexxus (D) was concerned that Sally Beauty (P) would not have used its "best efforts" to promote its products, its remedy was not to cancel the contract, but under U.C.C. § 2-609 to demand assurances of due performance, or under common law to sue for breach of the implied "best efforts" clause of the distributorship agreement. The merger of Best into Sally Beauty (P) did not represent an inability to perform and an anticipatory repudiation. It is commonplace and legitimate for businesses to sell or distribute a competitor's products.

EDITOR'S ANALYSIS: Of course, an obligee's intention that the duties under a contract not be delegated may be expressly set forth in the contract; terms prohibiting or restraining delegation will always be enforced. Further, and as mentioned in J. Posner's dissent, U.C.C. § 2-210 expressly provides that in a contract for the sale of goods, delegation is a reasonable ground for insecurity which can warrant a demand for assurance of performance.

[For more information on restraints on delegation, see Casenote Law Outline on Contracts, Chapter 5, § III, The Delegation of Contract Duties.]

NOTES:

JOHNSON v. HOLMES TUTTLE LINCOLN-MERCURY

160 Cal.App.2d 290, 325 P.2d 193.

NATURE OF CASE: Appeal from award of damages to third-party beneficiaries of an oral agreement.

FACT SUMMARY: Johnson (P) and Jones (P) brought suit to recover damages upon an auto insurance policy that Holmes (D) had promised to obtain for its customer, Caldera, who collided with Johnson (P) and Jones (P).

CONCISE RULE OF LAW: It is not necessary that the beneficiary be named and identified as an individual; a third party may enforce a contract if he can show he is a member of a class for whose benefit it was made.

FACTS: Caldera purchased a new car from Holmes (D) through its salesman, Rozany. Rozany agreed with Caldera to procure, at the time the car was purchased, "full coverage" auto insurance for Caldera, including public liability and property damage. The premium cost was figured into the monthly payments due on the car. Holmes (D), which had a full insurance department, failed to procure coverage for Caldera. Three weeks after purchasing the car, Caldera was involved in a collision with a car driven by Johnson (P), who, along with a passenger, Jones (P), was insured. Johnson (P) and Jones (P) sued Caldera and obtained judgments of $4,413 and $2,070, respectively, the judgments going unsatisfied. Johnson (P) and Jones (P) then brought suit on their judgments against Holmes (D), alleging that they were third-party beneficiaries of the promise to obtain insurance for Caldera. From judgment for Johnson (P) and Jones (P), Holmes (D) appealed.

ISSUE: May a third-party enforce a contract if he can show that he is a member of a class for whose benefit it was made?

HOLDING AND DECISION: (Vallee, J.) Yes. It is not necessary that the beneficiary be named and identified as an individual; a third party may enforce a contract if he can show that he is a member of a class for whose benefit it was made. The action by a third-party beneficiary for the breach of the promisor's agreement does not rest on the ground of any actual, or supposed, relationship between the parties but on the broad and more satisfactory basis that the law, operating on the acts of the parties, creates the duty, establishes a privity, and implies the promise and obligation on which the action is founded. It is no objection to the maintenance of an action by a third party that a suit might be brought also against the one to whom the promise was made. Clearly, the agreement between Caldera and Holmes (D) was not for Caldera's sole benefit but that it was intended to protect third persons who might be injured in an auto accident. This was what Caldera wanted as a means of obtaining a benefit for himself. It was reasonable for a jury to infer that Caldera, in making the agreement with Holmes (D), desired and intended that such persons be protected in case of an accident involving his new car. Affirmed.

EDITOR'S ANALYSIS: Johnson is just one of a number of cases applying this view. Although some liability policies contain terms limiting payment only to the insured, states generally require that liability insurance provide for the protection of third parties.

[For more information on the rights of an intended beneficiary, see Casenote Law Outline on Contracts, Chapter 5, § I, The Status and Right of an Intended Beneficiary.]

NOTES:

HALE v. GROCE

Or. Sup. Ct., 304 Or. 281, 744 P.2d 1289 (1987).

NATURE OF CASE: Appeal from dismissal of third-party beneficiary action for breach of attorney-client agreement.

FACT SUMMARY: Groce (D) failed to make a testamentary bequest to Hale (P) as requested by Groce's (D) client.

CONCISE RULE OF LAW: A third party intended by a testator to be the beneficiary of a bequest by will or trust may sue, in contract or tort, the lawyer who failed to include the bequest.

FACTS: Groce (D), an attorney, was directed by a client to prepare testamentary instruments including a bequest of a specified sum to Hale (P). After the client's death, it was discovered the gift was not included in the testator's will or a related trust instrument. Hale (P) sued Groce (D) in contract as the intended beneficiary of the testator's professional contract with Groce (D) and in tort based on Groce's (D) breach of professional duty. The lowest court dismissed both claims, but the appellate court allowed the negligence claim.

ISSUE: May an attorney employed to draw a will be liable to a third party deprived of the portion of the estate which the testator instructed the attorney should be given in the will to the third party?

HOLDING AND DECISION: (Linde, J.) Yes. A third party intended by a testator to be the beneficiary of a bequest by will or trust may sue, in contract or tort, the lawyer who failed to include the bequest. Groce (D) was an "intended" third-party beneficiary of Hale's (P) promise to his client that he make a will or trust including the gift to Groce (D). Failure to include the bequest may give rise to a claim either for breach of contract or in tort for failure to use best professional efforts to accomplish a testator's desired result with the skill and care customary among lawyers in the relevant community. Hale's (P) contract claim should not have been dismissed. Reversed in part.

EDITOR'S ANALYSIS: Despite this holding, a majority of courts hold that the lack of privity between the attorney and the third party bars a beneficiary's recovery against attorneys. The court also refers to a "balancing test" adopted by the California courts which examines six factors to determine negligence: (l) whether the contract was intended to benefit plaintiff; (2) foreseeability of harm to plaintiff; (3) certainty of plaintiff's injury; (4) how closely plaintiff's injuries and defendant's conduct are connected; (5) moral blame of defendant's conduct; and (6) public policy in avoiding similar harm in the future.

[For more information on the rights of an intended beneficiary, see Casenote Law Outline on Contracts, Chapter 5, § I, The Status and Right of an Intended Beneficiary.]

ZIGAS v. SUPERIOR COURT

Cal. Ct. App., 120 Cal. App. 3d 827 (1981).

NATURE OF CASE: Petition for a writ following a demurrer to breach of contract action.

FACT SUMMARY: Certain owners of rental property charged rents in excess of amounts that they contracted with HUD that they would charge.

CONCISE RULE OF LAW: When the federal government has contracted with landlords to provide apartment financing in return for rent ceilings, tenants have standing to seek enforcement or damages.

FACTS: HUD helped finance certain apartments. In exchange, the landlords contracted that they would adhere to certain rent schedules. The landlords did not so adhere, charging rents in excess of the schedules. Several tenants (P) brought a class-action suit seeking enforcement and damages. The trial court sustained a demurrer predicated on lack of standing, and the tenants (P) petitioned for a writ.

ISSUE: When the federal government has contracted with landlords to provide apartment financing in return for rent ceilings, do tenants have standing to seek enforcement or damages?

HOLDING AND DECISION: (Feinberg, J.) Yes. When the federal government has contracted with landlords to provide apartment financing in return for rent ceilings, tenants have standing to seek enforcement or damages. Where a contract is made specifically for the benefit of a third party, that third party may enforce it any time prior to rescission. Where the benefits are incidental, the third parties may not so enforce the contract. The question, therefore, is whether the plaintiffs are intended to be beneficiaries. Here, there can be no doubt that this is the case, as the possible rationale for the contract would be to benefit them. Reversed.

EDITOR'S ANALYSIS: To reach the result it did, the court here had to distinguish between two somewhat conflicting cases. Shell v. Schmidt, 126 Cal. App. 2d 279 (1954), would have permitted recovery here; Martinez v. Sucoma Companies, 11 Cal. 3d 384 (1974), would not have. The court here held that Martinez only involved incidental beneficiaries, as opposed to the intended beneficiary situation of Shell.

[For more information on the rights of an intended beneficiary, see Casenote Law Outline on Contracts, Chapter 5, § I, The Status and Right of an Intended Beneficiary.]

TWEEDDALE v. TWEEDDALE

116 Wis. 517, 93 N.W. 440.

NATURE OF CASE: Action on a bond and mortgage by a third-party beneficiary.

FACT SUMMARY: After Daniel Tweeddale (D) gave a bond for support secured by a mortgage which provided that if the mortgaged land was sold, certain sums would be due to Edward Tweeddale (P) and others, the land was sold and the mortgage discharged before Edward Tweeddale (P) knew about the provision.

CONCISE RULE OF LAW: A third-party beneficiary to a contract has an immediate right of action upon the contract that does not depend upon his acceptance, nor may the contract be rescinded while he is still ignorant of it and before he assents to it.

FACTS: Daniel Tweeddale (D) gave a bond for support to his mother secured by a mortgage on certain land. The bond provided that in case the land was sold, certain sums would be due to Edward Tweeddale (P), Daniel's (D) brother, and others. Daniel (D) sold the land, making the obligation to Edward (P) operative. However, before Edward (P) even knew of the bond and mortgage, the mother discharged Daniel's (D) debt to her and released the mortgage. Edward (P) brought a foreclosure action against Daniel (D), arguing that the release did not bar his recovery. Edward (P) appealed a judgment for Daniel (D).

ISSUE: Does a third-party beneficiary have an immediate right of action upon a contract that does not depend upon his acceptance?

HOLDING AND DECISION: (Marshall, J.) Yes. A third-party beneficiary to a contract has an immediate right of action upon the contract that does not depend upon his acceptance, nor may the contract be rescinded while he is still ignorant of it and before he assents to it. The law immediately operates upon the acts of the contracting parties to establish privity between the promisor and the third-party beneficiary so that the liability is at once binding. No party can thereafter change the situation without the consent of the third-party beneficiary. As such, the satisfaction of the mortgage is void as regards the third-party beneficiary, Edward Tweeddale (P).

EDITOR'S ANALYSIS: The view here is that a third-party beneficiary has an immediate vested interest in the subject matter of the contract when made. Such is contrary to the law in most jurisdictions which prescribes that the third party must have had at least notice of his rights whether or not he changes his position in reliance thereon. Because there was no notice until after the bond and mortgage were discharged, this case results in the anomaly of having the discharge declared void to a third-party beneficiary who never knew he was a beneficiary until the entire transaction was over.

[For more information on the rights of a third party beneficiary, see Casenote Law Outline on Contracts, Chapter 5, § I, The Status and Right of an Intended Beneficiary.]

NOTES:

Notes

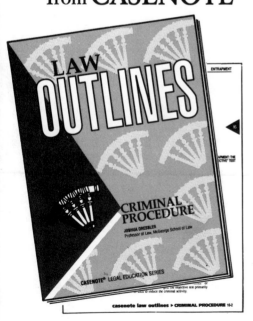